LABEL ME HUMAN:

Minority Rights of Stigmatized Canadians

For those on whom society pins harshly loaded labels, the struggle to overcome pervasive, institutionalized discrimination is a daily challenge. In this study of human rights issues for such minorities, Evelyn Kallen focuses on three categories of stigmatized Canadians: alcoholic, disabled, and gay/lesbian. She considers first the process by which stigmas are created and attached, and then the ways stigmas can be removed, including minority organization and the pursuit of human rights and liberation.

Applying internationally recognized principles of human rights, Kallen explores how violations of human rights help create and maintain stigmatized minority status, and how protection of human rights in law and public policy aids the destigmatization and liberation of long-debased and disadvantaged minorities.

Kallen addresses some of the current claims put forward by stigmatized minorities under human rights legislation and the Charter of Rights and Freedoms. She proposes strategies for change in law, public policy, and social practice designed to ensure full recognition and protection for the minority rights of stigmatized Canadians.

Evelyn Kallen is Professor of Social Science and Anthropology at York University, and author of *Ethnicity and Human Rights in Canada.*

EVELYN KALLEN

Label Me Human: Minority Rights of Stigmatized Canadians

/ 6

UNIVERSITY OF TORONTO PRESS

Toronto Buffalo London

© University of Toronto Press 1989
Toronto Buffalo London
Printed in Canada

ISBN 0-8020-2696-6 (cloth)
ISBN 0-8020-6664-x (paper)

∞

Printed on acid-free paper

Canadian Cataloguing in Publication Data

Kallen, Evelyn, 1929–
  Label me human

  Includes bibliographical references and index.
  ISBN 0-8020-2696-6 (bound). – ISBN 0-8020-6664-x (pbk.)

  1. Minorities – Canada. 2. Stigma (Social psychology)
  3. Human rights – Canada. 4. Minorities – Canada –
  Political activity. I. Title.

  JC599.C2K3 1989   323.1'71   c88-095156-7

Contents

APPENDICES

Charts and tables

For D, B, and J

Acknowledgments

Research for this book was conducted with the aid of a sabbatical-leave fellowship (1983–4) from the Social Sciences and Humanities Research Council of Canada.

The helpful comments of Professor Judith Posner on an early draft of the manuscript for this book were much appreciated. The insightful comments and questions of the many students in my undergraduate course on Stigmatized Minorities and Human Rights in Canada, in which over a period of four years, drafts of the manuscript were utilized extensively in lectures, contributed significantly to the final shape of this book.

Above all, I wish to express my gratitude to the members and spokespersons of minorities upon which this book focuses, without whose co-operation my research for it would not have been feasible.

This book has been published with the help of a grant from the Social Science Federation of Canada, using funds provided by the Social Sciences and Humanities Research Council of Canada.

Preface

From a human-rights perspective, it may be argued that the tradition of social-scientific inquiry designed to further the scholarly understanding of stigmatized non-ethnic minorities is flawed with an abiding tendency (however unintentional) to 'blame the victim.' Theoretical models that have conceptualized stigmatized-minority status as a function of 'deviancy' almost invariably have had the unintended consequence of reinforcing prevailing prejudices and stereotypes underlying minority stigmata. While the social-deviance model, which conceptualizes deviancy in terms of non-normative attributes, represents a theoretical leap forward from the medical model, which defines deviancy in terms of abnormal (pathological) attributes, both models tend to focus scholarly attention on the stigmatized attributes of minorities labelled as deviant.

Over the last decade or so, spokespersons for various stigmatized minorities have argued that the concept of deviance is not, indeed cannot be, value free. Even in the seemingly innocuous concept of statistical deviation from a societal norm, 'deviant' serves to mark the labelled attribute as less socially acceptable, less worthy, than the norm from which it is perceived to deviate. Accordingly, the stigma persists, while the legitimacy of the norm itself and the justness of its arbitrary imposition upon minorities by majority authorities remain unquestioned.

By way of contrast, this book adopts a 'deviance-free' approach that deflects scholarly attention away from the stigmatized attribute and focuses instead on the fundamental human rights of the bearer of the stigma. From a human-rights view, the legitimacy of established majority norms may be called into critical question. Further, and most important, the arbitrary imposition of norms that protect the values and interests of powerful majorities at the expense of those of vulnerable minorities is seen to constitute categorical discrimination – an explicit violation of the fundamental human rights of stigmatized-minority members.

Under the various articles of the International Bill of Human Rights (United Nations, 1978) and related human-rights covenants, freedom to decide, equality of opportunity, and dignity of person are held to be inalienable human-rights principles. These fundamental rights can be claimed by all human beings *as such*: they do not have to be earned, and they apply equally to all, regardless of differences between individuals or groups in the nature of their human attributes. As moral principles, human rights are unconditional; in their exercise, however, they are not absolute, for each person's rights are conditional upon non-violation of the rights of others. Human rights, then, entail social responsibilities.

From a human-rights approach, restriction or denial of the exercise of human rights of any individual or group can be justified only in instances where violations of the human rights of others can be fully substantiated. In such cases, restrictions justifiably may be imposed on the violator's exercise of human rights, but only to the extent necessary to prevent further violations of the rights of others.

The bearing of stigmatized human attributes does not in itself justify the imposition of restrictions on the exercise of human rights by the bearer of stigmata. Stigmatized and non-stigmatized persons alike may violate the rights of others. Should they do so, restrictions on the exercise of their human rights justifiably may be imposed. Alternatively, the imposition of restrictions on the exercise of human rights of minority members on the arbitrary basis of the presumed nature of their stigmatized attributes constitutes categorical discrimination, in direct violation of their human rights. Insofar as such human-rights violations can be documented, stigmatized minorities can put forward justifiable claims for redress against the disadvantageous effects of categorical discrimination upon minority members. Such claims may be conceptualized as *minority-rights claims*.

The internationally recognized basis of justification for minority-rights claims rests on the premise that human-rights principles are prior to law. As codified in the human-rights instruments of the United Nations, these principles represent globally endorsed moral guide-lines, which ratifying states are morally (but not legally) obliged to follow in enacting human-rights legislation. When such legislation is enacted, however, human rights also become legal rights that can justifiably be claimed by any member of the society who can provide evidence of human-rights violations.

Insofar as stigmatized minorities, by definition, are collectivities whose members' human rights have been categorically violated, claims put forward by or on behalf of minority members are best conceptualized as minority-rights claims.

The reader may ask: is it necessary to make a conceptual distinction between human rights and minority rights? Are these not one and the same? My response is twofold. Assuredly, minority rights are human rights. Nevertheless, it is essential to make the conceptual distinction.

The minority-rights concept is important because it focuses attention on the *categorical* nature of the human-rights violations underlying minority claims. The basis of minority claims, whether they are put forward individually or collectively, is not discrimination against individual members as unique persons, but categorical discrimination against minority members *as such*. Categorical discrimination does not recognize individual differences among minority members, for it is premised solely on stigmatized attributes that all minority-group members are assumed to share. The concept of minority rights is also important because it draws attention to the *necessity* of making claims. Insofar as stigmatized minorities are perceived by majority authorities as substandard beings undeserving of full human rights, minority members' human rights will not become legally recognized and protected without some form of intervention on the minority's behalf. Accordingly, minority rights will have to be claimed by minority representatives and/or by other advocates acting on behalf of minority members.

The minority-rights concept, then, particularizes the concept of human rights as applied to minorities by incorporating the postulate of categorical discrimination and by highlighting the necessity for putting forward minority-rights claims designed to attain legal and other protection for the human rights of minority members.

A theoretical framework informed by the foregoing perspective on minority rights was developed and applied in the analysis of racial and ethnic minorities in my earlier book, *Ethnicity and Human Rights in Canada* (1982). In the present book, the original conceptual design is broadened and applied in the analysis of stigmatized non-ethnic minorities and human rights in Canada.

The interdisciplinary scheme of this book builds upon key concepts derived largely from ethnic-relations and social-deviance theories and reconceptualized from a human-rights perspective. The conceptual framework is designed to provide a scholarly understanding of the social processes underlying the acquisition of stigmata, the creation and perpetuation of stigmatized-minority status, the shedding of stigmata, and the liberation of long-degraded minorities. Central to the conception of the design is the part played by human-rights violations in the genesis and maintenance of stigmatized-minority status and the part played by human-rights protection in the discarding of stigmata and in the human liberation of minorities.

For heuristic purposes, the sequential conceptual scheme may be divided into three phases.

In the first phase (becoming a minority or going into the closet), the conceptual framework builds primarily upon ideas derived from labelling theory, reconceptualized from a human-rights view. In this phase I analyse a / the social processes of stigmatization and categorical discrimination responsible for the creation of stigmatized-minority status, b / the processes of involuntary and voluntary social seclusion through which stigmatized minorities go 'into the closet,' c / the psycho-social ramifications of a closeted existence and the social mechanisms adopted by minorities in order to cope with the pain of stigma, and d / the self-fulfilling prophecy of stigmatization through which minority stigmata become internalized and through which stigmatized self and group identities are generated.

In the second phase (destigmatization or coming out of the closet) the scheme builds primarily upon concepts from ethnic-relations and social-deviance theories, informed by a human-rights perspective. In this phase I analyse a / the social processes of delabelling and relabelling through which stigmatized identities come to be rejected and through which new and positive minority identities are created and b / the development of minority self-help groups and support networks that serve to bolster positive identities and to raise collective consciousness of human-rights violations.

The concept 'coming out' bridges the transition from the second to the third phase of the framework. The set of concepts relating to the 'closet syndrome' has been drawn largely from the social-scientific literature on the homosexual minority. In the present scheme, these ideas have been extended so as to apply generally in the analysis. 'Coming out' is conceptualized as a rite of passage through which stigmatized-minority members come to shed their cloak of shame and secrecy; begin to emerge from their self-created (invisible) closets or from majority-imposed (institutional) closets; and endeavour to reintegrate within the majority community.

In the third and final phase (towards minority rights and cultural liberation), the conceptual design builds predominantly upon theories from the ethnic-relations and social-movements literature reconceptualized with a human-rights approach in my earlier book (1982). In this phase I analyse a / the social processes involved in the progression from closeted (secretive) to open and activist minority organization, b / the development of minority organization predicated on a goal of contention (social-reform movement), c / the development of minority organization predicated on a goal of cultural liberation (revitalization movement), and d / the growth of minority advocacy and the putting forward of minority-rights claims for constitutional and statutory legal protection for the individual and collective rights of minority members.

The empirical focus of this book is on disabled, alcoholic, and homosexual minorities. Several considerations influenced my selection of these particular populations. One important consideration was the directing of scholarly attention towards those minorities whose members had suffered the most profound stigmatization and the most flagrant human-rights violations. Another, theoretical, consideration was to focus scholarly attention upon target groups not commonly conceptualized or understood as minorities. A more pragmatic consideration was to focus scholarly concern upon stigmatized minorities that were not among the target populations currently singled out for specialized (area) studies. Taken together, these considerations led me to choose these target groups over such other non-ethnic minorities as women, children, and the aged.

The decision to limit the focus of analysis to three target populations was also a function of time considerations. Research for this book spanned a period of more than two years, including an entire year during which I was on sabbatical leave. In addition to conducting library research, I collected data on the three target populations from human-rights commissions, citizens' rights groups, and minority organizations. These data I supplemented by means of interviews with selected minority spokespersons and participant observation at a number of minority-organized events. The time-frame for this research project precluded the extension of the investigation to other target groups.

Behind all of the foregoing considerations was the necessity to obtain documentation for each of the three phases of the conceptual framework that could best elucidate the book's sequential scheme. In the case of the alcoholic minority, there was a wealth of substantive material on Alcoholics Anonymous that could well illustrate the closeted phase of minority self-help. Materials on the deinstitutionalization and normalization movement among Canada's disabled minorities could well illustrate the phase of coming out, with specific reference to the 'institutional' closet. Additionally, materials on the consumer movement of the disabled provided ample documentation for the phase of contention, especially with regard to social-reform movements predicated on a goal of community integration. Materials on the homosexual minority provided unparalleled substantiation for the culminating phase of the theoretical design, the putting-forward of minority-rights claims for protection of the individual and collective human rights of minority members. Further, documentation on this minority could be provided to represent the entire sequence of phases in the conceptual scheme; thus, a continuity of illustration not possible in the other minority cases was afforded by this singular case.

The selected target groups may be held to represent comparable, but quite different minority experiences of stigmatization and discrimination. For example, the closet of secrecy in which homosexual and alcoholic minorities attempt to hide their stigmata is an invisible and voluntary (self-created) enclave. By way of contrast, the 'disabled' closet, that of the total institution (Goffman, 1961), is a tangible enclosure, complete with walls and (sometimes) guards, created by majority authorities for the involuntary confinement of minority members. Again, for the disabled, coming out of the closet through the process of deinstitutionalization is a different, yet comparable, experience to that for homosexuals or alcoholics who do so through open disclosure of minority stigmata. Differences in minority experiences of human-rights violations through denial of opportunity afford another basis for comparative analysis. To varying degrees, homosexuals and alcoholics have been able to 'pass' (assume pseudo-identities as majority members) and thus avail themselves of educational and occupational opportunities for participation and advancement in public life. For most members of disabled minorities, social isolation in total institutions, lack of appropriate educational opportunities, inaccessibility of many public buildings, and employer discrimination have provided insuperable barriers, making economic independence, for the majority of Canada's disabled, an unattainable goal.

The comparative thrust of the differential minority experiences of these target populations affords the analysis a dynamic dimension and, at the same time, serves to dispel the myth that all minorities are alike.

While the empirical focus of this book is on three minorities, it is my hope that readers will find the conceptual framework that informs the analysis to be useful well beyond the limited parameters of the target groups selected for illustrative purposes.

The principal scholarly aim of this book is to contribute to the social-scientific understanding of stigmatized minorities and human rights. Substantively the book focuses on the minority experience within the Canadian context, but the applicability of the theoretical framework is far broader. The design of the book is informed by a set of key concepts derived from international human-rights principles. Accordingly, the scheme may be usefully applied in cross-cultural analyses of stigmatized minorities. The interdisciplinary nature of the framework also extends its scholarly value beyond the bounds of a single area of concentration.

The unique contribution of the book, however, lies in the application of an original, non-legal human-rights approach to the social-scientific analysis of stigmatized non-ethnic minorities. Stigmatized-minority status is seen to derive from demonstrable human-rights violations, and the process of minority liberation is conceptualized as one through which minority members become collectively conscious of majority abrogation of their human rights and organized and politicized in order to put forward minority-rights claims.

In developing the theoretical framework for the book, my aim was to inform the scheme with a human-rights perspective that would enable it to serve not only as a 'model of reality' but also as a 'model for reality.' By building human-rights principles into the theoretical framework, I hoped that the book would contribute not only to social-scientific scholarship, but also to the realization of this country's human-rights mandate as articulated and constitutionally entrenched in the Charter of Rights and Freedoms (Constitution Act, 1982). The broader vision, then, was to provide a work that could reach out beyond the academic context, to governments, to human-rights advocates, and to the community at large, in order to increase public awareness of, sensitivity to, and support for minority rights in Canada.

E.K.

Abbreviations

AA	Alcoholics Anonymous
BCHRC	British Columbia Human Rights Commission
BOOST	Blind Organization of Ontario with Self-Help Tactics
CFOCCF	Concerned Friends of Ontario Citizens in Care Facilities
CGRO	Coalition for Gay Rights of Ontario
CHRA	Canadian Human Rights Advocate
CHRC	Canadian Human Rights Commission
CNIB	Canadian National Institute for the Blind
COPOH	Coalition of Provincial Organizations of the Handicapped
CRF	Charter of Rights and Freedoms (Constitution Act, 1982)
IBHR	International Bill of Human Rights
IC	concept of 'institutional completeness'
ICCPR	International Covenant on Civil and Political Rights
ICESCR	International Covenant on Economic, Social, and Cultural Rights
LAR	Lesbians against the Right
MHRC	Manitoba Human Rights Commission
MLA	Meech Lake Accord (The Constitutional Amendment, 1987)
NACOVA	National Advisory Council on Voluntary Action
OHRC	Ontario Human Rights Commission
QHRC	Quebec Human Rights Commission
RCMP	Royal Canadian Mounted Police
SH	concept of 'self-help'
SHRC	Saskatchewan Human Rights Commission
TI	concept of 'total institution'
UDHR	Universal Declaration of Human Rights
UN	United Nations
UNGA	United Nations General Assembly

Key definitions and concepts

I. Alcoholic Minority

Alcoholism – condition of addiction to/dependency on alcohol.
Active alcoholic – the person who is addicted to alcohol and whose compulsive and repetitive use of alcohol interferes in any major area of his or her life.
Inactive alcoholic – the person who is remaining free of alcohol dependence; the person whose drinking habit has been arrested, permitting his or her physical and mental health, skills, and job performance to return to a normally functioning level.
Recovering alcoholic – the person who is actively seeking, taking, or has taken treatment, is following a prescribed rehabilitation course, and is continuing to have his or her recovery monitored by a treatment centre or other bona fide self-help recovery program.

II. Disabled Minorities

Disabled person – any person unable to ensure by himself or herself wholly or partly the necessities of a normal individual and/or social life, as a result of an impairment,[2] either congenital or not, in his or her physical or mental capabilities.

---

1 These definitions represent my adaptations of current terminology derived from medical, legal, and human-rights sources.
2 'Impairment' is a generic term that embraces any disturbance of or interference with the normal structure and functioning of the body, including the systems of mental function. It is characterized by a permanent or transitory psychological, physiological,

Physical disability – any degree of physical impairment, infirmity, malformation, or disfiguration, regardless of cause, that impedes the ability of the bearer to ensure by himself or herself the necessities for a normally functioning life as a member of society at large.

Mental disability – any degree of mental impairment, regardless of cause, that impedes the ability of the bearer to ensure by himself or herself the necessities for a normally functioning life as a member of society at large (includes mental retardation and mental illness).

Mental retardation – significantly subaverage general intellectual functioning existing concurrently with deficits in adaptive behaviour, and manifested during the developmental period: where 'general intellectual functioning' is defined as the results obtained by assessment with one or more of the individually administered general intelligence tests developed for that purpose; 'significantly subaverage' is defined as IQ more than two standard deviations below the mean for the test; 'adaptive behaviour' is defined as the effectiveness or degree with which an individual meets the standards of personal independence and social responsibility expected for age and cultural group; and 'developmental period' is defined as the period of time between birth and the eighteenth birthday.

The degree of mental educational retardation is classified as follows:

A, MILD: educable; IQ 50–70

B, MODERATE: trainable; IQ 35–50

C, SEVERE: untrainable; IQ 20–25

D, PROFOUND: custodial; IQ below 20

The assumptions of the professional (majority) – caretakers/educators – are as follows:

A Can usually achieve social and vocational skills adequate to minimum self-support.

B May achieve self-maintenance in unskilled or semi-skilled work under sheltered conditions.

C May contribute partially to self-maintenance under complete supervision.

D Some motor and speech development; may achieve very limited self-care. Needs nursing care.

Mental illness – this concept knows no precise boundaries and has *no* universally accepted definition.

or anatomical loss or abnormality, and includes the existence or occurrence of an abnormality, defect, or loss in a limb, organ, tissue, or other structure of the body, or in a functional system or mechanism of the body.

xxiii Key definitions and concepts

Mentally ill persons – persons professionally diagnosed as having some
type of psychological or psychiatric mental disorder (includes organic
mental disorders, substance- use disorders, for example, abuse of
alcohol and other drugs; paranoid, schizophrenic, and neurotic disorders).

Handicap – the cumulative result of the obstacles that disability interposes
between the individual person and his or her maximum functional
level.

Handicapism – negatively prejudiced feelings, attitudes, beliefs, and
discriminatory behaviours (practices, policies, laws) towards disabled
minorities based on untested, categorical assumptions about the
inferiority, incompetence, and/or dangerousness of their members'
defining characteristics.

III. Homosexual Minority

Sexual orientation – affectional and sexual preference by a person for
another person regardless of the sex of either person involved.

Homosexual (orientation/person) – affectional and sexual preference by a
person for another person of the same sex.

Heterosexual (orientation/person) – affectional and sexual preference by a
person for another person of the opposite sex.

Homophobia – irrational/morbid fear and hatred of homosexuals.

Ambisexual/Bisexual (orientation/person) – alternations in affectional and
sexual preference by a person between other persons of the same sex
and of the opposite sex.

Gay – term applied to homosexual persons who openly accept their
sexual orientation. (Applies to males and females, but the term may be
rejected by some females in favour of the more specific term 'lesbians.')

Lesbian – homosexual female.

KEY CONCEPTS

Human rights – The social-scientific concept of human rights refers to just
or justifiable claims for specified kinds of treatment made by or on
behalf of individuals or collectivities against other individuals, collectivities, or the state (Kallen, 1982).

Minority status – From a human-rights perspective, the concept of
minority status refers to the social position of any human population
whose collective, disadvantaged and subordinate status in society

derives from categorical discrimination – violations of minority members' human rights in the political, economic, social, and/or cultural
spheres of public life.

Stigma – The social-scientific concept of stigma refers to the phenomenon
of deep discreditation (Goffman, 1963). Stigma derives not from the
quality of a given human attribute, but from the discrediting label
imposed upon the assumed bearer of the negatively evaluated attribute
by societal authorities. Once imposed, the stigmatizing label brands the
assumed bearer as a less-than-human being, a virtual social outcast.

Stigmatized minority status: the process – Societal authorities with the power
to stigmatize also have the power to act upon their discrediting labels,
however erroneous and/or prejudicial these may be. Those in power
thus are able to violate the human rights of the stigmatized with
impunity, by defining them as less than human, hence unworthy of the
fundamental rights of full human beings.

Stigmatized minority status: the outcome – The long-term outcome of
human-rights violations – categorical denial of political, economic,
social, and/or cultural opportunities to members of stigmatized populations – is the social creation of stigmatized-minority status, characterized by group degradation, disadvantage, and subordination.

LABEL ME HUMAN:

Minority Rights of Stigmatized Canadians

Introduction

For the most part, human-rights issues pertaining to the conditions and claims of minority groups have been approached by social scientists from a negative stance, that is, with a view to exposing (and, ultimately, persuading majority authorities to eradicate) the insidious forms of prejudice and discrimination that underscore and sustain minority status. By way of contrast, this book will adopt a positive approach, emphasizing the inalienable individual and collective human rights of stigmatized minorities.

From a human-rights perspective, the eradication of existing prejudices and forms of discrimination is a necessary, but not sufficient, condition for the equalization of minority opportunities and for the protection of minority rights. To these ends, public policies, laws, and social practices need to be critically assessed and appropriately amended so as to provide minorities with suitable forms of redress against the long-term inequities and indignities they have suffered as collective victims of systemic discrimination. Additionally, in order to secure permanent guarantees for minority rights, specified provisions protecting the individual and collective rights of all minority groups need to be entrenched in constitutional and statutory law. In order to clarify this position for the reader, in the following pages I will present a brief overview of the juridical aspects of human rights.

Juridical aspects of human rights: international, constitutional, and statutory law

International law provides the norms of conduct or moral guide-lines governing the relationship of states and world organization in the international community (Binavince, 1987). However, as there is no international legislature, executive, or judiciary in the international community, international law lacks the authoritativeness and coercive sanctions found in domestic law. For this reason, some legal scholars argue that international law is not law at all, but simply a set of guiding moral principles to which laws, at every level, should conform.

In the enforcement of international law in Canada, a further difficulty lies in the fact that international law is not a part of the law of the land (as it is in the United States) but must be translated into Canadian law by the enactment of appropriate statutes. Ratification of international treaties and conventions by Canada, therefore, implies only an expression of *intent* to comply or enforce international law unless statutes are enacted to make them part of the law at some level of Canadian jurisdiction.

Constitutional law provides the ground rules directing the activities of the state and its government (Binavince, 1987). These rules fall into two broad categories: 1 / rules that establish the constitutional structure of the state and 2 / rules that mark out that area of 'ethical minimum of human personality from which powers of government are banned from intruding' (ibid: 9). These constitutional rules provide safeguards against state action towards the individual. Such limitations on state action are necessary because the state possesses a monopoly on authority and coercive sanction. The CRF (Constitution Act, 1982) is an example of these rules.

With specific regard to Canada, under the constitutional regime prior to 1982, the state operated under a recognition of parliamentary sovereignty. As long as provincial legislatures and the federal parliament followed the constitutional rules that governed their respective jurisdictional powers they could validly deny or infringe upon any right of anyone, 'from free speech to racial dignity' (Binavince, 1987: 10). This regime ended in 1982 when the CRF was adopted. However, it can be argued that the CRF is not, in fact, a charter of that 'ethical minimum of human personality and dignity' (ibid), for it contains two escape clauses to justify arbitrary state power. First, Section 33 of the CRF permits legislative override of Sections 2 and 7–15 (fundamental freedoms, legal rights, and equality rights). Second, Section 1 provides that all CRF rights are subject to such 'reasonable limits' prescribed by law as can be demonstrably justified in a free and democratic society. Because of this provision, no fundamental right is beyond encroachment by state action.

Statutory law regulates actions between individuals (in Canada, under federal and provincial jurisdictions) within the state. Human-rights statutes are designed to regulate the discriminatory actions of individuals against other individuals. Although these laws are simply statutes enacted by provincial legislatures and the federal parliament, the accepted view is that they have a higher status than ordinary statutes, meaning that, in cases where human-rights legislation conflicts with other statutes, the former is ordinarily enforceable (Binavince, 1987: 16).

There are other 'quasi-constitutional' statutes, such as the Canadian Bill of Rights at the level of federal jurisdiction, that afford protections for human rights. Additionally, statutory laws of general applicability often contain regulations prohibiting discrimination, for example, the provisions of the Criminal Code relating to hate propaganda (Binavince, 1987: 17).

In the Canadian context, the juridical dictates for human rights provide a three-tiered system of norms of conduct governing human relations within the state. International human-rights instruments provide the global standards to which all state legislation should conform. Constitutional rules, under the CRF and related constitutional provisions, provide the national standard to which all statutory laws (federal and provincial human-rights codes as well as laws of general applicability) should conform.

International law: global human-rights principles

Insofar as Canada has ratified the provisions of United Nations human-rights instruments, legal guarantees for the protection of human rights in this country are based upon the human-rights principles that inform the various articles of these international treaties and covenants. The three central principles behind fundamental human rights articulated in current, international human-rights instruments are those of freedom, equality, and dignity. Article 1 of the Universal Declaration of Human Rights (UDHR) (see Appendix A) states that all human beings are born free and equal in dignity and rights. Put another way, freedom, equality, and dignity are *natural rights* that accrue to every human being simply by virtue of belonging to the human species, *Homo sapiens*. From this vantage point, what becomes clear is that it is the essential biological oneness of humankind that provides the scientific underpinnings for the concept of fundamental, universal human rights (Hughes, 1982: 11).

Insofar as fundamental human rights are natural rights, ascribed to all human beings *as such*, they do not have to be earned. That is to say, fundamental human rights are inalienable rights that can be claimed equally by all human beings, regardless of demonstrated or assumed differences in talents, abilities, skills, and resources of individual persons and regardless of their membership in different human groups. As moral principles, fundamental rights can be said to be unconditional individual rights, with one important proviso: in the exercise of his or her fundamental rights, each human being must not violate, indeed must respect, the fundamental human rights of others.[1]

The content of human-rights provisions

The bulk of the articles included in the International Bill of Human Rights (IBHR, 1978) as well as in the parallel codes adopted by various national and subnational governments throughout the globe address a common, threefold theme: the right of every human being to participate in the shaping of decisions affecting his or her own life and that of the society to which he or she belongs; reasonable access to the economic resources that make that participation possible; and affirmation of the essential human worth and dignity of every person, regardless of individual qualities and/or group membership. Phrased succinctly, in sociological terms, the central or guiding principle of fundamental human rights holds that every human being qua human being has the inalienable right to equal

1 As set out under the covenants of the International Bill of Human Rights (IBHR) some of the human rights specified are subject, in practice, to certain restrictions. By and large, the IBHR provides that rights shall not be subject to any restrictions except specific legal restrictions deemed necessary to protect national security, public order, public health, or the rights and freedoms of others. Such limitations apply under the International Covenant on Civil and Political Rights (ICCPR), to the rights to liberty of movement, to freedom to leave any country, to a public hearing, to freedom of expression, to manifestation of religion or beliefs, to peaceful assembly, to freedom of association, and to form and join trade unions. In time of public emergency, which is officially proclaimed as such and in which the life of the nation is threatened, states may take measures derogating from the obligations under the Covenant, but only to the extent strictly required by the exigencies of the situation, and provided that such measures are not inconsistent with other human-rights obligations and do not involve discrimination on prohibited grounds.

There are, however, some human rights whose obligations may not be derogated, even in time of public emergency. These include the right to life; the right not to be subjected to torture or to cruel, inhuman, or degrading treatment or punishment; the prohibition against slavery or servitude; the prohibition against imprisonment solely for non-fulfilment of a contractual obligation; the prohibition of the application of ex–post-facto criminal law; the rights of every human being to be recognized as a person before the law; and the right to freedom of thought, conscience, and religion.

access to decision-making power (political rights), life-chance/opportunity (economic rights), and human dignity (social rights).

Clearly, the single most basic human right is the right to life. The fundamental principle behind the human right to life requires that every human being have access to the economic resources that maintain life. For without adequate economic maintenance – work, food, shelter, clothing – all other rights and freedoms are virtually meaningless.

Under the International Bill of Human Rights and associated human-rights instruments, the human right to economic maintenance includes not only the right to the minimal, life-maintaining essentials (which were even provided to 'chattel,' under slavery) but also the right to a decent standard of living, and to the kinds of public services – that is, medical and health care, social services, and, especially, education – that afford the institutional supports for a proper living standard in modern society. The denial of the fundamental right of economic maintenance constitutes neglect.

Freedom to decide and to determine one's own destiny is another fundamental human-rights principle. Indeed, the right to self-determination of all individuals – regardless of their race or class – was one of the earliest of the fundamental human rights to gain universal recognition, for it provided the corner-stone of the early movement to abolish slavery. The exercise of this right requires access to political power; hence, within the context of the political process, it translates into the right to the franchise. But beyond the political process, this right extends into decision-making in all life spheres: home and family, work, school, church, club, and choice of life-style. The denial of the right of individual decision-making and self-determination constitutes oppression.

The right to human dignity is another fundamental human-rights principle. It embodies the right of each individual to be held worthy, and to feel worthy, to be held in esteem and accorded respect by others, and to experience a personal sense of self-esteem and self-respect. The denial of the right to human dignity constitutes diminution (literally, to be 'made small,' to decrease in worth).

Many of the derogatory labels commonly used in identifying members of stigmatized minorities – for example, the term 'invalid,' used to describe very sick or severely disabled persons – can be seen to violate the labelled's right to human dignity. 'Invalid' (literally, 'in-valid') connotes worthlessness, uselessness, and lack of dignity; this label, and others like it (cripple, moron, idiot, faggot, dyke, drunk, junkie), serve to diminish and to deny the very humanity of their bearers.

The human right to dignity is inextricably linked with the fundamental right to economic maintenance and the fundamental freedom to decide. Without these, dignity ceases to exist. The social conditions of slavery in the United States provides a case in point.

Before the abolition of slavery in the southern United States all persons legally classified as 'Negroes' on the basis of racial criteria were defined as 'chattel' (things) and were bought and sold on the open market. As the legal 'possessions' of their white masters, Negro slaves were kept illiterate; they were summarily denied freedom to decide, and they were stripped of all vestiges of human dignity. Yet, they were provided with the basic life necessities – food, clothing, and shelter – for their labour was essential to the white-controlled plantation economy. Moreover, they were treated kindly – in the fashion of children – as long as they 'knew their place and stayed in their place' (Van den Berghe, 1967).

This kind of paternalistic treatment of an entire class of human beings constitutes a classic example of wholesale violations of human rights: oppression, neglect, and diminution. Yet, as this book will demonstrate, paternalistic policies and practices – especially towards institutionalized minorities – continue today in Canada and elsewhere.

The right-to-equality principle is probably one of the most misunderstood (and variously interpreted) of all tenets of fundamental human rights. The right to equality essentially represents equality of opportunity. Equality does not necessarily mean sameness. What it does imply, from a human-rights view, is equal concern for all. Equal concern, in some instances, may be appropriately expressed in equal (standard) treatment, but in other instances, equivalent (special) compensatory treatment may be required.

In those instances where standard treatment of members of different populations affords true equality of opportunity, application of the principle of equal (same) treatment is required. Openly gay persons, recovering alcoholics, and members of other stigmatized minorities must be afforded the same opportunities as their equally qualified majority counterparts to enter the professional fields of their choice, to obtain jobs commensurate with their skills, to obtain deserved promotions, and so forth.

Alternatively, in those instances where standard treatment denies true equality of opportunity, application of the principle of equivalent treatment is required.

For example: Equal concern for the educational opportunities of the wheelchair-bound, as well as for the ambulatory members of Canadian society, would be expressed architecturally, where educational facilities are equipped with ramps and handrails as well as with stairs. In this particular example, the provision of equal (standard) treatment for all, in the form of access to the facility by open stairways only, would not provide equal opportunity for the mobility-impaired minority members. Access to the facility for persons disabled with unstable gait and for the chair-bound disabled would be seriously impeded, if not entirely prevented. This example is but one of the multitude of documented instances, where, in order to offset the handicapping effects of a disability, special compensatory measures (e.g., architectural modifications to buildings) must be provided. In these cases, equivalent, rather than equal (standard) treatment is required to ensure real equality of opportunity.

The two forms of equality of opportunity are reflected in the respective provisions of Sections 1 and 2 of the equality-rights clause (15) of the CRF. The first, the non-discrimination provision, guarantees the principle of standard treatment; the second provision (notwithstanding the first) guarantees the principle of equivalent treatment, where necessary.

The foregoing conceptualization of individual human rights is summarized in the following scheme:

Societal sector	Human rights	Human-rights violation
Political	Freedom of choice/ self-determination	Oppression
Economic	Equal/equivalent opportunity	Neglect
Social	Human dignity	Diminution

In the following section of this chapter, I will briefly address the development of these principles in international human-rights instruments.

The International Bill of Human Rights: an overview

On 10 December 1948, the United Nations General Assembly proclaimed the Universal Declaration of Human Rights (UDHR), a declaration that represents a statement of principles or moral guidelines for the recognition and protection of human rights throughout the globe. Since its proclamation, the Universal Declaration has had international impact, influencing national constitutions and laws, as well as international resolutions such as the Declaration on the Rights of the Child (1959) and the Declaration on the Rights of Disabled Persons (1975). Its impact notwithstanding, the UDHR represents only a general statement of ideals: it is morally but not legally binding on member states of the United Nations. Some countries, seeking a more forceful agreement, accordingly pressed for a treaty that would establish binding obligations on the part of member states. As a result, two additional covenants were drawn up and came into force in 1976. Their provisions, however, apply only to those member states that have decided to ratify them. To date, some 70 of the UN's 155 members, including Canada, have ratified each one.

The first covenant, the International Covenant on Economic, Social, and Cultural Rights (ICESCR), deals primarily with collective rights – defined as rights due to all people of a society that are the responsibility of governments to provide. The second covenant, the International Covenant on Civil and Political Rights (ICCPR), deals with individual rights – freedoms and responsibilities that all individual citizens must be allowed to exercise.

The International Covenant on Economic, Social, and Cultural Rights adopts a collective societal or nation-wide perspective, putting the onus on governments to provide adequate living conditions for all persons. The covenant recognizes that all persons have a right to work, to fair wages, to social security, to freedom from hunger, to health and education, and to form and be members of trade unions. While considerable time may be required, especially for developing countries, to implement all of these rights, nations choosing to ratify the covenant are expected to undertake appropriate efforts following ratification.

The International Covenant on Civil and Political Rights adopts an individual perspective, placing the onus on nations and judiciaries to protect all individual citizens against cruel, inhuman, and degrading treatment. This covenant recognizes the right of every person to life, liberty, security, and privacy. It prohibits slavery, guarantees the right to a fair trial, and protects against arbitrary arrest or detention. It recognizes freedom of expression, freedom of association, and the right to peaceful assembly and emigration.

These rights and freedoms that guarantee protection to the individual include protection from abuses by governments. The burden of responsibility to uphold individual freedoms, therefore, lies not with governments but with the judicial system.

Nations that ratify this covenant are expected to introduce laws that will reflect its provisions. Canada has taken measures to fulfil its

Enforcement

commitment by enacting human-rights legislation at both provincial and federal levels of jurisdiction and by entrenching the Charter of Rights and Freedoms (CRF) in the Canadian Constitution (1982).

The Optional Protocol to the ICCPR provides individual citizens with direct recourse to the United Nations. Persons who believe that their rights as specified in the covenant have been violated can state their case before the UN Human Rights Committee. Such persons must first have exhausted all legal avenues within their own country. To date, Canada is one of only twenty-eight of the nations signing the covenant that have ratified the Optional Protocol.

Canada's response to the IBHR

Since the proclamation of the UDHR, Canada has made significant progress in promoting the full recognition and protection of human rights throughout the country. As indicated previously, Canada's legal measures for the protection of human rights and freedoms fall into two categories: constitutional law and statutory law.

The 1982 Charter of Rights and Freedoms, which is entrenched in Canada's Constitution and binding on all levels of government, generally follows the model of the ICCPR. The constitutional CRF limits the power of the state to take action, such as arrest, against individual citizens. It also limits the scope of legislation that the state can pass. Laws that violate fundamental human rights, for example, laws denying freedom of association or freedom of speech, are not permissible.

Anti-discrimination legislation in the form of human-rights codes or acts has been enacted by the federal and all provincial governments. These statutory laws apply to private transactions, such as employment and the renting of accommodation, and to governments, as in the case of public-service employment or the provision of social assistance. Most provinces also have an ombudsman's office that investigates individual complaints against the government.

Internationally, Canada has ratified numerous conventions through the United Nations and other international organizations, such as the International Labour Organization. These include the UN Declaration on the Elimination of All Forms of Racial Discrimination (1963), the Declaration on the Rights of Mentally Retarded Persons (1971), the Declaration on the Rights of Disabled Persons (1975), and the Convention on the Elimination of All Forms of Discrimination against Women (1981). Canada is one of few countries to have acceded to the UDHR, the two covenants, and the Optional Protocol under the IBHR. The East European nations have all signed the Covenant on Civil and Political Rights, but none has signed the Optional Protocol. The United States has signed neither of the covenants. Because Canada has chosen to ratify the IBHR as a whole, it is incumbent upon this country to bring its constitution and its federal and provincial laws into line with the moral guide-lines of all of the provisions of the IBHR. It is important to note, however, that Canada's adoption of the declaration, covenants, and protocol does not automatically update the rules, policies, and laws of every company, organization, and level of government in the country. At every level of Canadian society there are formal regulations and informal practices that are contrary to the principles of human rights. Violations of omission and commission in the innumerable laws and regulations enacted in the past require considerable time and attention in order to be properly redrafted so as to conform fully with international human-rights principles.

As articulated in the provisions of the IBHR and associated covenants, international human-rights principles represent the global standards to which the laws of all ratifying states should conform. Universal human-rights principles should not, however, be confused with legal rights, that is, rights recognized as such in law. Fundamental human-rights principles may become incorporated into various national and international legal statutes (human-rights legislation); then again, they may not (discriminatory legislation). One of the most important points to be made about fundamental human rights is that they are prior to law. Laws themselves may violate human rights.

Human rights as minority rights

In no known human society have the laws of the nation served to guarantee equal protection for the human rights of all individual persons and all human groups within the society. Indeed, throughout human history, majorities typically have used legal discrimination as one of their most effective techniques of domination, persecution, and even extermination of stigmatized minorities.

Today, however, minorities can seek to alter this situation. In order to secure protection for their individual and collective human rights, minorities may now invoke national and international human-rights instruments. As will be shown in the following pages, however, there is far less protection afforded for the *collective cultural rights* of minorities than for minority members' individual human rights. Indeed, the notion of collective rights under the IBHR is used primarily to refer to the right of a national population as a whole to be provided by its government with adequate living conditions and associated economic rights. The collective rights of minorities as distinctive cultural groups *within states* are afforded only negative protection (under Article 27, ICCPR).

Collective human rights

Scholarly critics of current, internationally recognized human-rights instruments – especially the UDHR, which sets out in detail the various individual human rights and freedoms – have argued that these instruments, with their highly individualistic focus, clearly reflect the Western liberal-democratic ideological bias of their drafters and supporters. Thus, they promote individual rights and freedoms at the expense of any real guarantees for collective rights. Put another way, the argument put forward by critics is that, in these instruments, the principle of human unity clearly is given priority over the principle of cultural diversity.

This criticism notwithstanding, there are at least two articles with direct implications for collective rights that may serve as guiding principles for our purpose of conceptualizing minority rights.

The first article to be considered is the only one that specifically addresses minority rights. Article 27 of the ICCPR speaks directly to the rights of minorities within states where they exist: 'In those States in which ethnic, religious or linguistic minorities exist, persons belonging to such minorities shall not be denied the right, in community with other members of their group, to enjoy their own culture, to profess and practice their own religion, or to use their own language' (United Nations, 1978: 30).

Whether or not this article can be interpreted as providing a basis for collective minority claims remains a matter of some debate among legal scholars. Some suggest that the wording refers to individual members of minorities rather than to minorities as collectivities. A great many scholars, however, seem to be of the opinion that the article should be interpreted collectively (Leavy, 1979).[2]

Legal invocation and interpretation of the minority-rights article clearly reveal that it is the ethnocultural underpinnings of minority status that

2 The July 1981 decision by the United Nations Human Rights Commission, in support of Canadian Indian Women's rights (in the Sandra Lovelace case) invoked Article 27 in a collective, cultural sense and thus lent strong support to the interpretation favouring collective minority rights.

provide the recognized grounds for minority-rights claims. Yet, insofar as the article addresses 'culture' as a category distinct and separate from language and religion, I will argue that, *in principle*, the concept of culture could be interpreted so as to include all minority subcultures and alternate life-styles whose values are consistent with human-rights principles. This broader, social-scientific interpretation of culture could afford protection to ethnic and other minorities for their collective cultural and/or subcultural rights.

Even more problematic than Article 27 (ICCPR), with regard to its potential for offering protection to *non*-ethnic minority groups, is Article 1 of the ICESCR, which provides the international norm for the right of self-determination of peoples. It reads as follows: 'All peoples have the right of self-determination; by virtue of that right they freely determine their political status and freely pursue their economic, social and cultural development' (United Nations, 1978: 10).

Legal invocation and interpretation of the peoples'-rights article (ICESCR) indicates that the concept of 'peoples' has been very narrowly defined so as to support the right to self-determination only in the cases of 'nations' formerly under colonial rule by overseas states (Wiberg, 1981). This very limited definition excludes both ethnic and non-ethnic groups living within sovereign states from making claims for autonomy. Yet, in principle, the concept of people's rights, like the concept of minority rights, could be more broadly defined so as to afford both ethnic and other minority groups recognition for their collective right to some form and degree of group autonomy.

Minority rights: international and national bases for minority claims[3]

The international human-rights instruments that I have drawn upon in my discussion provide the current guiding principles upon which minority collectivities throughout the globe may justifiably base their claims. Yet, given the narrow sense in which these documents have been legally interpreted, it seems clear that they cannot, as yet, be counted upon to provide protection for the collective rights of stigmatized non-ethnic minorities.

In Canada, as internationally, human-rights instruments provide a

3 The social-scientific concept of minority claims, as used in this book, refers to just or justifiable claims for distinctive or specialized kinds of treatment made by or on behalf of minorities as individual members or as groups against other individuals, social collectivities, or governments.

clearer and more comprehensive basis for individual rights claims than for collective cultural claims. Nevertheless, I will argue that, in accordance with the guide-lines afforded by CRF provisions, two kinds of minority-rights claims may be put forward collectively under the provisions of constitutional and statutory law. These two types of claims may be conceptualized as *categorical* and *collective* rights claims.

Categorical claims may be brought forward by minority representatives under the equality-rights provisions of the CRF (Section 15(2)) and under parallel statutory provisions. Categorical-rights claims seek collective forms of redress to counter the adverse impact of systemic discrimination against the minority as a collective entity. Categorical claims may be put forward by minority representatives as group-oriented claims, but such claims should not be confused with group claims based on collective cultural rights. In order to make this distinction clear, I will refer to minority claims for collective redress against systemic violations of members' *individual* (political, economic, and/or social) human rights as claims based on categorical rights. Forms of redress sought in categorical claims may involve special measures such as job recruitment or special training programs. These programs of 'affirmative action'[4] entail temporary or permanent measures of special treatment (positive discrimination) towards minorities. Such measures are allowed by the Charter as justifiable means of working towards the actualization of the ultimate goal of equity of opportunity and treatment.

Insofar as categorical claims do not address collective cultural rights, they can justifiably be put forward by minorities with or without a viable cultural base. Alternatively, collective-rights claims seek redress against cultural discrimination. Accordingly, these claims can justifiably be put forward under constitutional and statutory legal provisions only by minorities with distinctive subcultures or life-styles. In the case of those non-ethnic minorities that have developed viable and legitimate subcultures, I will argue that claims for collective cultural rights parallel to claims of ethnic minorities can justifiably be brought forward under the guide-lines of the CRF (Section 27).[5] In this connection, my argument

4 For a detailed account and critique of the present state of affirmative action in Canada, see chapter 7.
5 Canadian legal scholars are divided in opinion with regard to the interpretation of Section 27 of the CRF. Some argue that it is only an interpretive provision, which can serve to reinforce other substantive constitutional provisions, but which cannot stand on its own. Others argue that it may afford protection for collective cultural rights (see Beckton, 1987; Sanders, 1987; Magnet, 1987).

parallels that of the case made for collective subcultural rights under the concurrent provisions of Section 27 of the ICCPR. I will elaborate, at a later point in this book, on the ways in which Section 27 of the constitutional CRF can provide an important legal resource for the protection of both ethnic and non-ethnic minority subcultures in Canada.

Special mention: human rights of disabled minorities

While the fundamental human rights of disabled minorities are recognized and protected under the framework of international instruments protecting all human beings, it has long been evident that these instruments were not designed to meet the special needs of disabled persons. Accordingly, in the last decade two international proclamations have been declared by the United Nations General Assembly: one, specifically designed to protect the rights of the mentally retarded, and the other, more broadly designed to protect the rights of all physically and mentally disabled persons (see Appendices C and D). These instruments make it very clear that in the case of disabled minorities standard (equal) treatment is insufficient and that equivalent (compensatory) treatment, geared to the special needs of disabled minorities as distinct human collectivities, is required, in some cases, on a permanent basis.

Under Section 15(2) of the CRF (Constitution Act, 1982), the provision that allows measures of affirmative action, mentally and physically disabled minorities are included in the enumerated grounds (see Appendix B). For disabled minorities, this Charter provision is critical, for it affords constitutional sanction for equivalent treatment, geared to special needs. The inclusion of disabled minorities under this CRF provision represents a monumental constitutional breakthrough, and one that marks the successful end of a long and hard-fought struggle beset by seemingly insurmountable obstacles.

However, for the disabled and for other stigmatized minorities in Canada, the battle is not yet won. As will be shown in the following pages, the current picture of human-rights protection under constitutional and statutory law in Canada reveals marked inconsistencies. The task of bringing all Canadian legislation into conformity with international human-rights guide-lines so as to provide equity for minorities remains a formidable one.

Constitutional and statutory protection for minority rights in Canada

While Canada has ratified all of the international human-rights instruments drawn upon thus far in this discussion, the fulfilment of governments' obligation to develop and/or to modify legislation in conformity with these moral guide-lines has proceeded slowly and unevenly throughout the country. The inclusion of the CRF in Canada's constitution (Canada Act, 1982) was designed, in part, to remedy this situation by providing a nation-wide standard to which all statutory law should conform. Yet, the provisions of the Charter itself afford differential and unequal protection for minority rights across population categories.

My earlier discussion of Section 27 of the CRF notwithstanding, the most crucial section of the Charter for non-ethnic minorities is Section 15, under equality rights. The enumerated non-discriminatory grounds of this provision include only race, national or ethnic origin, colour, religion, sex, age, and mental or physical disability (see Appendix B). Legal opinion, however, strongly supports the position that the provisions of Section 15 are 'open': that is to say, they are not limited to the enumerated grounds. Thus, minorities not included under the provision's enumerated grounds (for example, homosexuals and recovering alcoholics) also should be able to claim protection against discrimination under Section 15 of the CRF (Beckton, 1987). Legal scholars also seem to agree, however, that the potential claims of non-enumerated minorities are seriously weakened by the constitutional act of omission. Insofar as the CRF provides the constitutional standard to which all statutory law should conform, legal opinion supports the argument that it is a flawed instrument insofar as it does not provide for equality for all. Under its designated 'equality rights' provisions, it provides a stronger basis for the claims of enumerated minorities than for the parallel claims of non-enumerated minorities.

The current picture of statutory human-rights legislation in Canada exhibits even greater disparities in its protections across minority categories, particularly with regard to the enumerated, prohibited grounds of discrimination and to the societal sectors in which non-discriminatory provisions apply. Some statutes have closed clauses that limit their sphere of jurisdiction to enumerated non-discriminatory grounds, while others are more open and can include minority claims based on non-enumerated grounds under such general grounds as 'social condition' or 'reasonable cause.'

A brief glance at the two charts 1 and 2, documented by the Canadian Human Rights Foundation, reveals that the more traditional non-discriminatory grounds – race, colour, religion, religious belief, ethnic and national origin, and sex – have become publicly and legally recognized as 'legitimate' prohibited gounds virtually everywhere

SCHÉMA 1
L'énumération des motifs de discrimination dans les divers Codes et Chartes des droits de la personne au Canada +

| | Juridiction/ | | | | | | |
MOTIFS MENTIONNÉS	F*ÉD.	C.-B. B.C.	A.	S.	M.	O.	Q.
Race	X	X	X	X	X	X	X
Couleur	X	X	X	X	X	X	X
Religion	X	X	X	X	X		X
Croyance						X	
Nationalité			X	X			
Origine nationale	X		X		X		X
Ascendance		X	X	X	X	X	
Origine ethnique	X				X	X	X
Lieu d'origine		X	X	X		X	
Citoyenneté						X	
Sexe	X	X	X	X	X	X	X
Orientation sexuelle					[X]	[X]	X
Grossesse	X		X	X			X
Âge (1)	X	X	X	X	X	X	X
Handicap physique	X	X	X	X	X	X	X
Handicap mental	X	X			X	X	X
État civil							X
Situation de famille (2)	X				X	X	
État matrimonial	X	X	X	X	X	X	
Convictions politiques (3)		X			X		X
Origine sociale							
Condition sociale							X
Provenance des revenus (4)					X	X	
État de personne grâciée	X						
Casier judiciaire (5)		X				X	X
Langue							X
Sans motif raisonnable (6)					X		
Notamment (7)							

(+) Schémas conçus et annotés par Daniel Proulx, professeur à la Faculté de droit de l'Université d'Ottawa.

(*) Le Yukon et les T.N.-O. étant soumis à la *Loi canadienne sur les droits de la personne*, les *Fair Practices Ordinances* de ces deux territoires ont été omis, d'autant plus qu'ils n'ajoutent pas significativement aux motifs énumérés dans la loi fédérale.

CHART 1
Enumerated grounds
of discrimination in
Canadian human-rights
legislation +

| Jurisdiction | | | | | ENUMERATED GROUNDS |
N.-B.	N.-É. N.S.	Î.-P.-É. P.E.I.	T.-N. N.	CONST.	
X	X	X	X	X	Race
X	X	X		X	Colour
X	X	X	X	X	Religion
X	X	X	X		Creed
					Nationality
X	X	X	X	X	National origin
X					Ancestry
	X	X	X	X	Ethnic origin
X					Place of origin
					Citizenship
X	X	X	X	X	Sex
					Sexual orientation
					Pregnancy
X	X	X	X	X	Age (1)
X	X	X	X	X	Physical disability
				X	Mental disability
					Civil status
					Family status (2)
X	X	X	X		Marital status
		X	X		Political convictions (3)
			X		Social origin
					Social condition
	X				Source of income (4)
					Pardoned conviction
					Record of offences (5)
					Language
					Without reasonable cause (6)
			X		In particular (7)

(+) Charts conceived and annotated by Prof. Daniel Proulx, Faculty of Law, University of Ottawa.

(*) The Yukon and Northwest Territories are governed by the federal *Canadian Human Rights Act*, to whose enumerated grounds their *Fair Practices Ordinances* add little. They are thus omitted in the Chart.

[X] Recent amendments (added by author)

SCHÉMA 2

Les domaines d'activité proteges contre la discrimination par les divers Codes et Chartes des droits de la personne au Canada*

DOMAINS PROTEGÉS	F E D.	C.-B. B.C.	A.	S.	M.	Juridiction/ O.
Publicité						
Affichage, annonces écrites	X	X	X	X	X	X
Messages radio ou télé				X	X	
Propogande téléphonique	X					
Louage						
Logement (1)	X	X	X	X	X	X
Local commercial	X	X	X	X	X	X
Biens, services et lieux publics (2)	X	X	X	X	X	X
Emploi						
Embauche et conditions de travail (3)	X	X	X	X	X	X
Formulaires de demande d'emploi	X		X	X	X	X
Annonces (4)	X	X	X	X	X	X
Enquêtes et entrevues	X		X	X	X	X
Bureau de placement		X	X	X	X	X
Salaire égal	X	X	X			
Harcèlement (5)	X					X
Liberté d'association						
Association partonale ou professionnelle		X	X	X	X	X
Association de salariés	X	X	X	X	X	X
Liberté d'entreprise				X		
Instruments juridiques						
Contrats mobiliers (6)				X	X	X
Contrats immobiliers (7)		X		X	X	X
Actes juridiques (8)						
Accès à l'éducation (9)				X	X	

* Etant formulé comme une norme generale d'egalité devant la loi, l'art. 15 de la Charte canadienne ne protège pas certains domaines d'activité de manière expresse.

CHART 2

Activities in which discrimination is prohibited in Canadian human-rights legislation*

Q.	N.-B.	N.-É. N.S.	Î.-P.-É. P.E.I.	T.-N. N.	ACTIVITIES COVERED
					Advertising
X	X	X	X	X	Signs, symbols, notices
	X	X	X	X	Radio or television messages
					Telephone messages
					Leases
X	X	X	X	X	Dwellings (1)
X	X	X	X	X	Commercial premises
X	X	X	X	X	Public goods, services and facilities (2)
					Employment
X	X	X	X	X	Hiring and conditions of employment (3)
X	X	X	X	X	Job application forms
	X	X		X	Advertisements (4)
X	X	X	X		Enquiries and interviews
X	X	X	X	X	Employment agency
X			X	X	Equal pay
X				X	Harassment (5)
					Freedom of association
X	X	X	X		Professional or employers' associations
X	X	X	X	X	Employees' associations
					Free enterprise
					Legal documents
X	X				Contracts (6)
X	X	X	X		Purchase of real property (7)
X					Juridical acts (8)
X					Education (9)

Jurisdiction

* Excluding the Canadian Charter, whose s. 15 is a general rule of equality before the law without specifying particular activities.

SCHÉMA 1 – NOTES

(1) L'âge signifie 18 ans ou plus en Ontario; 19 ans et plus au N.-B.; entre 18 et 65 ans en Sask., à l'Î.-P.-É. et, dans l'emploi seulement, en Ontario; entre 19 et 65 ans à T.-N.; entre 40 et 65 ans en N.-É. et entre 45 et 65 ans en C.-B. Seuls le Québec et le Manitoba n'ont pas donné de définition visant à restreindre le sens de ce motif. Par ailleurs, l'âge n'est interdit que dans l'emploi en C.-B., en Alberta, en N.-É. et à T.-N. Toutes les juridictions, à l'exception du Québec et du Manitoba, prévoient que la retraite forcée en vertu d'un régime de pension n'est pas discriminatoire. La loi peut aussi, au fédéral, au Québec, au Manitoba, en Sask. et à l'Î.-P.-É. fixer un âge minimal pour l'accès aux services et lieux publics ou à certains emplois.

(2) Les motifs de «*marital status*» et de «*family status*» ne sont définis, de façon différente d'ailleurs, qu'en Ontario et au Manitoba. En outre ces deux motifs ne sont interdits que dans le secteur de l'emploi en Alberta et en N.-É.

(3) En C.-B. et au Manitoba, ce motif n'est interdit que dans l'emploi.

(4) Ce motif, exprimé de manière différente dans les trois provinces qui le mentionnent [ex.: "source of income" (Manitoba); "receipt of public assistance" (Ontario); "receipt income maintenance payments from ... government or ... under the terms of a court order or separation agreement" (N.-É.)], semble surtout destiné à protéger les «assistés sociaux» et son application est limitée au domaine du logement.

(5) Interdit dans l'emploi seulement.

(6) Dans le logement, les services et lieux publics, mais non dans l'emploi, toute discrimination est interdite au Manitoba "*unless reasonable cause exists*".

(7) Contrairement aux Codes et Chartes statutaires qui énumèrent exhaustivement un certain nombre de motifs discriminatoires interdits, l'art. 15 de la Charte constitutionnelle n'est pas limité aux neuf motifs qui y sont mentionnés.

SCHÉMA 2 – NOTES

(1) Au fédéral, au Québec, en Ontario et à T.-N., on interdit en plus le «harcèlement» dans la fourniture de logements ou de locaux commerciaux. Les Codes de l'Ontario et de T.-N. définissent le «harcèlement» ainsi: "engaging in a course of vexatious comment or conduct that is known or ought reasonably to be known to be unwelcome".

(2) Alors que la Charte québécoise semble limiter ce domaine à l'entreprise privée (art. 15), la loi manitobaine l'étend expressément aux institutions municipales et scolaires, aux régies et autres organismes gouvernementaux (a. 3). Ailleurs, il est question, sans plus de précision, de biens, services et commodités «destinés au public» ("*customarily available to the public*") sauf en Ontario où cette expression consacrée a été retranchée en 1982. Le «harcèlement» dans ce domaine n'est interdit qu'au Québec et au fédéral.

(3) La Charte québécoise étend le champ protégé à la période d'apprentissage, de probation et de formation professionnelle. En N.-É. et à l'Î.-P.-É., la loi protège spécifiquement les bénévoles mais à condition qu'ils travaillent dans un organisme public comme un hôpital ou un service de pompiers.

(4) Au Québec et en C.-B., les offres d'emploi discriminatoires dans les journaux ou ailleurs sont visées par l'interdiction de la discrimination dans l'affichage et les annonces.

(5) Le harcèlement dans l'emploi fondé sur tout motif discriminatoire est prohibé au Québec, au fédéral, en Ontario et à T.-N. De plus, la loi fédérale tient à préciser que le harcèlement sexuel est «réputé être fondé sur un motif de distinction illicite» et les Codes d'Ontario et de T.-N. ajoutent que les «avances sexuelles» ("*sexual solicitation*") sont interdites de la part des supérieurs hiérarchiques.

(6) Ces contrats sont visés à condition de n'être pas de nature purement privée (soit "*offered to the public*"), sauf au N.-B. en on Ontario où cette condition n'existe pas.

(7) Domaine limité aux contrats de vente d'une propriété ou de l'un des ses démembrements.

(8) Cette notion inclut mais déborde celle de contrat. Les clauses discriminatoires sont prohibées dans tous les actes juridiques (a. 13), mais ces derniers doivent porter sur des biens ou services ordinairement offerts au public pour qu'il soit interdit de refuser de le conclure avec un individu pour cause de discrimination (a. 12).

(9) Au Québec, l'éducation publique est non seulement un secteur d'activité exempt de discrimination en vertu de la Charte, mais un droit comme tel (a. 40). La Charte québécoise a en effet la particularité de proclamer un catalogue complet de droits et libertés et, par surcroît, de prévoir que leur jouissance est garantie en pleine égalité (a. 10.).

CHART 1 – NOTES

(1) "Age" means age of 18 or over in Ont.; 19 or over in N.B.; between 18 and 65 in Sask., P.E.I. and, only with regard to employment, Ont.; between 19 and 65 in Nfld; between 40 and 65 in N.S.; and between 45 and 65 in B.C. Only Que. and Man. do not qualify the term "age" with a definition. B.C., Alta., N.S. and Nfld. apply this ground only to employment.
All jurisdictions but Que. and Man. provide that forced retirement within a pension scheme is not discriminatory. The fed., Que., Man., Sask. and P.E.I. legislation may set a minimum age for access to certain types of employment or goods and facilities available to the public.

(2) Only Que. and Man. define "marital status" and "family status", and they do so in different ways. In Alta. and N.S. these grounds apply only to employment.

(3) In B.C. and Man., "political convictions" applies only to employment.

(4) This ground is expressed differently by each of the three jurisdictions that include it: "source of income" (Man.), "receipt of public assistance" (Ont.), "receipt of income or maintenance payments from ... government or ... under the terms of a court order or separation agreement". (N.S.). It appears to be aimed particularly at beneficiaries of social assistance, and applies in each case only to dwelling leases.

(5) "Record of offences" applies only to employment.

(6) Under Man. legislation, any discrimination in dwelling leases and in services and facilities available to the public is forbidden "unless reasonable cause exists". This does not apply to employment.

(7) Section 15 of the Canadian Charter, unlike all the statutory Codes and Charters, provides expressly that its coverage is not limited to the nine grounds it enumerates.

CHART 2 – NOTES

(1) "Harassment" also applies to leasing, of dwellings and of commercial premises, in fed., Que., Ont. and Nfld. legislation. The Ont. and Nfld. Codes define "harassment" as "engaging in a course of vexatious comment or conduct that is known or ought reasonably be known to be unwelcome".

(2) Que. seems to limit this activity to the private sector (s. 15); Man. extends it expressly to municipal corporations, educational institutions, and to boards, commissions, and other agents of the Crown (s.3). Elsewhere this activity is described only as services, goods and facilities "customarily available to the public", except in Ont., where those qualifying terms have been removed. "Harassment" in this activity is prohibited only by fed and Que. legislation.

(3) This activity includes apprenticeship, probation, and vocational training in Que.; N.S. and P.E.I. specifically cover volunteers working for agencies carrying out public functions (e.g. fire protection, hospital services).

(4) In B.C. and Que., employment ads are also covered by the prohibition of discrimination in "signs, symbols, notices".

(5) "Harassment" in employment, on any ground, is prohibited by fed., Ont., Que. and Nfld. legislation. In particular, under fed. legislation sexual harassment "shall be deemed to be harassment on a prohibited ground of discrimination", and distinct provisions in Ont. and Nfld. forbid "sexual solicitation" by a "person in a position to confer, grant or deny a benefit or advancement".

(6) Except in Ont. and N.B., where all contracts are covered, this activity includes only contracts "offered to the public".

(7) "Purchase of real property" includes the purchase of any interest in land.

(8) "Judicial acts" includes, but is not restricted to, all contracts. Discriminatory clauses are prohibited in all juridical acts, in Que. The refusal to contract with a person on a discriminatory ground, however, is forbidden only insofar as the contemplated contract concerns a service or good ordinarily offered to the public.

(9) Under the Quebec Charter, public education is not only an activity in which discrimination is prohibited, but a service to which access is itself a right (s. 40). It is its complete catalogue of fundamental rights, including a general equality provision, which distinguishes the Quebec Charter from other human rights legislation.

throughout the country. What also is clearly revealed, however, is that grounds such as sexual orientation and history of alcohol abuse, which could protect the fundamental human rights of two of the most deeply stigmatized minorities – homosexuals and recovering alcoholics, respectively – are far less commonly recognized and protected. Indeed, to date, despite almost continuous lobbying efforts and despite numerous recommendations by various human-rights commissions for amendments to legislation, 'sexual orientation' is specified only in the Charter of the Province of Quebec, in the Ontario and Manitoba human-rights codes, and under the prohibited grounds of the new (1987) Human Rights Act of the Yukon Territory. With regard to history of alcohol abuse, only the federal government and that of Prince Edward Island, in recent amendments to their acts, afford protection for recovering/recovered alcoholics (under the general rubric of physical disability).

Despite the fact that mental disability is included in the enumerated non-discriminatory grounds of the constitutional CRF, under statutory human-rights legislation, only the federal and Yukon governments and the provincial governments of the British Columbia, Manitoba, Ontario, and Quebec, thus far, have specified this ground.

At present, among the most complex and variable provisions in the area of human-rights protection are those afforded in the case of physically disabled minorities. While virtually all Canadian human-rights legislation currently lists physical disability among the enumerated prohibited grounds, the exact disabling conditions covered, as well as the particular sectors and services in which the legislation applies, vary considerably from one constituency to another.[6]

The foregoing overview of the protections afforded minority rights in Canada under the provisions of constitutional and statutory law reveals marked disparities across diverse population categories. While barriers to the acceptance of some minorities as full and equal human beings appear to have been removed, such is clearly not so for others. For many deeply stigmatized minorities in Canada, tenacious barriers rooted in public prejudice and fed by unwarranted, yet persistent, derogatory minority stereotypes continue to impede public acknowledgment of minority members as full and equal human beings.

6 The reader should note here that virtually all legislation lists 'exceptions,' and that some statutes vary their specified grounds with reference to different sectors of application (e.g., public signs and notices vs housing or employment). For exact details on any given piece of legislation, the reader is strongly advised to consult the primary source.

The breaking of these remaining barriers will not occur without a fundamental change in Canadian public attitudes and practices towards stigmatized minorities. It is my hope that this book will shed light on the role of public prejudice and discrimination in perpetuating the stigmatized status of Canadian minorities and that it will contribute to a growing, public acknowledgment of minority rights in this country.

Quebec
Charter of Rights + Freedoms

1

Deviance and ethnicity: social-scientific approaches to the study of minority groups

My experience over more than fifteen years of teaching a social-science course on minorities and human rights in Canada revealed that there was a real need for a theoretical framework that could facilitate the analysis of human-rights issues pertaining to both ethnic and non-ethnic minorities. Traditionally, social scientists have focused their analytic attention upon one or the other of these two types of minorities. Accordingly, their analyses have been informed by somewhat different conceptual perspectives. Racial and ethnic minorities have been analysed from the approach of ethnic relations and social stratification: from this view, these populations have long been conceptualized as 'minorities.' Non-ethnic minorities have been analysed from the approaches of medical pathology and social deviance: from this view, these populations have long been conceptualized as 'deviants.'

In the attempt to teach an undergraduate course that addressed human-rights issues germane to both types of minorities, I deemed it essential to develop a conceptual design that would integrate pertinent aspects of both theoretical approaches. My formulation of such a design is represented in the theoretical framework of this book.

In this chapter, a historical overview of the theories drawn upon in the development of the conceptual framework for this book will be presented.

FROM DEVIANCE TO MINORITY THEORY

The social-scientific study of majority/minority relations traditionally has focused upon racial and ethnic minorities. Accordingly, early definitions and explanatory models of majority/minority relations were not designed to include non-ethnic population categories within their purview. Sagarin (1971) was among the first social scientists to argue that the themes of negative, group-based judgments; collective discrimination; collective consciousness of oppression; and subordinate social status – commonly found in prevailing definitions of racial and ethnic minorities – were equally applicable to similarly disadvantaged and stigmatized non-ethnic collectivities. Following from this assertion, Sagarin argued persuasively that women, children, aged, homosexuals, alcoholics, mentally and physically disabled, and so forth, could be conceptualized and analysed as minorities.

The non-ethnic minorities that have provided key target populations for social-scientific research have been analysed for the most part from the perspective of deviance theory. The traditional sociological approach to deviance orginated in social pathology and was concerned primarily with an etiological explanation for deviant behaviour. Heavily influenced by the medical model, traditional theory and research focused on the individual 'deviant' (rather than on the category of deviant persons), for it was in individual pathology that the source (cause) of the deviance was assumed to be located. The medical model of deviance – whether derived from psychological, psychiatric, or psychoanalytical theories – assumes that some identifiable psychological abnormality or mental disorder in the individual is the determining cause of the deviant behaviour.

Over time, social scientists became increasingly critical of this approach, arguing that it is based on tautological reasoning. The medical model, they pointed out, 'diagnoses' deviant behaviour as evidence of psychological disturbance (its assumed cause) without being able to measure the cause independently of the behaviour itself (Conrad and Schneider, 1980). Further, the medical model fails to take into serious account the social nature of deviance. The critical role of the social audience with its norms and sanctions against deviance, the political processes of defining and controlling deviant behaviour, and even the possibility of learning deviant life-styles – all of these social factors are overlooked (or discounted) in the preoccupation with internal medical causes (ibid).

In reaction against and in contradistinction to the medical model, social scientists, in recent years, have developed a number of alternative models of social deviance based on conflict theory and labelling theory. Labelling theorists, such as Becker (1963), are among the most vehement opponents of the medical model of deviance. They argue that the approach derived from social pathology obscures the value judgments that form a crucial part of the social process of creating deviance. Becker (among others) contends that when social scientists fail to question the label 'deviant,' they are *ipso facto* uncritically accepting the values of the labellers, that is, the majority authorities making the judgments.

The shift in theoretical focus from etiological to sociological determinants of deviance paved the way for the development of conceptual designs applicable in the analysis of both ethnic and non-ethnic minorities. Models derived from conflict theory represent one such approach.

The conflict approach to minorities

Conflict models posit the social creation of deviance by majority authorities with the power to define, treat, control, and punish what they view as social deviancy. Majority authorities create society-wide policies and laws that reflect their own moral and ideological values and serve their own instrumental interests. In their role as official gatekeepers for society-wide norms, majority authorities are able 'officially' to label non-conformist behaviour as socially deviant. Once deviant labels are imposed, majority authorities can discredit and control 'deviant' (non-conforming) behaviour, which is perceived to threaten their moral, ideological, political, and economic hegemony.

Among the leading theorists of this school is Kinloch. He defines a minority as '. . .any group that views itself and/or is defined by a majority power elite as different and/or inferior on the basis of assumed physical, cultural, economic and/or behavioral characteristics and is subject to exploitation and discrimination' (1979: 36).

Kinloch's definition of minority extends the concept of social deviance beyond the traditional parameters of non-conformist *behavioural* characteristics to include *assumed* physical, cultural, and economic characteristics as well as *assumed* behavioural characteristics. This definition, Kinloch points out, clearly focuses on power relations and labelling. It implies, further, that majority groups relate to minority groups on the basis of control, exploitation, and discrimination, for the minority is itself a social creation of the majority, and, as such, reflects the vested political, economic, and social interests of the majority (Kinloch, 1979: 44). In Kinloch's scheme, minority group relations are seen to evolve out of macro-level demographic and economic developments in which assumed physical and/or psychological inferiority is used by the majority (or majorities) to legitimize material inequality and thereby to maintain their own position of dominance in the institutionalized hierarchy of power, privilege, and prestige (ibid: 205–6).

Conflict theory, as exemplified in Kinloch's scheme, provides a useful beginning for the integration of social-deviance and ethnic-relations perspectives by explaining how majority authorities create, define, and control minorities whose characteristics are assumed to deviate in unacceptable ways from majority norms. However, this macro-level approach has limited usefulness at the micro level of social-psychological analysis. It is not designed to explain the processes through which individuals acquire deviant identities and, given similar social circumstances, why some persons embrace deviant life-styles while others do not (Clinard and Meier, 1979).

In recent years, the model of social deviance that has been most widely adopted by North American social scientists is the one based upon labelling theory. Labelling theory is designed for micro-level analysis. Accordingly, it focuses analysis on the processes through which a deviant identity is created and a deviant life-style is embraced.

Labelling theory: the social creation of minority status

Labelling theory incorporates some of the basic assumptions of conflict theory, such as the relativity of deviant labels to an individual's status in the stratified social order, but it goes farther in analysing the psycho-social consequences of negative labelling for the individual upon whom the label is imposed.

Central to labelling theory is the concept of stigma, originally defined by Goffman (1963) as deep discreditation. Labelling theorists, following Goffman's seminal conceptualization, argue that stigma has its roots not in the particular characteristic singled out for deep discreditation, but in the discrediting label imposed upon assumed bearers of the attribute by majority authorities (discrediting sources). Those with the power to stigmatize others presumed to deviate from established societal norms in unacceptable ways also have the power to discriminate against stigmatized persons and social categories. Majority authorities thus are able to violate the human rights of members of stigmatized population categories by defining them as somewhat less than human and hence unworthy of the full exercise of the fundamental rights of humankind.

For the individual bearer of stigma, Goffman argues, the psycho-social ramifications are so profound that the shattering effects of stigmatization on one's personal identity are almost irreversible. One's stigma becomes the key to one's whole persona: the key to personal discreditation. At the group level, the long-term consequence of stigmatization and collective discrimination is the social creation of a minority category characterized by collective disadvantage, subordination, and degradation.

Briefly, this is how it happens. Majority labelling creates minority status by the act of officially defining persons as deviant (primary deviance). Once labelled as deviant, minority members are subject to degrading experiences on virtually every occasion in which they come into confrontation with majority authorities (degradation ceremonies). Majority authorities acting on their own definitions of deviance proceed to prescribe 'appropriate' social placement and treatment (control) for minority members. 'Deviant' minorities are assumed to be dangerous and unstable, and/or inferior and incompetent. Accordingly, social placement by majority authorities – for the 'protection' of minorities and/or for the 'protection' of society at large – customarily takes the form of incarceration of minority members in a socially and spatially isolated 'total institution.' Within institutional confines the lives and destinies of minority inmates are formally administered and comprehensively controlled by majority caretakers (societal reactions). Acting upon prejudicial assumptions of minority unworthiness, majority authorities are able to rationalize everyday violations of inmates' human rights. Thus, the treatment of minorities within a total institution is characterized by oppression, neglect, and diminution.

Within or outside of the context of a total institution, stigmatization leads to minority ostracization, discrimination, and degradation. Thus, a self-fulfilling prophecy of stigmatization is set in motion, whereby the systemic denial of opportunities and of human dignity blunts capabilities, breeds apathy, and eventually creates dependency. Minority members come to accept their stigmatized, majority-imposed label (primary deviance), which becomes central to their stigmatized self-identity. They begin to 'act out' their deviant roles (secondary deviance) and to develop deviant careers. The self-fulfilling prophecy of stigmatization reaches fruition when minority members come to embrace a 'deviant' minority subculture as a personally appropriate, alternative life-style.

In recent years, labelling theorists, following Goffman and Becker, among others, have been sharply criticized for their contention that the fulfilment of the self-fulfilling prophecy of stigmatization is almost inevitable. The assumption that labelling as deviant sets up a process of deeper and deeper involvement in deviance has been called into critical question by increasing numbers of scholars. One of the most vehement of these critics is Prus (1983: 137) who contends that 'deviance is problematic and negotiable in definition, participation and regulation.' Prus points out, in this connection, that even Lemert (1967), the originator of the concept of 'secondary deviations,' does not view subsequent involvement in deviance as inevitable, but argues that the likelihood of this happening and the extent to which it occurs are related to the formality and intensity of societal reactions and to the perceived availability and desirability of other options, by minority members.

Prus (1983: 129) builds upon Lemert's position and addresses a number of further social conditions that can impact upon the minority member's deviant behaviours and social involvements over time. Further involvement in deviance, says Prus, is more likely when the discrediting sources define members of deviant minorities as inherently dangerous and persistently threatening and when the discrediting sources themselves have a high degree of power and prestige with which to wield control over public opinion, social policy, and community practice pertaining to the deviant minority. With regard to the latter point, I might add the observation that the discrediting sources must themselves have a high degree of public credibility, if their definitions of deviance are to achieve and sustain the stamp of community-wide legitimacy.

Other key factors that can impact significantly upon subsequent involvement in deviance include the minority member's prior experiences and affiliational networks. Prus argues that the extent of involvement in deviant (non-conventional) as opposed to conventional prior experiences as well as the extent of involvement in deviant as opposed to conventional affiliational networks will markedly affect subsequent involvement in deviance.

Using Becker's (1963) organizing concept of 'career contingencies' as a starting-point, Prus goes on to elaborate upon the kinds of personal and social factors that can impact upon a deviant career over time. How persons become defined as deviant; how they become involved in deviant activities and groups; how they cope with the stigma of deviance; how they avoid conventional options (and, I might add, how they 'pass' for majority members when they choose to pursue conventional options); how they become disinvolved/reinvolved in deviant networks and life-styles – all of these 'career contingencies,' says Prus, must be examined in order to account fully for the degree of a person's subsequent involvement in deviance and the particular pattern of his/her deviant career.

Prus's approach to the study of social deviance reveals some of the inherent limitations not only of traditional labelling theory, but also of one of its central concepts, the notion of 'master status.' In its traditional usage (Becker, 1963), the concept denoted the comprehensive stigmatizing effect of deviance definitions on the person as a whole. The effect of stigma deriving from a single 'deviant' attribute or behaviour was said to 'infect' all other attributes and behaviours with its discrediting 'poison.' Like a rampant cancer, stigma was held to spread throughout the bearer and to render the bearer as a whole 'untouchable' – a social outcast, a being 'not quite human' (Goffman, 1963: 5).

Prus, alternatively, suggests that the stigmatizing effects of deviance definitions in any given case may or may not be as overwhelming as traditionally suggested by labelling theorists. Rather, he argues, the stigmatizing effects of deviance definitions can be moderated by other, positively valued attributes and involvements. Insofar as the 'deviant' person may harbour other socially valued attributes (e.g., political influence, economic wealth, family prestige) and insofar as he or she may be involved in socially valued, conventional roles and activities (e.g., member of parliament, chairperson of a corporate board, university president), these attributes and involvements can serve to moderate the stigmatizing effects of deviance definitions. In Prus's view, then, a given minority member's 'multiple involvements' can play a significant role in accentuating or dissipating the degree of discreditation (stigmatization) effected by deviant definitions.

Another important variable affecting the discrediting impact of stigmatizing (deviant) definitions on bearers of stigma lies in the conceptual distinction between 'discredited' and 'discreditable' (Goffman, 1963: ch. 1). This distinction, largely overlooked in the analyses of labelling theorists, has important implications for coping with stigma through the strategy of 'passing.' The discredited bearer of stigma, says Goffman, assumes his or her non-conformist attribute is known about or immediately visible. Alternatively, the discreditable bearer of stigma assumes that his or her non-conformist attribute is neither known about nor immediately perceivable. Insofar as the stigmatized attribute is discreditable, rather than discredited, the bearer of stigma may attempt to avoid discreditation by others through passing – creating a conventional (normative) façade in the presence of (assumed unknowing) others.

The strategy of passing has been well documented in the ethnic-relations literature (Kallen, 1982), but it is the literature on the homosexual minority that has most adequately conceptualized the nature and magnitude of the deceptive mechanisms employed by stigmatized-minority members in order to hide stigmata (discredited or discreditable) from public view. Plummer (1975), Ponse (1978), and other scholars have demonstrated the ways in which stigmatized-minority members engage in secretive identity-management strategies in order to prevent personal and 'official' discreditation. These theorists also have shown how the employment of such strategies leads to the creation of a minority 'closet,' an invisible, private, life-sphere where stigmatized-minority identities may be revealed and where non-conformist minority life-styles may be developed and embraced.

As a 'sensitizing concept' (Becker, 1963) labelling theory has contributed much to the social-scientific understanding of the processes underlying the creation of non-conformist (minority) identities, careers, and life-styles. Yet, like the other theories of deviance considered earlier, it has some serious shortcomings. Most important, from a human-rights perspective, this approach is not designed to address fully the processes of delabelling and relabelling at the group level. The focus is on the individual 'deviant' and on the individual 'deviant career.' No systematic effort has been made by labelling theorists to identify the social mechanisms that might serve to destigmatize minorities *at the group level* and to reintegrate their members into the conventional (majority) community (Trice and Roman, 1970).

Delabelling and relabelling: the process of destigmatization

Trice and Roman (1970) outline three types of social mechanisms through which successful delabelling and relabelling of stigmatized minorities, at the group level, can occur:

1 Minority organizations designed to change majority norms so as to render normative whatever characteristic was previously labelled as deviant. For example, homosexual organizations can carry out a public-education mandate to teach children that homosexual and heterosexual life-styles represent equally legitimate human expressions of sexual and affectional preference.
2 Status-return ceremonies created by professional labellers (discrediting sources) designed to legitimate re-entry into the community at large of 'officially' delabelled/destigmatized minorities. For example, army-prison officials can restore an inmate to active duty with the potential for an honourable discharge, and administrators of mental hospitals can discharge inmates with a clean bill of health, as 'cured.'
3 Minority mutual-aid (self-help) organizations designed to discourage

non-conformist behaviour and, through intensive peer support, to encourage the embracement of new, positive self and group identities and life-styles, in conformity with majority norms. This mechanism is best exemplified by Alcoholics Anonymous, and international organization of self-help groups for members of the alcoholic minority.

This conceptualization of delabelling and relabelling shifts the focus of analysis from the level of the individual 'deviant' to that of the minority group, and from the self-fulfilling prophecy of stigmatization to the social mechanisms behind successful delabelling/destigmatization and relabelling rehumanization of 'deviant' minority groups. This approach, with its emphasis on strategies for change, invites comparison with ethnic models predicated upon similar kinds of goals. At this juncture then, it may be appropriate to begin an examination of some comparable conceptual designs found in the deviance and the ethnicity approaches to the study of minority groups.

Total institution and alternative models

A concept of central importance in labelling theory is that of the 'total institution,' originally developed by Erving Goffman (1961) with specific reference to hospitals, mental institutions, and prisons. These 'asylums,' he argues, treat special forms of deviance: they are designed to protect both the incarcerated population and the outside community from the assumed dangerousness associated with the inmates' deviancy. While the alleged goal of the total institution is the 'cure' or rehabilitation of the inmates and their return to society at large, in reality what is often created within institutional confines is just the opposite: a syndrome of psychosocial dependency and the realization of the self-fulfilling prophecy of stigmatization.

Upon assuming the role of inmate, says Goffman, all vestiges of one's previous social status, roles, and personal identity are stripped away, to be replaced by a common, ascribed, and stigmatized master status, that of anonymous deviant, symbolized by a standard-issue uniform. Life within the institution, for the inmate, consists of an ongoing series of degradation ceremonies through which majority caretakers effectively expunge the inmates' sense of self-worth and human dignity. Under the total bureaucratic control of majority authorities, inmates are expected to give unquestioned obedience to the rigid set of prescriptions and proscriptions governing institutional life and designed by the majority for the purpose of curbing deviant behaviour. Ironically, however, total subservience to majority caretakers, in all facets of everyday existence, nourishes deviancy and dependency among inmates. Over the long term, Goffman contends, the almost inevitable result is a kind of minority backlash – the development of a deviant, inmate subculture predicated upon minority norms and mores that run counter to the rules of the majority-dominated institution. Finally, says Goffman, even in the event of a discharge, the stigma attached to having been in an asylum results in permanent deviant-minority status.

The previously discussed limitations of this classic labelling model notwithstanding, it may be useful to consider it here, in comparative perspective. Before doing so, however, I wish to draw attention to the intrinsic discriminatory underpinnings of the total institution (hereafter, TI) as a model for and of societal reality. The categorical abrogation of minority inmates' fundamental right of self-determination (freedom of choice, freedom to decide) – without reference to and regardless of individual attributes and capabilities – represents one of the most inhumane forms of institutional discrimination. That this kind of collective violation of human rights tends to go hand in hand with other violations – daily assaults on inmates' sense of human dignity; neglect of inmates' physicial and material well-being – lends strong support, from a human-rights perspective, for the consideration of more humane, alternative models.

To begin my comparative assessment of models dealing with social deviance and minority status, I will briefly examine the 'self-help' model (hereafter, SH) proposed by Gellman (1964: 153–8) as an alternative to the total institution (TI).

Total institution versus self-help model

In contrast to the TI model, with its hierarchical structure in which subservient minority inmates are dominated and controlled by majority authorities, the SH model is egalitarian in organization, with all members sharing a common, minority status. While the TI model is designed to isolate inmates from contacts with the outside, conventional (majority) members of society, the SH model is designed to facilitate the process of integration of minority members into the community at large. Whereas, in the TI model, the inmate is stripped of personal identity and becomes, in effect, a dehumanized ward of the majority-controlled organization, in the SH model, not only is the personal identity of minority members maintained, but also, through the committed support of peers, their self-identity becomes destigmatized and their self-worth is enhanced. In contradistinction to the TI model, in which the self-fulfilling prophecy results, over time, in a syndrome of psycho-social dependency, among inmates, in the SH model, the personal and social independence of members is actively promoted. Finally, while the TI model leads to the development of a deviant subculture and life-style, the SH model produces a parallel structure, an analogous life-style within the normative parameters of majority society.

The foregoing comparison draws attention to:

1 The failure of the TI to translate majority rhetoric (treatment and cure of inmates) into empirical reality (normative or 'conventional' behaviours and reintegration of inmates into society at large), and
2 the potential for success in the SH option whereby members of stigmatized minorities take over the reins of their own destinies and organize themselves in a co-operative effort to regain positive self-identity, human dignity, and independence.

As conceptual designs for organizations dealing with social deviance, the TI and SH models can be seen to share a number of important features with parallel models of ethnic organization. In the following section, I will briefly compare some of the key features of the TI model with those of the model of institutional completeness (hereafter, IC) as originally outlined by Breton (1964) with specific reference to immigrant ethnic communities.

Breton's seminal notion of 'institutional completeness' referred to the comprehensiveness of ethnic institutions that provide the structural and cultural framework of the internal social organization of immigrant ethnic communities. Breton was concerned with the relationship between the degree of institutional completeness of a given immigrant ethnic community and the direction of integration of its members. His research findings supported his central thesis that the greater the degree of IC, the greater the centripetal attraction of the immigrant ethnic community, and the greater the probability that members of the community will sustain positive in-group identities, loyalties, and attachments. Breton's findings suggested, moreover, that ethnic organizations were capable of providing a locus for the raising of collective-minority ethnic issues, prior to public debate, and also of generating an internal, organizational basis for minority 'unity in defence' against discriminatory attacks from the 'outside.' In short, in Breton's conception, a high degree of IC not only meant that a given immigrant ethnic community could provide its members with a wide range of essential services and that it was well-equipped to satisfy members' expressive, group-identity needs, but also that it could provide the immigrant minority group with an organizational basis for the politicization of ethnicity and for the formulation of collective human-rights claims against outside majority bodies.

I will now turn attention to a comparative assessment of the models of institutional completeness (IC) and total institution (TI).

Total institution versus institutional completeness:
involuntary versus voluntary minority 'closet'

While neither of these models has been explicitly conceptualized in the literature as a form of minority 'closet,' I will argue that key boundary-maintaining mechanisms shared by both models support my reconceptualization. Both schemes posit a holistic institutional framework designed to meet virtually all life-needs of the minority community served. Both models require a substantial degree of population concentration and geographical segregation/isolation as a safeguard for boundary maintenance between majority and minority communities. The two schemes also posit the development of a collective sense of minority identity and the embracing by substantial numbers of minority members of alternative or parallel minority life-styles and subcultures. Finally, both models, in their operational intent, posit long-term goals of integration or reintegration of minority members into society at large.

While both models share features that enable their reconceptualization in terms of the closet concept, they also differ in several important ways. One critical difference between the TI and IC models lies in the criteria for membership and means of recruitment of members. In the TI model, membership of inmates is largely involuntary, and placement within the TI may involve some degree of coercion on the part of majority authorities. Further, membership within the TI may involve a status change, from majority to minority, for some inmates, as well as a general uprooting from previous social roles and a stripping away of personal identities. Within the hierarchical structure of the TI, ordinary members/inmates constitute a subservient minority totally controlled by majority caretakers.

In the IC model, by comparison, membership for both ordinary members and leaders tends to be ascribed at birth. Thus, while recruitment to the community is essentially involuntary, it does not (as in the TI model) involve a major status change for members, nor does it entail a disruption of previous social roles and a stripping away of previous identities. Within the IC community, leaders and ordinary members share a common social status, that of an ethnic minority. In contrast to the TI, with its intrinsic abrogation of inmates' right to self-determination, the IC allows minority members as a collectivity to determine their own destinies within its structure. Yet, like the status of TI inmates, the status of IC members within society at large remains that of a somewhat stigmatized minority.

From a critical stance, these two seminal models – TI, derived from deviance theory, and IC, derived from ethnic-relations theory – can be seen to share a common bias, that is, their underlying assimilationist premise. Both schemes conceive of the holistic institutional apparatus serving the minority group as a 'half-way house,' a service centre that caters to the needs of a particular clientele (immigrant/deviant) during that transitory period of time in which the minority population is being remodelled (acculturated/rehabilitated) so as to conform with the majority-created norms and life-styles of society at large. Further, neither model provides for the possibility of internal transformation of the institutional structure of the minority community or for the creation of alternative social arrangements by majority or minority members. The only long-term options presented are maintenance of a deviant subculture/minority ethnoculture or abandonment of same in the inter-ests of embracing majority values and norms and full integration into society at large.

In the foregoing section of this chapter, I have critically reviewed some of the main theoretical models presented as alternatives to the total institution and designed to aid in the analysis of minority destigmatiza-tion. These models address an important transitional stage in the process of minority liberation, a stage where the focus of minority attention is on presenting a normative (conventional) front in order to avoid majority discrimination and to justify minority claims for equal treatment. The limitation of these conceptual schemes, however, is that they are not designed to aid in the analysis of the processes whereby alternative (non-conventional) minority life-styles and subcultures can gain societal legitimation. Insofar as behavioural conformity to majority norms implies rejection by minority members of the legitimacy of minority cultural alternatives, social mechanisms (such as minority self-help groups) predicated on dominant conformity are not designed to promote a goal of minority cultural liberation. In order for minorities effectively to put forward claims for collective cultural rights, substantial numbers of minority members must demonstrate their commitment to their minority subculture as a genuine and distinctive design for living affording a legitimate, alternate life-style. From a human-rights approach, the distinction between the assimilationist and the cultural-pluralist models of minority organization is that the former allows only for the development of categorical minority-rights claims, while the latter allows for the development of both categorical and collective (cultural) minority-rights claims.

Models of ethnic organization: constraints on group priorities

Over the last two decades, social-scientific research in the area of ethnic relations has led to an elaboration of theory in the area of ethnic organization that may facilitate my analysis of the social processes whereby minority organizations become oriented towards the pursuit of legal and other protections for individual and collective minority rights. A recent typology of ethnic organizations developed by Baureiss (1982) may provide a helpful beginning for this analysis.

Baureiss builds upon some of the seminal ideas of earlier ethnic-relations theorists, in particular, the distinction between 'alternate' and 'parallel' types of minority organization conceived by Shibutani and Kwan (1965) and elaborated upon by Hughes and Kallen (1974).

Alternate minority institutions are those that differ in value-orientation (cultural non-conformity) and in organizational form (institutional non-conformity) from majority norms. In the Canadian societal context, communal societies (e.g., Inuit and Hutterite) whose value-orientations favour the group over the individual, and whose organizational forms are predicated on economic co-operation and political consensus, can be seen to deviate markedly from the individualistic ethos and bureaucratic structure of majority social formations. In Baureiss's (1982) scheme, such alternate institutions are both 'collectivist' and 'adhocratic' in type.

Parallel minority institutions are those that share the value-orientation (cultural conformity) and organizational form (institutional conformity) of majority social formations. In the Canadian societal context, ethnic organizations found in many European immigrant communities can be seen to conform with majority Canadian norms. In Baureiss's scheme, such parallel institutions are both 'democratic' and 'bureaucratic' in type.

Baureiss's scheme assesses the form and the viability of ethnic organizations in relation to the nature of the larger societal system in which they are imbedded (advanced capitalist market economy/established ethnic hierarchy of opportunity). He views the particular type of ethnic organization (i.e., collectivist, adhocratic, or bureaucratic) at any given time as a variable, dependent upon minority resilience (cultural and institutional distinctiveness) and majority discrimination. This model, at a macro level of analysis, is able to account for structural changes in ethnic organizations that reflect shifts in ethnic-group priorities, from the politicization of ethnicity at one pole to the revitalization of ethnic identity at the other.

The explanatory value of this model, from a human-rights approach, lies in its demonstration of the way in which internal and external variables interact to constrain ethnic-group priorities relating to the pursuit of human-rights claims. In the application of this model to stigmatized minorities, one may argue that as long as the external variable of majority discrimination presents formidable barriers to visible and cultural non-conformity, minority organizational priorities will favour closeted strategies.

The limitations of Baureiss's scheme lie in its failure to address the microlevel processes whereby shifts in identity, interests, and life-styles occur among individual members of (ethnic) organizations, and whereby protest movements are generated. For an analysis of these psycho-social processes, I will draw upon the literature on the homosexual minority which provides the seminal models of the 'coming out' process.

Coming out and the development of activist minority organization

A central thesis of this book is that, in order to convince majority authorities of the legitimacy of minority non-conformity (whatever its assumed basis), minority members must come out of the closet and openly lobby for minority rights. This thesis is strongly supported by the literature on stigmatized minorities, particularly the substantial recent literature on the homosexual minority.

However, Plummer (1975), among others, argues convincingly that, for stigmatized minorities, coming out of the closet is far easier said than done. The cloak of secrecy provided by the closet enables minority members to develop alternative subcultures and to engage in non-conformist life-styles that, exposed publicly, would bring majority condemnation and harassment, if not more severe punitive measures. Nevertheless, Plummer points out, closeted life is not without its own negative psycho-social consequences, for it is dependent upon the constant protection of a fragile façade of secrecy. Minority members may 'pass' (hide or disguise their minority identity and assume a majority pseudo-identity) in public life in order to maintain chosen careers. At the same time, they may engage in minority relationships and life-styles in their private lives. This 'double life' syndrome involves a constant preoccupation with identity-management and a constant employment of strategies of deception in order to hide stigmatized identities. Yet, fear of exposure of the secret is ever present, and a life built upon layer after layer of pretense can lead to intolerable feelings of shame and guilt. Minority members may thus be propelled out of the closet in order to seek professional guidance or they may seek psycho-social support from minority self-help groups.

Stigmatized minorities may develop different kinds of organizations designed to afford emotional and social support to members during the difficult process of coming out. Ponse (1978) differentiates between two principal types of minority organization: 'secretist' (closeted) and 'activist' (open). Ponse argues that, in the early phase of coming out, minority members may be willing to make disclosures about their stigmatized identities only to a few, trusted insiders (members of the same stigmatized minority). In this intitial phase of coming out, secretive (sometimes, anonymous) minority organizations provide critical support in the development of positive minority identity. In the second phase of coming out, activist organizations that encourage members to come out publicly provide necessary, successful role-models and support systems, which facilitate the development of personal pride in openness and enable minority members to make open disclosures of their minority identity. Activist groups also undertake lobbying activities; thus, they are designed to effect social changes that serve to strengthen legal and customary protections for minority rights.

Minority protest movements

Activist organizations play a central role in the evolution of minority protest movements. However, the potential for such organizations to attract and maintain a stable and committed membership and to achieve collective goals depends on a number of key variables. In order to analyse the social processes through which minority members become organized and politicized in their pursuit of human-rights protections, I will draw upon conceptual schemes derived from the social-scientific literature on social movements and minority ethnic protest.

Numerous studies of minority protest movements (see, especially:

Clark, Grayson, and Grayson, 1975; Killian, 1968; Klapp, 1969; Lincoln, 1961; Rioux, 1971; Turner and Killian, 1972; Wallace, 1956) lend strong support to Baureiss's (1982) view that discrimination alone is not the determinant of effective activist minority organization. What also is shown to be necessary is the heightening of in-group consciousness of injustice and the mobilization of minority discontent towards a clearly defined goal.

Clark et al (1975: Introduction) define a social movement as a social process through which substantial numbers of participants attempt to bring about or to resist social change. It is a conscious effort to create new social and cultural frameworks or designs for living, or to restore old ones. Following the approach of the 'Chicago School' (Turner and Killian, 1972, in particular) these scholars argue that minority discontent is rooted in profound dissatisfaction with prevailing life conditions, arising out of perceived value inconsistencies. Discontent may arise from a perceived conflict between values, from a perceived discrepancy between values and their implementation, from a perceived gap between expectations and achievements, from status inconsistency, and from a host of similar variables. Whatever its perceived source, discontent is expressed in a rejection of societal values, norms, and/or leaders and an attempt to find meaningful alternatives.

The process of organization of the minority in order to achieve better life conditions involves the formulation of guide-lines for new life-styles (group ideologies) and the gaining of the commitment of the discontented to the new designs for living. Central to this initial phase of activist minority organization are the processes of delabelling and relabelling whereby positive group identity is generated and minority-group resilience is fortified. Slogans provide important symbols, here: Black is beautiful; Gay is good; Fat is where-it's-at – all provide affirmation of the legitimacy of minority-group distinctiveness. Thus, they spur the process of in-group coalescence around alternative minority ideologies and goals.

A second and critical phase of minority protest movements is the mobilization of members to participate in activities designed to effect social change. Clark et al (1975) posit four key variables affecting the potential for success of a social movement in the mobilization of members: the development of a unifying ideology; the recruitment of willing, able, and representative leadership; the availability of channels for communication; the existence/cultivation of networks of co-operative relationships; and the development of an autonomous organizational base. Another important factor affecting the effective organization of minority protest movements is the nature and extent of social segmentation (cleavages between groups) in the society. Minority discontent is more likely to give rise to protest movements in stratified societies marked by great disparities in cultural values and in political and economic power between groups. Further, in stratified societies, minorities will be more likely to have a heightened sense of collective consciousness, agreed-upon group values and goals, existing channels of communication, and networks of co-operative relationships with which to build an organizational base for protest movements.

The conceptual distinction between 'communal' and 'associational' forms of minority organization (the *Gemeinschaft/Gesellschaft* typology) has important implications for mobilization and retention of members of protest movements (Clark et al, 1975; Oberschall, 1973). Communal groups are based on traditional cultural and kinship linkages between people (ethnicity). Associational groups are based on special interests (political, economic, religious, civic). Communal groups are more likely than associational groups to have value consensus beyond one set of issues, and are more likely to have developed an organizational base for a protest movement.

These observations relate importantly to the conceptual distinction between (ethnic) *group* and *category*, which I have emphasized in earlier works (Hughes and Kallen, 1974; Kallen, 1982). Members of minority *groups* with the requisite institutional infrastructure for maintenance and transmission of a distinctive subculture or ethnoculture are more likely to have and/or to develop the collective consciousness and the organizational basis for a successful protest movement than are members of minority *categories*. A minority category represents a conceptual or statistical classification of a population based on one or more criteria (race, age, sex, sexual orientation, history of alcohol abuse) that may or may not give rise to a sense of collective consciousness or to minority organization. Minority categories are more likely than minority groups to be represented empirically by dispersed, fragmented population aggregates whose members' only common attribute is the stigmatizing label imposed upon them by majority authorities. The propensity for factionalism to impede organization for minority protest is, therefore, much greater within minority categories than within minority groups.

The course and potential success of a minority protest movement is determined by the continual interaction of internal (minority) and external (majority) forces as well as by changes in the broader environment. A crucial task for minority leadership is to create and maintain in-group solidarity. Lines of fragmentation based on differences in values, interests, priorities, and sources of discontent among minority members must be contained through the development of a strong collective commitment to the ideology and goals of the movement. Rivalries among minority leaders must be resolved so that leadership is perceived by both insiders and outsiders as representative of the membership of the movement. Lobbying efforts by minority representatives must convince majority authorities that minority demands are valid and must be dealt with.

The response of majority authorities (in most instances, governments) to minority protest may take the form of indifference, accommodation, and/or obstruction (Clark et al, 1975). A response of indifference is most likely when the movement is not perceived as a threat of any kind by governments (e.g., Jesus Freaks). Accommodation implies a willingness of governments to negotiate, based upon the recognition of some minority demands as valid and also upon the perception of the minority movement as non-threatening, provided that its demands are addressed (e.g., the aboriginal movement). A response of obstruction is most likely if the success of the movement is perceived by governments to threaten the social order (e.g., the FLQ). While these conceptual distinctions are important for analytic purposes, in reality a combination of responses may occur. A government may accommodate a minority protest movement (or be indifferent) but it may obstruct particular tactics (e.g., Hippies and the use of psychedelic drugs).

Minority protest movements frequently fail to achieve their original ideals, but some succeed at least in part by compromising often unrealistic goals and by adapting group ideologies and strategies in order to gain acceptance by insiders and outsiders. When movements succeed, they become 'routinized' (in Weber's classic term): they become institutionalized in a stable organizational form. They may become absorbed through legislation as part of the majority society; they may develop organizational bases independent of the majority society; they may overthrow the majority order and establish their own organizational base as dominant. Whatever happens, minority protest movements leave their mark on society. They identify an area of perceived human-rights violation needing redress, and even if they fail to achieve such redress, they provide the inspiration for future movements that may arise to revitalize the quest.

Minority-rights movements

Minority-rights movements represent a particular form and direction of collective minority protest. This type of social movement is most likely to emerge when minority discontent focuses on the inconsistency between declared societal ideals endorsing human-rights principles and the non-implementation of these ideals in public institutions and in public practice.

Ironically, as pointed out more than a century ago by Alexis de Tocqueville (quoted in Clark et al, 1975: 11): '. . . generally speaking, the most perilous moment for a bad government is one when it seeks to mend its ways.' When governments begin to replace discriminatory social policies and laws with anti-discriminatory human-rights instruments, the expectations of minorities, the targets of discrimination, begin to rise. When minority expectations rise at a faster rate than actual achievements, the gap between expectations and achievements widens, and minority discontent escalates.

When human-rights principles become constitutionally entrenched, it follows that minority expectations will reach new heights. Minority expectations for explicit constitutional recognition of minority rights and for actual equality of societal opportunities may then come to outstrip the manifest increase in achievements. When this happens, minority discontent rises palpably.

The emergence and proliferation of minority-rights movements in Canada over the last two decades provide evidence for this theoretical position. Minority protest on the part of both ethnic and non-ethnic groups initially focused on policy changes. In the 1970s (the 'human-rights decade') protest came increasingly to incorporate demands for legal changes, such as enumeration of the minority-status criterion in the non-discriminatory grounds of statutory human-rights instruments. Since the advent of the CRF in 1982, minority-rights issues have become constitutionalized, and minority protest has focused on constitutional changes designed to guarantee minority rights. However, actual achievements have lagged behind soaring minority expectations; hence, expressed minority discontent (in the form of continued lobbying for change) has increased. These general observations will be documented with specific reference to disabled and homosexual minorities in chapter 6.

Minority protest in pursuit of human rights may be organized around expressive/cultural and/or instrumental/empowerment types of goals. When empowerment demands take precedence, minority protest may take the form of *contention*, seeking social reforms that will recognize and protect the individual human rights of minority members and will enhance their political, economic, and social opportunities. When demands for cultural legitimacy and equality take precedence, minority protest may take the form of *revitalization*, seeking structural changes designed to recognize and protect the collective (cultural or subcultural) rights of the minority as a collectivity.

In light of Baureiss's typology of ethnic organizations, I posit that contention will be most likely to develop within bureaucratic organizations (parallel institutions), whereas revitalization will be most likely to develop within collectivist organizations (alternate institutions).

Minority-rights movements and human-rights claims

The conceptual distinction between contention and revitalization as forms of minority-rights movements has important implications for the nature of human-rights claims that can justifiably be put forward by minority organizations. Drawing upon the typology of human-rights claims developed in my earlier work (Kallen, 1982: 75–7) and addressed briefly in the introduction to this book, I will argue that contention focuses on individual- and categorical-rights claims, while revitalization focuses on collective-rights claims.

Individual-rights claims represent demands for recognition and protection of the individual human rights of minority members. Such claims may seek specified changes in constitutional and/or statutory law. Categorical-rights claims represent demands for collective redress against the adverse impact of systemic discrimination upon the minority as an entity. Such claims may seek the implementation of affirmative-action programs designed to remedy group inequities. Categorical claims do not rest on assumptions about cultural distinctiveness or alternative lifestyles; thus, they can justifiably be put forward by representatives of minorities with and without a viable cultural base. Accordingly, blacks, ex-convicts, women, alcoholics, children, homosexuals, mentally and physically disabled, aged, as well as ethnic minorities may put forward categorical-rights claims.

Alternatively, collective-rights claims contain the underlying assumption of the right of a minority as a collectivity to express and perpetuate a distinctive ethnoculture or subculture. Accordingly, collective-rights claims may only be justifiably put forward by representatives of minorities with a viable ethnocultural or subcultural base.

While a fuller argument in this connection will be developed in the course of this book, at this juncture I shall posit two basic conditions for collective claims based on subcultural rights: 1 / that the alternative minority-group values/life-styles do not directly threaten the peace and order of society at large or present a real and present danger to any members thereof and 2 / that the minority collectivity is both able and willing to provide the institutional framework necessary for the transgenerational continuance of the alternative subculture.

Caveats
The reader may be concerned here that I – by way of the conceptual scheme – am condoning illegal activities undertaken within the normative rubric of alternate subcultures (e.g., heroin trafficking and use, delinquent youth gangs). This, most definitely, is not the case. The first condition was not posited as 'illegal' acts because some prevailing, discriminatory laws, in Canada (as elsewhere), continue to exist in contravention of international and national human-rights principles. Thus, until the discriminatory provisions of such legislation (e.g., Elections Act, against the mentally retarded; Criminal Code, against homosexuals; Family Law, against women) are removed, the legal system cannot unconditionally be assumed to protect minority rights.

A second caveat relates back to the concept of institutional completeness and its implications for my second condition, regarding the transgenerational continuation of minority subcultures. Current human-rights instruments, both international and Canadian, continue to be rooted in the traditional, family-oriented model of ethnoculture and enculturation. Accordingly, they tend to discriminate, in various ways, against assumed non-reproductive subcultural minorities. From a social-scientific perspective, however, the concept of institutional completeness can provide the basis for an alternative model, one that is designed to recognize and protect non-ethnic subcultural minority rights. Insofar as non-ethnic minorities develop the requisite organizational base for cultural maintenance, the transmission through time of viable, alternative subcultures is empirically possible. Insofar as minority subcultures do not present a real and present danger to the society at large, alternative forms of cultural expression and cultural transmission may be seen as morally justifiable, from a human-rights perspective. In sum, insofar as the two conditions posited have been met, I will argue that the minority subcultures of non-ethnic collectivities should be afforded the same protections as their ethnic counterparts under the provisions of international, constitutional, and statutory law.

A SCHEME FOR THE ANALYSIS OF STIGMATIZED MINORITIES
AND HUMAN RIGHTS IN CANADA

Drawing upon key concepts derived from the theoretical designs presented throughout the discussion in this chapter, I have developed a

TABLE 1

Stigmatized minorities and human rights: the conceptual framework – a sequential scheme

Phase One Becoming a minority or going into the closet	Phase Two Destigmatization or coming out	Phase Three Towards minority rights and cultural liberation
Labelling and stigmatization (primary deviance)	Individual delabelling and relabelling	Individual disclosures to trusted others
Discriminatory treatment and placement (the closet)	Positive minority identity	Group mobilization for minority protest
Internalizing stigma as minority identity	Group-level stigma conversion	From secretism to activism
Acting out (secondary deviance)	Group consciousness-raising	Coming out publicly
Coping mechanisms (hiding stigmata)	Minority self-help	Contention: individual rights claims
Minority subculture (alternative life-style)	Minority support systems	Revitalization: collective rights claims

sequential conceptual framework that will inform the analysis through-out this book. The development of this scheme has been addressed earlier, in the preface to this book. For heuristic purposes, a synopsis of the theoretical design is presented in the form of a table (see table 1).

In the next chapter, I will turn my attention to the first phase of this scheme: becoming a minority. In the pages to follow, I will differentiate among various types of minorities and assess the social and legal implications of these differences from a human-rights perspective.

2
The social creation of minority status

Minorities are not 'natural' entities: they are socially created population categories. From a human-rights perspective, a minority may be conceptualized succinctly as any social category whose subordinate and disadvantaged status in society is a result of categorical violations of the individual and/or collective human rights of its members by majority authorities.

Majority/minority relations are intergroup relations predicated on demonstrable disparities in political, economic, and social power. They are *not* necessarily predicated on disparities in population numbers. This point differentiates the social-scientific concepts of majority and minority from their political counterparts. The reader is cautioned to note this distinction, for the analysis throughout this book rests on the social-scientific conception (power disparities) and not on the political conception (numerical disparities).[1]

MINORITY AND MAJORITY: DEFINITION OF THE CONCEPTS[2]

In order to make clear to the reader the way in which concepts of majority/minority relations are employed in this book, the following comprehensive definitions are offered.

1 The classic case that well exemplifies this conceptual distinction is that of South Africa, under the government policy of apartheid. While the 'white' social category is far smaller in numbers than the 'black,' whites constitute a powerful ruling majority able to impose its racist jurisdiction through law, policy, and social practice in flagrant violation of the human rights of the black minority.
2 Definitions of minority and majority have been adapted from my earlier work (Kallen, 1982: 109–11).

The concept 'minority' refers to any social category within a society 1 / that is set apart and defined by the majority as incompetent/inferior or abnormal/dangerous on the basis of presumed physical, cultural, and/or behavioural differences from majority norms; 2 / that is categorically and systemically discriminated against by majority authorities and is thereby subject to some degree of oppression (denial of political rights), neglect (denial of economic rights), and/or diminution (denial of social rights/ human dignity); and 3 / that, as a consequence of the self-fulfilling prophecy of systemic or structural discrimination, comes to occupy a socially subordinate, disadvantaged, and stigmatized position within the society.

MAJORITY/MINORITY RELATIONS

The minority concept is a relative notion that is meaningful only in relation to a corresponding majority. With regard to any given human attribute (age, sex, sexual orientation) the majority or dominant population is the social category whose members enjoy the greatest degree of political, economic, and social power in the society, and whose particular physical, cultural, and behavioural attributes provide the recognized institutionalized norms for all social groups in the society. Insofar as a majority or majorities have the power to entrench their own values and to safeguard their own interests at all institutional levels within the society, it follows that the human rights of majority members will be recognized and protected through society-wide policy, law, and custom. Further, insofar as the majority or majorities have the power to define the normative order in society, for any socially significant human characteristic, the majority attribute will provide the referent in relation to which minority differences are defined as deviant.

The concept 'majority' refers to any social category within a society 1 / that has the recognized power (or authority) to define itself as normal and superior and to define all minorities presumed to deviate from its physical, cultural and behavioural norms as abnormal and/or inferior; 2 / that has the power to rationalize violations of minority rights through the use of invalidation mythologies (e.g., handicapism, heterosexism, and ageism) that draw upon prevailing public prejudice in order to create 'evidence' for the inherent inferiority and/or dangerousness of minority stigmata; 3 / that has the power to impose its will, norms, and laws on society at large and to deny/suppress the expression of alternate, minority ideas and life-styles; and 4 / that exercises the greatest degree of political, economic, and social power in the society and is thereby able to control the life-destinies of minorities.

Because minorities are assumed to harbour characteristics that differ from the norms of the majority or dominant group(s) in undesirable ways, minority members tend to be regarded and treated by majority powers as undeserving of equal societal opportunities. It follows from this premise that the deeper the discreditation of minority stigmata the more pernicious the forms of discrimination against minorities by majority authorities, and the greater the violations of minority rights.

Stigmatization and minority status[3]

(The process of stigmatization plays a central role in the social creation and perpetuation of minority status.) Public repudiation of minority stigmata facilitates justification of the flagrant abuse of minority rights by majority authorities. The concept of stigma, therefore, is pivotal for the under-standdding of majority/minority relations.

According to Goffman (1963) the term 'stigma,' in its orginal, Greek meaning, referred to a forcibly imposed bodily mutilation (e.g., a cut or burn) that publicly announced that the bearer was a morally blemished (or ritually polluted) person – a slave, criminal, or traitor – to be shunned by members of society at large (and, I would add, to be summarily denied human rights). Today, in social-scientific parlance, the term generally refers to any deeply discrediting attribute (e.g., criminal status), rather than to any visible bodily evidence of it.

While minority stigmata are by definition deeply discrediting attributes, some stigmata are more pervasive in their discrediting proclivity than others. When minority stigmata are deemed 'unnatural' (contrary to human nature) by majority authorities, the discrediting tendency may be so overwhelming that it serves to dehumanize the minority in the eyes of the majority audience. Once minorities are categorized as less than human, majority authorities are able to rationalize flagrant minority-rights violations with impunity.

Whatever the extent of their discrediting tendencies, stigmatizing labels – cripple, idiot, loonie, faggot, drunk, dyke – conjure up insidious stereotypes in which the entire mental image formed of the minority is that of a blemished person or group. This effect can be explained, in part, with reference to the nature of stigma. A central quality of stigma is that

3 The argument in this section on *stigma* is adapted from Goffman (1963: ch. 1).

of contagion: a stigma deriving from one discrediting characteristic tends to spread to other characteristics. Thus, the imputation of a wide range of discrediting attributes evoles on the basis of the original one: cripples are morons, faggots are sex maniacs, junkies are thieves and prostitutes, and so on. In this way, a highly distorted and wholly discrediting group stereotype is generated. It is this grotesque caricature of the stigmatized population that provides the legitimating grounds for categorical discrimination against the minority, for it is this deeply discrediting image that is used by majority authorities to justify policies and practices that violate minority rights. Over time, moreover, it is this pervasively stigmatizing group stereotype that tends to provide the overarching basis for the minority members' master status.

Master status and multiple-minority status

The concept of master status traditionally has been used by social-deviance theorists to refer to the phenomenon that occurs when the defining characteristic or cluster of characteristics singled out by the majority as 'deviant' and as the rationale for categorical discrimination against the minority becomes the bearer's overriding, defining characteristic. When this happens, the stigmatized characteristic that has assumed master status comes to mask all other human attributes. Put another way, the defining attribute (or cluster) that has achieved master status comes to assume precedence over and above all other statuses held by the minority members.

The reader should note that this definition of master status focuses on the way in which the majority creates stigmatized minorities through the processes of discrediting and discriminating against particular human populations.

Another way of looking at the phenomenon of master status is from the subjective view of the minority member. From this view, I may say that when a given human attribute (or cluster) becomes perceived by the minority member as most basic or central to his or her personal and social identity, then that attribute can be said to have assumed a master status for the individual bearer. For stigmatized minorities, the process of stigmatization (unless and until reversed) may be conceptualized as a process whereby the comprehensive, discrediting effects of stigmata become internalized by minority members and come to provide the overriding bases for minority members' self and group identity.

From a critical stance, this traditional usage of the notion of master status (as was pointed out earlier in this book) can be seen to have a number of limitations. Like the 'self-fulfilling prophecy' – a notion to which it is closely related – the concept is static: that is, master status, once achieved, brands an indelible stamp on one's persona and one's social placement. This conceptualization does not allow for the possibility of change through destigmatization, relabelling, and/or situational shifts in master status from one attribute to another, within varying social contexts.

In reality, the notion of master status is far more complex, and in order for the concept to be employed more fruitfully, it should be seen in relation to the bearer's multiple attributes, statuses, and social involvements. Insofar as several different human attributes may become stigmatized, and thus may come to provide socially recognized bases for differential treatment, a given individual can belong to several minorities at the same time. Such individuals may be said to have acquired multiple-minority status.

The social implications of multiple-minority status tend to vary with the particular social context and situation, depending, for example, on the relevant issues at hand and on the nature of the majority discriminator involved. A blind female alcoholic may be discriminated against on criteria of sightedness, sex, and sobriety, but which of these criteria will provide a catalyst for discrimination will vary with the nature of the majority discriminator in a given situation (in this example, sighted handicapist, chauvinist male, and/or teetotaller).

Whether or not multiple-minority statuses will overlap in their discriminatory implications also will depend on the relevant social issues at hand. For example, a black, elderly male homosexual may be involved in the Black Power movement, the movement for Grey Liberation, and a Gay Rights organization. In each situational context a different stigmatized attribute is at issue, and it is this discrediting label that tends to dominate other minority attributes.

Alternatively, the overriding master status of one stigmatized-minority characteristic may render it salient for a particular bearer in a great many social contexts, even when other minority attributes are singled out for discriminatory purposes by the majority. For example, for a given Canadian Indian, female homosexual, Indianness may provide the overriding attribute for self-identification. Accordingly, aboriginal status may come to assume a master status, which remains salient even in situations focusing on women's or lesbians' rights.

Within the context of majority/minority relations, the notion of master status provides a parallel to the notion of primordiality emphasized by some scholars (e.g., Isaacs, 1977) in connection with ethnicity and ethnic identity. These scholars take the view that one's ethnic identity is a person's most basic (primordial) group identity; accordingly, in a case of multiple-minority status, one's ethnic attributes would override other minority characteristics and would invariably provide the underpinnings for one's master status, at least from the subjective point of view. Alternatively, I will argue that the extent to which this holds true in a given empirical instance must be taken as problematic. Both ethnic and other minority-group identities, I assert, are highly contingent upon the value judgments surrounding the stigmata imposed by majority labellers on minority attributes at any given time.

Before closing this discussion of master status and multiple-minority status, I wish to remind the reader of the caveat, raised by Prus (1983), namely, that members of stigmatized minorities ('deviant' persons) may have socially valued attributes and that they also may play normative social roles. Accordingly, individual minority members may acquire majority status on the basis of these socially valued attributes and involvements. In other words, at the level of the individual bearer of a stigma or stigmata, persons may, at the same time, hold both minority and majority statuses, with regard to different human attributes and social involvements.

To the extent that majority attributes and statuses predominate, the descrediting effects of stigmata on the individual persona will be moderated. Moreover, I would add, the severity of discriminatory treatment accorded the bearer of a stigma will be muted.

I would suggest, for example, that a skid-row alcoholic is likely to be more severely stigmatized and more harshly treated than an alcoholic member of parliament. Similarly, a chair-bound resident of a home for the physically disabled is likely to bear a greater burden of stigma than is a chair-bound president of the United States (e.g., F.D. Roosevelt). Again, an illiterate and inarticulate black 'ghetto' resident is likely to suffer far greater discriminatory effects of a stigma than is a highly educated black university professor or a highly articulate black civil-rights leader (e.g., Martin Luther King).

In all of these examples, and many more that could be cited, the stigmatized person's majority statuses – deriving from the bearer's socially valued attributes and involvements – can be seen to offset and to attenuate the discrediting effects of minority stigmata.

Readers should note, however, that the foregoing refers only to the individual bearer of a stigma. Despite moderating influences on the effects of a stigma at the level of individual minority members, the categorical stigma imposed upon the minority at the group level remains unchanged. From the negatively prejudiced perspective of the majority audience, the recognized achievements of individual members of stigmatized minorities typically are regarded as 'exceptions.' The bias in this perspective is evident in such common rationalizations as the expression: 'One of my best friends is (black, gay, blind).'

It is not unless delabelling and relabelling of stigmatized minorities occur at the group level that the discrediting effects of stigmata on the minority population as a whole may become attenuated. Until this happens, and despite the singular achievements of some individual members, the minority collectivity will retain its stigmatized status and its (non-exceptional) members will continue to suffer the dehumanizing effects of majority-imposed stigmata.

TYPES OF MINORITIES: VARIATIONS IN THE SOCIAL IMPLICATIONS OF LABELLING

Multiple statuses and status shifts

At the level of the individual, shifts in status between majority and minority can occur on the basis of a number of different criteria. All persons, at some period of their lives – childhood and old age, for example – are members of one or more minorities. On the criterion of age, status shifts from minority (child) to majority (adult) and then to minority (aged) can occur in an individual's lifetime. Moreover, all persons can, through accident, disease, or design, lose their majority status and acquire minority status with regard to a wide variety of criteria. Members of majority ethnic or racial collectivities may become mentally or physically ill; they may lose their sight or hearing or their arms or legs; or they may perform a criminal act. Some may become addicted to alcohol and/or other drugs; others may openly embrace a gay life-style, and so forth. Whatever the cause of the change in the nature of their human attributes, the outcome, within the context of majority/minority relations, is the same, that is, a loss of majority status with regard to the 'damaged,' newly stigmatized attribute.

For example, a white, English-Canadian male who enjoys majority status with regard to the attributes of race, ethnicity, and sex may suffer severe eye damage, resulting in the loss or near loss of his ability to see.

When this happens, he loses his sighted-majority status and becomes a member of the blind minority. A similar shift of status from majority to minority would occur if our hypothetical male decided to 'come out of the closet' and to openly declare himself to be a homosexual. In this case he would lose his heterosexual-majority status and would become a member of the gay minority. In both of these examples, the white, English-Canadian male would retain his majority status with regard to the attributes of race, ethnicity, and sex; only his status with regard to the attributes of eyesight and sexual orientation would shift from majority to minority.

The foregoing examples of shifts in status between majority and minority over time demonstrate not only that a given individual may hold both minority and majority statuses at the same time, but also that a person's human attributes are vulnerable to stigmatization: thus a person may acquire multiple-minority statuses at various points throughout his or her life.

Criteria employed in stigmatization

The discriminatory implications of minority status vary with the nature of the stigma(ta) as well as with the degree of presumed deviance of the defining minority attributes from majority norms. Stigmata may brand the bearer as inherently inferior or dangerous, or both. In general, we may say that the greater the majority assumption of dangerousness, the harsher will be the discriminatory implications of minority stigmata. Another relevant distinction lies in the assumed degree of mutability of stigmatized characteristics and behaviours. Where majority authorities assume that non-normative behaviours have been voluntarily (as opposed to involuntarily) acquired by the minority member, and that the offending behaviours can be dropped or altered, sanctions, scaled to the severity of majority condemnation, will more likely be invoked as control measures.

In table 2 I have developed a scheme for classifying minorities according to the criteria emphasized by majority authorities in the process of stigmatization. In this typology I have arbitrarily divided minority groups into three broad categories, on the basis of their defining attributes, that is, physical, cultural, and behavioural stigmata.

I have positioned criteria-specific minority categories on the table along two continua: 1 / inferiority/dangerousness and 2 / involuntary/voluntary nature of stigmata.

TABLE 2
Types of minorities: criteria emphasized in stigmatization

	Involuntary physical attributes	Voluntary cultural attributes	Behavioural attributes
Inferior	Age (children, elderly)	Ethnicity (origin/identity)	Body weight image (obese, anorectic)
	Sex (women)	Religion (parental/chosen)	
	Race (non-white)	Language (native/acquired)	Sobriety (alcoholic)
	Bodily stature (dwarf, midget)	Sexual orientation (homosexual, transsexual, transvestite)	Subculture (gay/lesbian)
	Physical 'normalcy' (physically disabled)		Drug use (drug subculture)
			Criminal acts (criminal)
Dangerous	Mental 'normalcy' (mentally disabled, ill, or retarded)		Political acts (political dissident, terrorist)

While this scheme is designed to facilitate my analysis of types of minorities, it should not be taken to represent anything more than a heuristic device. As will be shown in the following pages, the specific categorization of any given minority rests largely on majority assumptions. Hence, as majority assumptions change, minority classifications may be revised. Further, minorities may be stigmatized on the basis of multiple criteria; hence, their placement at any one position in the scheme should be viewed only in relation to the specific criteria at hand.

Mutability of minority attributes: voluntary/involuntary criteria

Involuntary criteria for minority stigmatization tend to be applied to those attributes presumed by the majority to be ascribed (born into, inherent) or involuntarily acquired and essentially immutable. Ascribed attributes include age, sex, ethnic and racial origin, and some mental and physical abilities/disabilities. Because these attributes are assumed not to be amenable to change, whether or not a member of an ascribed minority positively or negatively evaluates/identifies with the defining attributes behind the minority stigmata has little or no influence on the categorical nature of discrimination against him or her by majority authorities.

Voluntary criteria, in contrast, tend to be applied to achieved attributes (acquired by choice), such as language, religion, political ideology, culture or subculture, as well as educational, occupational, political, and social skills. These attributes tend to be perceived as essentially mutable. Because they are assumed to be amenable to change, their valence (positive/negative valuation) for the minority member may have differential implications for delabelling and status improvement. Should minority members come to evaluate negatively the achieved attributes underlying their minority status, they may be encouraged, by majority authorities, to shed these stigmatized characteristics in order to reduce institutional discrimination against them and in order to increase their societal opportunities. To the degree that one's achieved attributes are altered/ transformed in the direction of majority norms – for example, by shedding one's native (ethnic) language and becoming a fluent speaker in one of Canada's two official/majority languages (English and French) – one's social status with regard to the relevant attribute (in this case, language) may shift from minority to majority.

Sagarin and Montanino (1977: Introduction), social-deviance theorists, distinguish between voluntary and involuntary stigmata on the basis of the assumed control of the bearer over alteration of stigmatized attributes. In their view, involuntary stigmata are assumed to lie beyond the capacity of the bearer to control. Involuntary minorities, accordingly, are not held to be responsible for their stigmata even though they may be ostracized by the majority for harbouring blemished characteristics.

Voluntary stigmata, however, are assumed to be under the control of the bearer. Voluntary minorities, accordingly, are held to be responsible for their stigmata (non-conformist behaviours), as it is assumed by majority authorities that such behaviours can be altered. Most important, in connection with our conceptualization of stigma, Sagarin and Montanino argue that voluntary minorities are subject to more profound stigmatization than involuntary minorities because majority authorities assume that voluntary stigmata *can* and *should* be changed. A further assumption is that, at the group level, social policies and sanctions designed to induce conformity to majority norms can be fruitfully implemented. Thus, non-conformist behaviour of voluntary minorities can be forcibly if not voluntarily controlled.

Critical comments
While the voluntary/involuntary dichotomy is a useful heuristic device,

the reader should be cautioned that the distinction postulated is somewhat arbitrary. Scientific evidence necessary to validate classification of stigmata as voluntary or involuntary has not (as yet) been forthcoming in many cases. Moreover, the voluntary/involuntary dichotomy postulated by majority authorities is not based on scientific evidence, but on prejudiced-majority *assumptions* about minority stigmata. Homosexual, alcoholic, and obese minorites, for example, have long been perceived and treated as voluntary non-conformists. While unsupported by corroborating scientific evidence, this authoritative majority classification has served to rationalize blatant violations of human rights ranging from coerced 'treatment' to involuntary incarceration to genocide.[4]

The foregoing critique notwithstanding, in cases where minority stigmata are in fact voluntary, the individual bearer of a stigma is faced with a number of options. He or she may seek to maintain, disguise, alter, or shed stigmatized attributes.

Passing: the closet syndrome

Where shedding the stigmatized attribute is not perceived to be a viable option, the minority member may adopt the strategy of 'passing,' that is, disguising or hiding the stigma from public scrutiny and assuming the public pseudo-identity of a majority member. This strategy is usually adopted in instances where minority members are unable and/or unwilling to shed or alter stigmatized characteristics, yet are able to disguise them, so as to render them invisible to the majority. The ethnicity literature is replete with examples here: Jews who change their surnames and have their noses bobbed; blacks of mixed ancestry who 'pass' for white; Chinese and Japanese who have their eyes straightened.

Turning to the area of social deviance, the phenomenon of passing has been found to be associated with the double-life syndrome: the maintenance of a closeted (secret) minority identity and life-style in private life and the simultaneous maintenance of a pseudo-majority identity and

4 Readers familiar with reported concentration-camp atrocities associated with Nazi policies during the Second World War will probably recall that members of the Jewish minority were compelled to wear a yellow star on their clothing in order to identify them as belonging to a 'defiled race,' marked for extermination (genocide). What is not well known is that members of the homosexual minority were similarly singled out as targets for genocide. They were forced to wear a pink triangle on their clothing to identify them as part of a despised and deeply condemned category of 'sexual perverts.' A shattering depiction of the experience of homosexuals in Nazi concentration camps is presented in M. Sherman's play *Bent*, first staged in 1980.

life-style in public life. Examples are manifold: the student/closet political activist, the politician/closet homosexual, the professional male athlete/ closet female – and so forth. Whether the stigmatized attribute is, in fact, mutable or immutable, the act of passing represents a conscious reaction to stigmatization. It represents the choice, by the minority member, of keeping the stigma 'in the closet' in order to avoid the anticipated discriminatory consequences of 'coming out.'

THE NATURE OF MINORITY STIGMATA: DANGEROUS AND INFERIOR LABELLING

The discriminatory implications of minority status can also be seen to vary with the nature of the stigmata imposed by the majority. In general, minorities presumed to be dangerous tend to be treated more inhumanely than those presumed to be inferior but relatively harmless. Dangerous minorities are those perceived by dominant populations to threaten their political, economic, and ideological hegemony, and/or to threaten the dominant racial, ethnic, cultural, and/or moral order of the society.

Table 2 (above) indicates that minorities may be classified as dangerous on the basis of physical attributes (e.g., race, physical/mental 'abnormalcy'), cultural attributes (alternative subculture), and/or behavioural attributes (e.g., sexual 'perversions,' criminal acts). The more dangerous the minority is presumed to be, the more likely that discriminatory treatment against its members by dominant powers will involve coercion in the form of punitive legal sanctions backed by armed force (military, police wardens, security guards).

During the Second World War, when Canada was at war with Japan, Japanese-Canadians – most of whom were Canadian-born citizens and many of whom had never seen Japan – were defined as dangerous enemy aliens. Under this definition, their fundamental human rights were systemically violated: their property was confiscated (neglect); they were interned, under armed guard, in Canadian-style concentration camps (oppression); and, forced to live in cramped and crowed quarters, without privacy, they suffered indignity after human idignity (diminution) for the remainder of the war (Krauter and Davis, 1978).

The justification given by majority authorities for abrogation of the fundamental human rights of 'dangerous' minorities (e.g., the Japanese in wartime Canada) is that such actions are taken in the public interest, that is, to protect the peace, security, and moral order of society at large.

While maintenance of peace and order is essential for the continued functioning and well-being of any society, from a human-rights view, the abrogation of human rights can only be justified in cases where there is concrete evidence of danger to society, and then only to the extent necessary to abort the danger. In the Japanese-Canadian case cited, no such evidence was ever presented by majority authorities.

The discriminatory treatment of alleged Japanese enemy aliens in Canada was far more severe than that accorded other wartime enemies, such as Germans and Italians. Clearly, the morbid fear of the Japanese (as compared with the 'white' enemies of Canada) reflected the racist assumptions of dominant Canadians, and the internment of Japanese-Canadians during the war period represented one of the most blatant, institutional forms of racial discrimination in Canada's history (La Violette, 1948).

The foregoing discussion draws attention to the way in which majority authorities can employ the notion of 'dangerousness' in order to rationalize discriminatory public policies and practices that entail pervasive violations of minority rights. It is important to differentiate here between 'real' and 'apparent' danger and to take into account the fact that what is 'real,' within the context of majority/minority relations, tends to be what is presumed/alleged to be real by majority authorities. Thus, for example, gays and lesbians, whose sexual preference for members of their own sex has never been demonstrated to pose a real danger to the heterosexual majority in Canada, nevertheless have been publicly perceived as dangerous and a threat to the established moral order. Homosexual-minority members, accordingly, have been subject to legal discrimination under various sections of Canada's Criminal Code. While it is not a crime to be a homosexual in Canada, pursuing one's homosexuality by way of engaging in prohibited sexual behaviours can result in criminal charges and the acquisition of a new stigma deriving from criminal status. While both heterosexuals and homosexuals may engage in illegal sexual acts, widespread homophobia among law enforcers has led to the imposition upon homosexuals of discriminatory legal sanctions far more severe than those imposed upon their heterosexual counterparts for the same offending behaviours (Jackson and Persky, 1982: 217).

Probably the most blatant example of a legal 'double standard' applied to homosexuals and not to heterosexuals is the section of the current Canadian Criminal Code that specifies age of consent for sexual acts between consenting adults in private. For both heterosexuals and homosexuals, the age of consent is twenty-one years. However, heterosexuals have the option of marriage, which legalizes sexual relations at an earlier age, while homosexuals do not. Further inequities result from other sections that specify various ages of consent for heterosexual acts between unmarried persons (Jackson and Persky, 1982: 218). The Criminal Code thus provides a form of legal discrimination used to criminalize and prosecute homosexual adolescents. It exacerbates the trauma experienced by vulnerable minority youths already burdened with the pain of a stigma and trying to come to terms with their sexual and affectional identities. From the minority (homosexual) point of view, this kind of legal double standard is seen to be rooted in majority (heterosexual) homophobia – morbid fear and hatred of homosexuals (Canadian Human Rights Commission, 1979).

At the time of writing, homophobia is on the upsurge in North America as a result of media attention to the 'spread' in the United States (and, to a lesser extent, in Canada) of the fatal disease AIDS (Acquired Immune Deficiency Syndrome). Male homosexuals (together with Haitians, haemophiliacs, and intravenous drug-users) have been identified as high-risk populations, and, as the disease is thought to be transmitted through the blood, these populations have been asked not to give blood for transfusions. The highly speculative and equally highly sensational media coverage of this as yet not well understood disease has focused public attention on male homosexuals as a dangerous minority, and has vastly heightened the salience of their stigmata. Fear of contagion through ordinary contact with persons with AIDS, while as yet unwarranted by any evidence, has become rampant. On the one hand, some health workers reportedly are refusing to treat AIDS patients; and on the other hand news reports from the United States indicate that the 'moral majority' is claiming that God is finally punishing the entire homosexual population for its sins, by inflicting its members with the deadly disease (*Globe and Mail*, 7 July 1983; *Time* magazine, 4 July 1983).

A similar kind of public paranoia prevailed in the 1960s when media attention focused on the 'danger' to society posed by the so-called hippies or flower children. Because the youthful hippie counterculture (presumably involving illegal drug-use and extramarital sex) was perceived to pose a threat to established adult moral and sexual values, many parents viewed their long-haired, teenaged offspring as potentially 'dangerous' (juvenile delinquents). Even more serious, police harassment of beflowered, barefooted young people, wherever they gathered together, was a common feature of the discriminatory treatment of this youthful minority in this era by the adult majority (Kallen and Kelner, 1976).

In contrast to the typically harsh, coercive treatment of presumed dangerous minorities, those minorities whose defining attributes mark them as inferior, but relatively harmless, tend to be treated less harshly/more paternalistically by dominant populations. Here, the majority concern is with protecting the minority, rather than with protecting the public peace and moral order of society at large. In historical context, women, children, elderly persons, and aboriginal peoples (Indians and Inuit) have been among those minorites stigmatized by their majority counterparts as inferior/incompetent – incapable of determining their own destinies. Today, mentally retarded and physically disabled persons also tend to fall into this social category. These 'inferior' minorities typically are denied fundamental human rights under a model of paternalism or benevolent despotism (Van den Berghe, 1967). That is to say, they tend to be viewed and treated as less than fully capable, less than fully responsible human beings – persons who 'need' institutional care and supervision under majority authorities. As long as members of inferior minorities stay in their place, that is, as long as they give unquestioned obedience to majority 'rules of the game,' and as long as they accept the restrictions on their fundamental rights and freedoms that accrue to their institutionalized minority status, they will be treated kindly by their caretakers, the majority authorities.

Children provide the archetypical minority for paternalistic policies and treatment. Indeed, the institutional placement of young people in the public schools under the policy of compulsory education originally was designed to keep them 'off the streets' and 'out of trouble' (West, 1978). Within the institutional confines of the early public school, as within the patriarchal parental home, children were to be 'seen but not heard.'

Children, however, grow up. Thus (as was pointed out earlier), their status as a youthful minority changes to that of adult majority. They can, however, acquire a new minority status, and one of the most ambiguous of these in Canadian society today is that of an alcoholic.

Because much of North American hospitality and social life involves alcohol provision and consumption, the line between acceptable and non-acceptable drinking behaviour is a most tenuous one, and one that varies considerably from one social group and from one social situation to another. Drinking on the job or when driving a car is generally considered to be unacceptable behaviour. By contrast, the 'happy hour,' when many bars offer cocktails at half-price – typically the time period between the end of the workday and the evening meal – has become almost institutionalized as 'winding-down time' and an acceptable daily drinking period. Even inebriety (drunken behaviour) meets with situational variations in terms of public reaction. Drunks can be regarded as 'funny' and even 'lovable' provided that their irrational behaviour is not seen as dangerous (to themselves or to others). The reaction of friends and observers to such persons, even habitual drunkards, may be 'kindly' paternalistic, rather than harshly condemnatory. (The hilarious 1980 movie *Arthur* epitomizes this situation.) However, the alcoholic who has reached 'rock bottom' – who has lost the last job, who has been deserted by family and friends, who has used up all sources of funding, and who winds up on skid row – typically suffers a long series of degradation ceremonies at the hands of majority authorities and, eventually, becomes a virtual social outcast (Giffen, 1966).

In the Canadian context, discriminatory treatment by majority care-takers against both 'dangerous' and 'inferior' minorities generally has involved involuntary confinement within a total institution – in the former instance, to protect society, and in the latter, to protect the minorities. However, the nature of institutional care and protection and, particularly, the degree of coercion utilized by dominant authorities to control the two types of minorities have differed. Assumed-dangerous minorities, such as criminals and juvenile delinquents, are more likely to have been incarcerated under lock and key and subject to brutal punishment than have assumed-inferior minorities, such as women, children, and mentally retarded persons.

In reference to the foregoing differences in the social implications of 'dangerous' versus 'inferior' labelling, it should be emphasized that stigmatized minorities frequently are viewed and treated by dominant populations as both dangerous and inferior. Here, I wish to draw particular attention to the notion of 'irrationality,' because a broad range of minority stigmata connoting inferiority and dangerousness rest, at least in part, on majority presumptions of irrationality.

Irrationality and minority stigmata

The ideological emphasis on the human attribute of rationality that permeates Western culture has long provided majority authorities with a publicly endorsed rationale for the stigmatization and social rejection of minorities. Stigmatized minorities presumed to be irrational tend to be feared because of the assumption that they are incapable of controlling their behaviour. The presumption of irrationality has thus carried with it the implication that persons so defined are dangerous both to themselves and to society at large. Concomitantly, treatment of 'irrational' minorities has typically taken the form of total institutionalization, a strategy allegedly designed to protect both the minorities and society at large.

Historically, the comprehensively discrediting attribute of irrationality or 'madness' provided the ideological rationale behind discriminatory policies towards and treatment of a wide variety of alleged mental incompetents. These presumably inferior and dangerous minorities included the mentally retarded and the mentally ill, the physically disabled and the physically deformed, as well as criminals, prostitutes, and paupers (Simmons, 1982). No distinction was made among these various categories of alleged mental incompetents in the nature of the social policies or the discriminatory treatment imposed upon them by the majority. All were defined as irrational, subhuman creatures ('wild beasts') and, accordingly, all were thrown together, locked up and shut away in subhuman, total institutions – 'loony bins,' 'crazy houses,' jailhouses, or poorhouses – where inmates were stripped of all vestiges of their basic human rights.

In the early insane asylums inmates were shackled, beaten, strapped to chairs, and often accorded less than the bare necessities for mere survival (Williams et al, 1972: 399). With advances in modern science and medicine, distinctions between the mental and other attributes of these (traditionally presumed) 'irrational' minorities increasingly became evident and professional/custodial treatment accordingly became both more diversified and more humane.

In conceptual terms, we may say that, in the past, the assumption of mental or intellectual irrationality provided an overarching stigma, and gave rise to a wholly discrediting master status rooted in the twin stigmata of abnormality/dangerousness and inferiority/incompetence. Thus, persons believed to be mentally inferior (idiots, imbeciles) were treated in the same way as those believed to be mentally deranged (lunatics, crazies). In the realm of Canadian public opinion, this association has not yet totally disappeared (Williams et al, 1972), but in professional circles (the realm of the official majority caretakers) the conceptual distinctions between mentally retarded (intellectually impaired) and mentally ill (emotionally impaired) persons has been formally recognized, and majority treatment of these two kinds of minorities (and the various subcategories of members within them) accordingly has become quite different. A major feature of this modern differentiation and its implications for treatment lies in the perceived/believed mutability or immutability of the defining attribute of minority status.

Mental illness is a concept that continues to defy precise definition; yet the human condition of mental illness tends to be perceived as a mutable disability that can be reduced or eliminated by appropriate majority treatment such as psychiatric care. Mental retardation (or 'developmental' disability), however, tends to be defined as a permanent disability. In the current Canadian context, mentally retarded (or developmentally delayed) minority members tend to be viewed and treated as more or less educable, depending on the perceived/believed degree of the disability. However, the disabling attribute itself is considered to be immutable.

Outside of professional, 'caretaker' contexts, majority treatment of minorities whose stigmata include presumed mental disabilities varies with the nature of the other defining attributes of minority status. Racially defined minorities such as blacks and Indians, as well as physically disabled minorities such as paraplegics and cerebral-palsy bearers – those whose visible, stigmatized attributes deviate most markedly from the bodily norms of the majority – have long been erroneously perceived/ treated as mentally inferior and/or impaired (Safilios-Rothschild, 1976). While these stereotyped perceptions are changing, they clearly have not disappeared.

COMMUNITY-WIDE MINORITY ORGANIZATION AND CULTURAL TRANSMISSION THROUGH TIME: FROM MINORITY CATEGORY TO MINORITY GROUP

A final distinction to be made among types of minorities relates to their capability for community organization and for cultural transmission through time. The key variable to be considered here is the degree to which the minority collectivity constitutes a social category or a social group.

If the minority exists as such only or largely in terms of the defining stigmata imposed upon its members by the majority, that is, if the minority consists of a loose aggregate of stigmatized individuals arbitrarily lumped together in a conceptual or statistical category by majority definition, then the potential for its members to mobilize and organize in pursuit of collective goals is weak.

Where group stigmata provide the basis for the master status of minority members, collective identification tends to be negative, and group commitment, low. Where feasible, the individual minority member will likely adopt a strategy of passing, accompanied by a deliberate dissociation from minority-organized groups or events. Thus, deeply closeted homosexuals, epileptics, or alcoholics, for example, not infrequently attempt to minimize or avoid those group situations that involve fraternization with minority members other than selected intimates.

It is not until minority members come to question and to reject majority-imposed stigmata that they may begin to develop a heightened consciousness of majority oppression, neglect, and diminution. When this happens, the valence of collective-minority identity may begin to shift from negative to positive. As positive group consciousness becomes intensified, leaders can begin to mobilize minority members into self-help groups designed to destigmatize minority identities and into pressure groups designed to combat collective discrimination and to bring forward minority-rights claims. Finally, when a minority collectivity develops that degree of institutional completeness that enables minority cultural transmission through time, then the minority collectivity becomes transformed from a minority category to a minority group.

Highly endogamous, institutionally complete, ethnoreligious communities (such as the Hutterites in Canada) provide the archetypical model of a transgenerational minority group. In general, it may be argued that highly endogamous minority cultural communities (e.g., the South Asian Sikhs, the Inuit of the Canadian Arctic, and the urban Chinese and Jews) have a far greater potential for transgenerational group persistence than have subcultural minority communities without sanctioned norms of endogamy such as those formed by gays, lesbians, alcoholics, blind persons, or elderly retirees.

Yet, as suggested earlier, insofar as minority collectivities that are neither endogamous nor family-based develop viable, subcultural, and institutional bases for transgenerational continuity, they also may become transformed from minority categories to minority groups. I might mention, at this point, that such a transformation already is well under way in the case of the gay/lesbian minority: this observation will be documented in some detail in later chapters of this book.

A final variable to be taken into account in assessing the potential for minority organization and for cultural transmission through time is that of the 'authenticity' of the disability behind the minority-group stigma. While the handicapping effects of authentic disabilities may be vastly exaggerated in stigmatizing minority stereotypes, this distortion does not belie the fact of their existence. Blind persons, for example, may not be deaf or mentally retarded, but they are visually impaired. In such cases, where minority status rests, at least in part, on real disabilities, the ability of the minority to mobilize collectively in order to combat discrimination may be restricted, in varying degrees. Thus, young children and the very old as well as the severely mentally or physically disabled, for example, are minorities who to some degree must enlist the help of concerned members of the majority in order to fight discrimination and in order to obtain protection for their fundamental human rights. In such cases, community advocacy can work together with minority advocacy to persuade majority authorities to provide whatever special measures are necessary in order to enable minorities to exercise their human rights as fully as possible.

The argument of the foregoing section delineates the following variables as key factors affecting the ability of a minority to perpetuate a distinctive culture and to organize on their own behalf to combat external discrimination:

1 the degree of community-wide organization (social category vs social group),
2 the scope and distinctiveness of the minority culture (ethnoculture vs subculture),
3 the degree of institutional completeness of the minority community,
4 the strength and valence of collective minority identity (strong vs weak; negative vs positive),
5 the authenticity of the disabilities of members (real vs apparent).

STIGMATIZATION AND MINORITY STATUS: CONCLUDING COMMENTS

In this chapter I have argued that stigmatized minorities are socially created entities whose disadvantaged social status derives from demonstrable human-rights violations based upon prejudiced majority assumptions about group attributes. While the discriminatory implications of stigmatization are ubiquitous, I have shown that the particular forms of discrimination, in any given social context, will vary with the nature of the stigmata and with the presumed degree of deviance of stigmatized-minority attributes from majority norms. Finally, I have postulated a number of variables affecting the collective ability of a minority to overcome stigmatization, to maintain a distinctive culture, and to develop the organizational base necessary for the pursuit of protections for minority rights.

In the next chapter I will focus attention on the forms of discrimination consequent upon stigmatization that serve to institutionalize and perpetuate disadvantaged-minority status. To support my analysis, I will provide empirical documentation for minority-rights violations on the basis of materials drawn from Canadian research findings and from selected, comparable data.

3

Categorical prejudice and discrimination: the subordination of stigmatized minorities[1]

In the last chapter, I argued that stigmatized-minority status represents a long-term outcome of violation of minority rights by majority authorities through acts and practices of categorical discrimination. My analysis demonstrated the way in which majority authorities are able to rationalize, indeed to 'justify,' discrimination against minorities, on the basis of prejudicial majority-created myths and stereotypes that provide pseudo evidence for minority stigmata of inferiority and/or dangerousness.

At this juncture, I will elaborate on the key concepts of prejudice, stereotype, and discrimination that inform the analysis of the social processes whereby stigmatized-minority status is created and sustained.

The concept of *prejudice* refers to biased attitudes, feelings, and/or beliefs towards particular human populations on the basis of unsubstantiated assumptions and *prejudgments* concerning the nature of members' collective, physical, cultural, and/or behavioural characteristics.

Prejudice can be positive or negative in thrust: the bias, that is to say, can be in favour of or against particular human groups. Prejudice also can vary in strength and salience. *Negative* prejudice, for example, may be expressed in a mild form, such as personal feeling of antipathy towards particular human groups and a desire to avoid contact with members of these populations. However, it may be manifested in a severe form such as a dogmatically held mythology of heterosexism, ageism, or handicapism through which ideas are manipulated and distored in order to justify the ideologue's prejudiced assumptions.

Positive prejudice is likely to be manifested towards social categories

---

1 The conceptualization of prejudice and discrimination for this section represents an adaptation of my earlier framework (Kallen, 1982: 28–30 and 35–41).

considered to be superior in human worth and whose members occupy positions of superior social status in society.

In the context of majority/minority relations, majority members are most likely to be prejudiced *towards* majority members and *against* minority members. For minority members, however, the situation is more complex and depends upon the degree to which minority members have internalized or have shed stigmatizing labels.

To clarify: in the case of majority/minority relations, where superior political power, social respect, and economic opportunities are majority prerogatives, the dominant populations tend to be highly ethnocentric and to be negatively prejudiced, in varying degrees, against stigmatized minorities. However, minority members, through the process of stigmatization, may come to identify negatively with their subordinate category. Accordingly, until the process of delabelling and positive relabelling occurs, they may come to be negatively prejudiced against members of their own minority group and positively prejudiced towards majority members.

Prejudice, whether positive or negative, consists of *unsubstantiated* beliefs and *biased* attitudes towards particular human groups. A negatively prejudiced person may come to harbour hostile emotions and defamatory group stereotypes about particular populations.

In relation to the concept of prejudice, the concept of stereotype can be said to represent the pictorial content of the prejudicial attitude or belief, the mental image of the population that is the target of prejudice. While stereotypes generally contain a 'kernel of truth' (Mackie, 1974), they invariably represent distorted images or caricatures that exaggerate some group attributes and disregard others. Not only do group stereotypes ignore the natural range of individual variation within all human populations, but also they overlook the strong, natural affinities in human attributes between populations. Group stereotypes, therefore, are rendered invalid by scientific evidence that clearly demonstrates that differences within human groups are far greater than differences between them (Hughes, 1982).

Insofar as minority stereotypes focus on stigmatized attributes, they serve to underscore negatively prejudiced feelings and attitudes towards target populations. It does not *necessarily* follow, however, that the bearer of prejudice will act upon his or her biased feelings and stereotyped images of particular populations. That is to say, prejudice does not necessarily lead to discrimination. Put simply, the distinction between prejudice and discrimination lies in the difference between what one thinks, feels, and believes, as against what one does.

The concept of *discrimination* refers to biased acts or practices towards particular human populations that afford categorical advantage or disadvantage on the basis of unsubstantiated assumptions about members' collective physical, cultural, and/or behavioural characteristics. Unlike prejudice, discrimination (whether positive or negative) invariably violates human-rights principles. Acts and practices that categorically privilege or disprivilege particular social groups violate the human right to equality/equivalence of opportunity.

Discrimination can be manifested in wide variety of forms. At the level of the individual, an act of discrimination may stem from conscious, personal prejudice. This form of discrimination may be termed *individual discrimination*. An employer who is prejudiced in favour of able-bodied and against disabled applicants for positions, and who thereby excludes *qualified* disabled applicants from job opportunities, provides a case in point.

Often, however, an act of discrimination does not derive from prejudice held by the bearer, but rather from the carrying out by an individual of the dictates of others who are prejudiced or of a prejudiced social institution. This form of discrimination may be termed *institutional discrimination*. To exemplify: an openly gay school teacher applies for a new post at a private boys' school. The headmaster is not homophobic (indeed, he happens to be a closet homosexual); yet, he refuses to hire the gay teacher, despite the applicant's excellent credentials, because of a 'gentleman's agreement' between the school-board and the pupils' parents barring homosexuals from staff positions.

The hypothetical case cited provides an example of institutional rather than individual discrimination. However, if we introduce a single change, namely, that the closeted gay headmaster is prejudiced against openly gay persons – and he fears that by hiring the applicant his own covert homosexuality may be discovered – then our case provides an example of both individual and institutional discrimination.

Individual and institutional forms of discrimination can ultimately be attributed to prejudicial attitudes: the actor either is prejudiced or conforms to the sanctions of other prejudiced persons or institutions. Yet, discrimination can occur even in the absence of conscious prejudice. Over time, a prejudiced *society* can become permeated with structural and cultural forms of discrimination.

The concept of *structural* or *systemic discrimination* refers to group inequalities that have become rooted in the system-wide operation of society as long-term consequence of institutional discrimination against particular human populations.

When members of stigmatized minorities have been categorically denied opportunities to acquire or to use political, economic, educational, and/or social skills and qualifications, as a long-term result the minority *category*, at the group level, becomes increasingly disadvantaged. The collective, adverse impact of group disadvantage becomes compounded through the self-fulfilling prophecy of stigmatization whereby minority members come to lose confidence in themselves and to give up hope of status improvement. Stigmatized minorities thus became locked into their increasingly disadvantaged minority status, excluded from significant social participation, and unable to regain their collective sense of human worth and dignity.

In the area of economic rights (equality/ equivalence of educational and work opportunities), the difference between institutional and systemic forms of discrimination is that the former denies equal chances for majority and minority members with equal qualifications, while the latter denies long-disadvantaged minorities the chances to acquire or reacquire skills and qualifications comparable to those held by majority members. Under the equality-rights provisions of the CRF, Section 15(1) protects all Canadians against individual and institutional discrimination, while Section 15(2) allows special measures of redress against the collective, adverse impact of systemic discrimination for disadvantaged Canadians.

Systemic discrimination probably has taken its greatest toll on disabled minorities in Canada. Because of ingrained majority stereotypes emphasizing and greatly exaggerating the handicapping effects of various mental and physical disabilities, social policies towards disabled minorities have tended to unnecessarily restrict their members' opportunities (Brown, 1977). For example, until recently most disabled children in Canada received minimal education or none at all, because of unfounded, paternalistic assumptions made by majority policy-makers about the inferior human capabilities of disabled persons *as a category*. Moreover, because of these same, negative prejudgments, teachers assigned to educate disabled children typically had little or no special training for the task. Today, despite the fact that educational exclusion is generally a policy of the past, the long-term effects of structural discrimination in education for the disabled are manifold: there are substantial numbers of disabled adults who received little or no education as children, and who must now be provided for from public funds. Included among these adults are those who, as children, had special educational needs that were never met (Brown, 1977).

Systemic or structural discrimination is not necessarily linked to prevailing prejudice (although it almost certainly can be traced to prejudice that existed in the past). The important point here is this: should all prevailing prejudice against a particular stigmatized minority suddenly be removed, the disadvantaged position of the minority category would in no way be improved, for the long-term effects of the self-fulfilling prophecy of stigmatization and denial of opportunity – lack of skills, jobs, and resources, apathy, self-hatred, psycho-social dependency – would remain. In order for status improvement to occur, a process of delabelling and relabelling, together with the provision of special opportunities to 'catch up' in the development of members' skills and resources, would have to be initiated. For example, minority self-help groups could offer minority members psycho-social support in the process of destigmatization, and affirmative-action programs could provide appropriate education, training, and job placement in order to redress long-term economic disadvantage. Further, programs of public education could be instituted in order to eradicate negative minority stereotypes and to pave the way for the participation of minorities in society at large on equal or equivalent terms with majority members. These or other forms of collective redress against long-term categorical discrimination are essential in order to provide long-disadvantaged minorities with the requisite means with which to exercise fully their fundamental political, economic, and social rights.

Like structural discrimination, *cultural discrimination* can produce long-term, system-wide inequities across groups. Cultural discrimination refers to the denial or restriction of the free expression of alternate (minority) cultural values and life-styles. When the moral and cultural values of majority group(s) become sanctioned in law and incorporated into public institutions, they come to provide the normative guide-lines for the whole society. Cultural discrimination occurs when *legitimate* alternatives – minority values and life-styles that are consistent with human-rights principles – are suppressed. *Cultural discrimination*, then, refers to the denial or restriction of the free expression by minorities of their legitimate alternate subcultures.

Cultural discrimination may violate fundamental freedoms – of conscience and religion, of expression, and of peaceful assembly – as in the case of the clash between the Catholic church (majority) and the Jehovah's Witnesses (minority) under the Duplessis government in Quebec. In the years between 1936 and 1959, church and state joined in persecuting Jehovah's Witnesses who carried their struggle for freedom of speech and religion again and again to the Supreme Court of Canada

(Berger, 1981: ch. 6). The Jehovah's Witnesses sought to establish their right, as a legitimate, alternate religious community, to seek converts from the Catholic church, and, to this end, they sought to establish their right to disseminate their religious literature in meeting halls and in the streets of Quebec. To challenge the Catholic church in Quebec, under the Duplessis regime, was not only an act of religious dissent, but also one of political dissent. That the Jehovah's Witnesses sought to campaign openly in the streets, and even on Parliament Hill, underscored the importance they placed on freedom of speech, without which their religious freedom was merely illusory.

Berger (1981) points out that assemblies, parades, and demonstrations may be the only mechanisms through which small, powerless minorities without easy access to media coverage can bring their grievances to public attention. To disallow minorities such activities is to violate their fundamental human rights.

Cultural discrimination may also be manifested in categorical violations of the fundamental right to security of person and the right to be secure against unreasonable search or seizure (not to mention the violations of human dignity that inevitably follow).

The continuing saga of police harassment of homosexuals in Canada is a case in point. In 1981, Metro Toronto police carried out a series of raids on gay bath houses in which private property was smashed, 'found-ins' were charged and exposed to public ridicule, and 'keepers' were dragged through the courts under antiquated 'bawdy house' laws.

Police harassment can be defined as the *selective* surveillance of persons (and cultural institutions) based not on realistic probabilities, but on the prejudices and stereotypes held by the majority community towards members of a particular minority group (Sepejak, 1977: 21).[2] Homosexual establishments – such as bars, baths, and discos – where clientele pursue an alternative sexual life-style – are frequently surveyed, not only for violations of sex laws, but under several other 'legitimate' pretexts such as the possession and display of liquor licences or the serving of alcohol to minors. Harassment as a form of cultural discrimination is involved where there is evidence that establishments catering to homosexuals are surveyed more frequently for possible legal violations than are parallel establishments catering to the heterosexual majority (ibid).

2 This definition relates to the specific context of police surveillance. Police harassment, as evidenced in the infamous bath house raids, extends well beyond surveillance and often entails far greater minority-rights violations.

Following the police raids on Toronto's gay baths, which took place on 5 February 1981, an editorial in the *Globe and Mail*, headed 'Heavy Hand of the Law,' pointed to the unusually large number of police involved in the raids, to the unusually large number of arrests, to the unnecessary violence and destruction involved in police use of sledgehammers and crowbars to smash doors and windows, and to the fact that no such raids had been made on heterosexual bawdy houses in Toronto. In closing, the editorial suggested that other minorities might wonder if 'so gross an action against so many citizens by such a large group of policemen with the support of the Chief of Police . . . means that no minority is safe from harassment in a city where it could happen' (*Globe and Mail*, Editorial, 9 February 1981).

DISCRIMINATION OF SILENCE: HUMAN-RIGHTS VIOLATIONS
BY ACTS OF 'OMISSION'

An important, covert, form of institutional and cultural discrimination that has only recently begun to receive the attention of scholars is the discrimination of silence whereby majority members – those with the legitimate power to do something – choose to say nothing and do nothing about discrimination against minorities in Canada. By such discriminatory acts of 'omission,' the human rights of minorities continue to be violated. Case (1977: 37) contends that silence can be a form of complicity in an act of violence. The fear of exposing invalidation myths and discriminatory public policies predicated upon them; the fear of teaching about minority-rights violations; the fear of engaging in face-to-face encounters with stigmatized minority members – all of these fears lead to discriminatory acts of 'omission' through silence. Discrimination by 'omission' may be deeply rooted in the fear of stigma by association, but whether or not this is so, it is in violation of fundamental principles of human rights.

In a 1982 report of the American Sociological Association's Task Group on Homosexuality, substantial evidence was provided to support the task group's research finding that stigmatization of homosexual minorities has led to widespread discrimination against homosexual professors and also against the undertaking by sociologists of academic research on homosexuality (American Sociological Association, 1982).

Findings, based primarily on three surveys conducted by the task group of sociologists, reveal that the vast majority of sociology department heads in American universities perceive real barriers to the hiring and promotion of known homosexual men and women (gays and lesbians). That this situation compels homosexual sociologists to remain 'closeted' is beyond doubt. Survey findings further reveal that the frequently expressed academic disapproval of homosexuality as a legitimate research topic appears to divert sociologists, heterosexual as well as homosexual, from pursuing research in this area. In this connection, a number of heterosexual sociologists reported personal stigmatization from their association with such research. Fear of stigmatization, then, is probably responsible at least in part for the reportedly small number of university courses dealing with homosexuality.

Insofar as fear of the discriminatory consequences of a stigma or of a stigma by association inhibits the productivity of the very scholars whose potential research and teaching in the area of homosexuality could contribute the most to the public understanding of homosexual (gay and lesbian) minorities, the prospects for reducing overt and covert discrimination against homosexuals are thereby diminished.

While social scientists and other educators, through their research, teaching, and public-speaking activities, could come to constitute a strong majority force towards destigmatization of minorities, this responsibility is not theirs alone. Besides these and other powerful majority authorities – policy-makers, judges, law enforcers, professional caretakers, and the like – there are also those among the families and close friends of stigmatized minority members who participate, often unwittingly, in the discrimination of silence. Well-meaning parents and spouses of homosexual, mentally ill, or alcohol-disabled persons, for example, can contribute to the discriminatory conspiracy of silence by engaging in the deceptive mechanisms designed to keep the stigmatized minority member in the closet.

In the case of the alcoholic minority, fear of the social consequences of alcoholism, such as loss of job and friends, together with fear of a stigma by association, can lead the family and friends of alcohol-disabled persons to engage in a multitude of acts of duplicity in their efforts to 'cover up.' Such closet mechanisms include lying to the boss about the reason for absence from work, paying the long overdue bills, refusing invitations to cocktail parties with friends, and searching for and getting rid of the liquor bottles hidden throughout the premises of home and office.

Because of their lack of understanding of the compulsive nature of the alcoholic's drinking pattern, close family members typically attempt to 'control' the situation. They may attempt to control the intake of alcohol (by hinding bottles or pouring their contents down the sink), they may attempt to control the alcoholic (through threats of breaking up a marriage or through demeaning name-calling to shame the alcoholic into sobriety), and they may attempt to control the alcoholic's behaviour when 'under the influence' (by driving the alcoholic home from a party, by plying him or her with black coffee, and so forth). Increasingly ashamed of the public scenes created by the active alcoholic, family members may retreat, more and more, to the privacy of their own homes where they try (usually unsuccessfully) to 'handle' the problem (*Al-Anon Family Groups*, n.d.: pamphlets 7 and 48). Alcoholism thus becomes a 'family disease' in which the families (and perhaps also close friends) of alcohol-disabled persons, in turn, go into the closet where their lives become a virtual 'merry-go-round' of cover-up activities centring on and catering to the alcoholic minority member (ibid).

The discrimination of silence engendered by the closet syndrome subtly infringes upon the human rights of alcoholic and other stigmatized minorities by helping to perpetuate the stigma. As long as minority members are kept in the closet and no attempt is made to address the handicapping effects of their stigmata, their fundamental (social) right to human dignity will continue to be violated. By doing nothing, or by 'covering up,' what majority members are really doing is protecting *themselves* from the anticipated, discomforting consequences of a stigma by association. At the same time, the closet syndrome impedes the process of destigmatization because it denies the public at large access to realistic information about alcoholism and thus indirectly perpetuates negative stereotypes about alcoholics.

CATEGORICAL DISCRIMINATION: SUMMARY DISCUSSION

All of the examples of discrimination against stigmatized minorities discussed in the foregoing pages can be seen to be *categorical* both in their conception and in their ultimate intent. That is to say, the real target of the discriminatory act, even when it is directed towards a given individual, is the minority *as a whole*. The erroneous underlying assumption behind categorical discrimination is that all members of the target population share the particular attribute(s) upon which differential treatment is predicated. In the case of discrimination against (presumed) members of a particular stigmatized minority, it is the minority as an entirety that bears the stigma(ta) triggering the discriminatory act or practice.

Thus, for example, when an employer arbitrarily discriminates against a female applicant for a job that requires the lifting of heavy objects, the discriminatory act is directed not against the particular female applicant – whose personal skills have not been tested – but against all females as a social category. (The underlying invalidation myth is that females are inherently weaker than males and that all females are incapable of lifting heavy objects.)

Similarly, when the manager of a restaurant or bar arbitrarily refuses to admit a physically disabled person in a wheelchair, the discriminatory act is not directed towards this particular disabled customer – who may be virtually unknown to the manager in question – but against the entire chair-bound disabled population as a social category. (The underlying invalidation myth is that the aberrant appearance and ungainly behaviour of disabled clients will spoil other clients' enjoyment and will therefore drive away customers.)

The categorical nature of discrimination against stigmatized minorities is important to understand because it provides majorities with one of their most powerful techniques of domination. By categorically denying equal/equivalent opportunities to entire minority populations, majorities are able to maintain their own political, economic, social, and cultural hegemony in the society.

Notwithstanding the latter observation, within the normative context of a democratic society, majorities must be able to 'justify' categorical violations of minority rights. They must provide 'evidence' to show that particular stigmata render their bearers unworthy and undeserving of social equality and full human-rights protections.

RATIONALIZING MAJORITY HEGEMONY: INVALIDATION MYTHS

In order to imbue their double standards with social legitimacy, majorities draw upon existing, deeply rooted public prejudices. Majority authorities use prejudicial invalidation myths to 'expose' minority stigmata and to 'prove' minority inferiority and/or dangerousness in order to justify discriminatory measures built into societal institutions.

Invalidation myths play an important part in maintaining majority hegemony by influencing public opinion in favour of discriminatory majority policies towards stigmatized minorities. Because of widely held public prejudice against particular minorities, public opinion may be *predisposed to accept* invalidation myths, despite their lack of scientific validity. Thus invalidation myths are endorsed *without question* as a legitimating basis for the unequal and inhumane treatment of stigmatized minorities.

TABLE 3
Survey on group differences

	Agree		
	1982	1984	1986
1. As a group, whites are smarter than blacks.	19 (16%)	10 (9%)	5 (8%)
2. Women are the weaker sex.	19 (16%)	18 (16%)	12 (20%)
3. Homosexuals have a stronger and more urgent sex drive than do others.	23 (19%)	16 (15%)	7 (11%)
4. You can always spot a Jew, because they stick to their own kind.	18 (15%)	25 (24%)	14 (23%)
5. Elderly people, compared to others, have little need for sex.	27 (22%)	31 (30%)	13 (21%)
6. As a group, young adults are more intelligent than elderly people.	15 (12%)	6 (5%)	9 (15%)
7. Native peoples (Indians and Inuit) tend to become alcoholics more frequently than do other Canadians.	42 (35%)	33 (31%)	29 (48%)
8. As a group, physically handicapped people tend to be mentally slower than physically normal people.	22 (18%)	12 (11%)	11 (18%)
9. Alcoholics tend to come from the poorer classes of society.	24 (20%)	16 (15%)	10 (17%)
10. Mentally retarded persons are easily distinguishable because they look different from others.	59 (49%)	47 (45%)	20 (33%)
11. Homosexuality is unnatural.	65 (54%)	63 (60%)	38 (63%)
All statements are incorrect (Nos. 1–11).	22 (18%)	16 (15%)	18 (30%)
	[N = 121]	[N = 108]	[N = 78]

The results of a survey on 'group differences' I administered to incoming classes of first-year undergraduate students at York University (North York, Ontario) may serve to illustrate.

In the opening lecture of a first-year social-science course, in each of three academic years (1982, 1984, 1986), students were asked to participate in a survey on 'group differences.' Students were then presented with a list of eleven statements, and were instructed to respond to each of these with a mark of agreement (Y) or disagreement (N). Each statement represented a prevalent invalidation myth.

Survey responses (see table 3) clearly revealed the continuing acceptance of minority-invalidation myths among these students. While some
minorities (homosexuals, mentally retarded, aboriginal peoples) were
found, consistently, to be more highly stigmatized than others, none of
the minorities depicted in the survey statements fully escaped stigmatizing assumptions. That is to say, not a single prejudicial statement about a
given minority was dismissed as incorrect by all (or even close to all)
student respondents in any of the three years that the survey was
administered.

Equally important, with regard to the foregoing survey responses, is
the fact that later discussions with students in small-group (tutorial)
format revealed that myths and stereotypes pertaining to particular
minorities tended, not infrequently, to be accepted not only by outsiders
(members of other [majority and minority] groups), but also by insiders
(members of minorities in question).

INSTITUTIONALIZED DISCRIMINATION: THE KEY TO MAJORITY
HEGEMONY

While invalidation myths that depict members of stigmatized minorities
as inferior in human capabilities and/or dangerous to society provide
important rationales for categorical (majority) discrimination, *in themselves* such myths are not sufficient to maintain majority hegemony in a
society. In order to understand the way in which majority authorities are
able to maintain their dominance and control over minorities in the long
term, attention must be directed to the mechanisms of *institutionalization*
of discrimination throughout the society.

Institutionalized practices of discrimination in the legal, political,
economic, social, and cultural spheres of societal life provide majority
authorities with legitimate, publicly recognized and supported techniques of domination and control of stigmatized minorities.

In the following section of this chapter, we will look at some of the
forms of institutional discrimination in Canada that have served to restrict
or deny the full exercise of the individual and collective human right of
stigmatized minorities.

Institutionalized spheres of discrimination

Denial of franchise
Denial of franchise is an institutionalized form of oppression; it denies
minorities their fundamental human right of access to political participa-

tion and power, and it infringes upon the right of minority members to determine their own destinies.

Historically, in Canada, a great many minorities including women, 'Orientals' (Chinese, Japanese, and East Indians), 'Negroes,' Anabaptists, Jews, aborginal peoples (Indians, Inuit, and Métis), as well as children, mentally and physically disabled, and a variety of incarcerated populations have been disenfranchised under provincial and federal legislation. Today, legal forms of disenfranchisement based on criteria of race, sex, and religion have all but disappeared. However, such discrimination continues to be considered legitimate when enacted to exclude those minorities deemed to be incapable of the 'rational,' 'mature,' 'responsible,' and presumably 'informed' exercise of the franchise: children under eighteen, the institutionalized mentally ill, and the mentally retarded minorities. The categorical assumption of human irrationality or incompetence underlying denial of franchise obscures and neglects the entire range of *individual variation* within these minority categories. Moreover, it also ignores the *parallel* range of variation among majority populations (over eighteen years, mentally healthy, mentally capable) whose members are categorically assumed to be rational and competent, hence capable of the responsible exercise of the franchise. That these contrasting assumptions are not (indeed cannot be) supported by scientific evidence goes without saying. Nevertheless, it is because of such prejudicial assumptions that minority members are categorically denied their fundamental right of political participation.

Legal denial of franchise also is deemed to be legitimate when it is enacted to exclude those institutionalized minorities deemed to be inherently dangerous and thereby undeserving of their right to exercise the franchise. Under the Criminal Code (Section 682) and the Canada Elections Act (Section 14), inmates of penal institutions are commonly disenfranchised, and under the latter piece of legislation, inmates of mental institutions are summarily denied their right of franchise (Mewett, 1979: 250). Prisoners identified as mentally ill are doubly stigmatized; they are assumed to be dangerous both to themselves and to society at large. Institutionalization within penal psychiatric facilities often results not only in denial of franchise, but also in other human-rights violations through cruel and degrading treatment of minority inmates.

In the case of denial of franchise for inmates of penal institutions, it can be argued, from a human-rights perspective, that the right to vote is not a reward for good behaviour; it is a fundamental human right that does not have to be earned and that should not be abrogated unless clear incompetence in rational decision-making ability can be demonstrated.

To deny penal inmates this right today can be seen as an act of 'archaic paternalism' (Mewett, 1979: 250).

While some victims of severe mental disease and some severely mentally disabled persons may, in fact, be (temporarily or permanently) incapable of the rational exercise of their right to vote, this clearly is not true for all. Yet the general wording of Section 14 of the Canada Elections Act *categorically* applies to all mental patients. There are no distinctions made among different kinds of mental disorders, among the different kinds of psychiatric facilities, among the different situations and conditions of the persons inhabiting these facilities. Accordingly, there are no clear criteria provided in the act for determining the specific cases of demonstrated incompetence where abrogation of fundamental human rights through the denial of franchise is absolutely justified (Canada, House of Commons, 1981: 24).

While members of physically disabled minorities face no legal impediments to their right to vote, in practice disabled persons in Canada may be prevented from exercising the franchise because the voting system makes it difficult for many members of this minority to travel to and to gain access to polls on election day. The prevailing policy of centralizing polling places, the practice of locating polls in premises inaccessible to persons with mobility problems, the unavailability of a postal vote-system option (except in the Province of Manitoba) – all of these obstacles restrict or entirely impede the ability of some disabled persons to exercise their franchise (Canada, House of Commons, 1981: 22).

Denial of public facilities/services and housing/ accommodation
Denial of equal access to public services and housing represents an institutionalized form of neglect; it denies stigmatized minorities their fundamental human right of economic maintenance. Some of the most blatant examples of this form of discrimination in recent years are found in cases involving gays and lesbians.

In a 1979 policy-planning report on 'sexual orientation' prepared for the Canadian Human Rights Commission (CHRC), the authors cite numerous instances of alleged discrimination against homosexuals (CHRC, 1979: 95–7).

In the area of public services, in Ontario, during 1974 – and with explicit reference to their sexual orientation – four lesbians were evicted from a tavern; several gay men were evicted from a delicatessen; a (male) gay couple was refused OHIP reimbursement; and the invitation extended to an openly gay speaker by a group of secondary-school teachers was revoked. In the area of housing, during the period from 1974 to 1977, a lesbian couple was refused a family unit by an Ontario Housing landlord; four lesbians had their rent increased by a landlord who told them that 'lesbians should pay more'; a gay man was evicted from his apartment; and one lesbian couple was denied accommodation on York University premises, while another lesbian couple was evicted from their apartment. From 1982 to 1986, five cases of discrimination on the basis of sexual orientation were reported in connection with the rental of apartment accommodation. In one case, a notice for shared accommodation in the University Centre (Guelph) read: 'NO GAYS! only stipulation' (Coalition for Gay Rights of Ontario [CGRO], 1986: 20–1). According to sources cited, the foregoing examples represent only a minor part of the cumulative evidence of widespread denial to gays and lesbians of equal access to public services and housing, throughout Canada.

The 1981 House of Commons report (*Obstacles*) provides compelling evidence for the contention that architectural inaccessibility is one of the most overt barriers to equal access for the mobility-disabled to public buildings, to transportation, to housing, and to other services. To cite but a few of the multitude of examples of architectural inaccessibility reported: the long series of steps restricting access to Parliament Hill; the inaccessibility at many public-transportation terminals of parking areas, toilets, ticket counters, baggage lockers, restaurants, telephones, and drinking fountains; the absence of mechanical facilities or services for lifting people in wheelchairs on and off vehicles; the extreme shortages of appropriate housing facilities adapted to the special needs of the disabled for independent living; and the similar shortage of group homes, suitable for the disabled who need respite care (Canada, House of Commons, 1981: chs. 5–8).

The *Obstacles* report also documents the discriminatory nature of barriers to equal access to information and communications, especially in the cases of the hearing-impaired and vision-impaired disabled minorities (Canada, House of Commons, 1981: ch. 4). In the case of vision-impaired persons, the paucity of radio reading services (special programs that provide in-depth reading of newspapers, periodicals, and popular books) impedes minority members' ability to receive current information and thus prevents them from keeping up to date in their understanding of life in their own and other communities. A similar shortage of general books, government documents, periodicals, and educational materials transcribed into Braille restricts the access to vital information of the vision-impaired. In the case of the hearing-impaired, a parallel situation has been documented. Here, barriers are posed, for example, by the paucity of captioned television programming and other visual media and by the widespread lack of provision in conference centres, theatre centres, and educational facilities of special equipment for the hearing-impaired.

The foregoing examples draw attention to the fact that, in the case of disabled minorities, realistic provision of equality of opportunity requires *special* (equivalent, compensatory) treatment rather than *standard* treatment (the same as for the majority). It requires special, compensatory mechanisms – architectural adaptations, such as ramps and handrails on buildings; and technological aids, such as books in Braille and captioned television programming – in order to overcome the handicapping effects of authentic disabilities. Continuing failure to provide appropriate special aids to the disabled indirectly perpetuates systemic barriers to participation in public life.

The *Obstacles* report included numerous, concrete recommendations to the federal government, designed to improve accessibility for the disabled to public institutions and designed to afford disabled Canadians equivalence of societal opportunity. None the less, in 1987, the Coalition of Provincial Organizations of the Handicapped (COPOH) was still trying to persuade the government to implement these, as yet largely ignored, recommendations (CHRA, III 5, May 1987).

The disadvantaging effects of systemic barriers to opportunity for disabled populations have long been compounded by ongoing instances of individual and institutional discrimination in everyday life. In 1975, a brief on human rights prepared by the Alberta Committee of Action Groups for the Disabled (cited in Brown, 1977: 447) revealed that handicapism was widespread throughout the province. Among the documented instances of discrimination against disabled minorities were the following.

A man confined to a wheelchair, together with his ambulatory friends, entered a tavern. The entire group was refused service by a waiter who said that it was house policy not to serve chair-bound persons.

A young man disfigured by a non-contagious skin condition was refused service in a restaurant. Even after his companion explained that the disfiguring condition was non-contagious, the disabled person was asked to leave on the grounds that he would infect the other customers and drive them away.

A young woman confined to a wheelchair was refused rental accommodation in three apartment buildings, all of which were easily accessible to chair-bound disabled persons. Three different excuses were used to justify the refusal by rental agents: the wheelchair would leave tracks on the rugs; the wheelchair would scratch the walls; and the rental policy excluded people in wheelchairs.

In a 1976 report on discrimination against the blind, Greenland (cited in Brown, 1977: 446) demonstrated that members of this minority were victims of some of the most patent forms of discrimination. For example, several blind couples reported that they had been refused rental accommodation above the ground floor in high-rise buildings, allegedly as a safety precaution. Refusals to provide mortgages and even insurance to blind householders also were documented.

Under Section 15 of the CRF, and under recent amendments to virtually all federal and provincial human-rights legislation, physically disabled minorities have gained and are continuing to gain legal protections against many of the forms of discrimination documented here and elsewhere in this book. Yet, public attitudes and institutionalized practices of handicapism are slow to change. New cases continue to come under consideration each year by various human-rights commissions and tribunals throughout Canada (see chapter 7).

Denial of employment opportunities
Denial of equal access to employment, wage, and/or promotion opportunities constitutes an overt violation of the fundamental economic rights of minorities. Without adequate jobs and earned income, minority members become economically dependent on 'benevolent' welfare hand-outs from the majority controllers of Canada's democratic welfare state.

Because majority myths of handicapism have long permeated Canada's economic institutions, examples of discimination against disabled minorities in the area of employment are rampant.

According to Greenland (cited in Brown, 1977: 446), blind people seeking employment, particularly in the public service and in industry, frequently are treated as 'pariahs.' For example, despite the fact that the safety records of (variously) handicapped workers have been found to be significantly better than the average, blind applicants continue to be refused employment on the grounds that they might harm themselves or others. Similarly, in some parts of Canada, blind persons reportedly have been refused employment in areas where food is prepared, on the alleged grounds that public-health laws prohibit hiring the blind. Yet no such discriminatory statutes have been found to exist (ibid).

As recently as 1986, the unemployment rate among disabled adults in Canada was estimated to be between 50 and 80 per cent (*Toronto Star*, 4 October 1986). In large part, this violation of disabled-minority members' economic rights has been a result of structural (systemic) discrimination – inadequate education and training and inaccessibility of educational institutions and employment facilities. Equally important, however, has been the widespread lack of understanding of disabled people's *capabilities* on the part of would-be employers. Equal employment opportunities have long been categorically denied to *qualified*, disabled persons.

A feature article in the *Toronto Star* (4 October 1986) profiled three disabled Canadians: Mike, who has a hearing and visual disability; David, who is legally blind; and Rose, who has cerebral palsy and is chair-bound. Mike has an honours degree in political science; David has a master's degree in political science and is finishing another in computer science; Rose has a diploma in business administration and is taking night courses in human-resources management. All three individuals are articulate, motivated, and highly skilled, and all three are unemployed. They are not exceptions to the rule: the estimated unemployment rate for disabled persons who have university education is 26 per cent, ten times that for the non-disabled. In light of this evidence for handicapism in employment, together with the previously documented evidence for handicapism in access to public facilities and services, it is not surprising that the largest number – nearly one-third – of discrimination cases heard by the Canadian and Ontario human-rights commissions are based in disability (ibid).

Where disabled minority members have been able to obtain employment, they have tended to be hired as cheap labour; hence, regardless of their skills, they have typically performed menial jobs for menial wages (*Toronto Star*, 4 October 1986). Thus, continuing institutional discrimination in employment compounds the disadvantaging effects of long-term, systemic discrimination against the disabled minority.

Sheltered workshops: institutionalized paternalism
Until very recently, disabled persons, if they were employed at all, were employed for the most part in *sheltered workshops*. In these special institutions for the disabled, employees receive well below minimum wages, in essence, 'pocket money.'

Sheltered workshops were originally designed as modes of vocational rehabilitation for *severely* mentally and physically disabled persons – those for whom regular jobs, realistically appraised, are not an appropriate long-range goal. The paid work experience, even at menial tasks (such as filling Christmas stockings), was designed to restore a sense of human dignity and usefulness to otherwise socio-economically dependent, severely disabled people. Sheltered workshops also were designed to provide an antidote to social isolation. They were supposed to afford severely disabled workers a community of peers and to foster in them a sense of community responsibility and group belonging (Feintuck, 1958).

In practice, however, as a result of continuing massive unemployment among members of disabled minorities, employees in sheltered workshops tend to be drawn from all ranks of disabled populations, including highly educated and skilled minority members. For the many *overquali-fied*, *non*–severely disabled employees, the sheltered workshop is a most *inappropriate* social placement. Rather than serving to restore employees' sense of self-worth and self-esteem it serves to degrade them, to violate their fundamental right to human dignity.

The traumatic effects of this experience are starkly depicted in the Canadian stage production *Creeps* (1972). The play's author, David Freeman, currently hailed as a brilliant young playwright, is a person disabled with cerebral palsy.

The setting of the play is in the wash-room of a Canadian-based sheltered workshop for persons disabled with cerebral palsy. The story unfolds as a series of degradation ceremonies experienced by disabled employees as a consequence of their inappropriate social placement and their paternalistic treatment at the hand of majority caretakers. The shattering psycho-social effects of the dehumanizing workshop experience are shockingly revealed in the comments of one of the play's key actors when he compares his own situation with that of a character in a book he is reading:

Tom: Anyway, it's about this guy who has this sickness that puts him into a coma every so often. And he's scared as hell someone's going to mistake him and bury him alive. Well, that's the way I feel about this workshop. It's like I'm at the bottom of a grave yelling 'I'm alive! I am alive!' But they don't hear me. They just keep shovelling in the dirt. (Freeman, 1972: 14)

While the play *Creeps* purportedly is a work of fiction, it represents the real-life experiences of a large sector of Canada's disabled population. A November 1987 report, detailing COPOH's preliminary position on fiscal arrangements affecting disabled Canadians (COPOH, 1987: 9–10), points out that a large proportion of the funds directed towards the needs of disabled Canadians go towards the support of sheltered employment. COPOH has developed policy initiatives designed to end the exploitation of disabled persons in these settings. Their ultimate goal is to terminate the sheltered-workshop system and to secure community-based employment for disabled Canadians. As an interim, short-term strategy, the adoption by all provinces of the Quebec model, which moves towards the payment of real wages to disabled persons engaged in sheltered employment and provides a realistic training option, is supported by COPOH (ibid).

Probably among the most controversial instances of discrimination in the area of employment are those involving the alcohol-disabled minority. Results of a 1974 national survey estimated that Canadian 'problem-drinking' workers cost industry about one million dollars per day. Yet, the stereotyped 'skid-row alcoholic' accounted for only 10 per cent of alleged problem drinkers (Calendino, 1975). The estimated costs to industry of widespread problem drinking among employees are exceedingly high, not only in dollars per day, but also in terms of decline or loss of productivity. Factors associated with problem drinking of employees include: on-the-job accidents, lateness, absenteeism, and poor morale affecting co-workers. As a result, a growing number of industries have launched employee assistance programs that employ coercion ('constructive confrontation techniques') as a technique for encouraging entry of problem-drinking employees into various alcohol-treatment programs. Where these programs have been instituted, the alcohol-disabled employee is presented with the option of entering the treatment program or being fired from his or her job on the grounds of alcohol abuse (Freedberg and Johnston, 1978).

Drinking on the job or inadequate performance on the job by an employee because of an alcohol-related problem or disability may threaten the safety of the employee, co-workers, and/or the public. In such cases, employers may, *justifiably*, invoke appropriate sanctions against alcohol-related behaviours.[3]

Alternatively, categorical discrimination occurs when employment opportunities are denied to *inactive*, recovered/recovering alcoholics (those minority members who are no longer drinking, including those seeking treatment at a recognized alcoholism facility). Inactive (recovering or recovered) alcoholics often are refused employment, based on their past problem rather than on their present condition (PEI Human Rights Commission, 1986: 31).

Institutionalized discrimination against the alcohol-disabled minority

---

3 From a human-rights view, 'coerced' treatment is problematic, because it may constitute oppression.

may also be found in the nature of the work environment itself. Among the many factors that have been found to trigger or exacerbate the condition of alcoholism, an unusually stressful work environment in which alcohol is readily available as an 'antidote' is prominent (Jenkins and Shain, 1982).

In a 1981 case brought before the commissioner of the Workman's Compensation Board of British Columbia, the plaintiff claimed that the conditions of his employment – namely, prolonged periods of isolation and loneliness in logging camps, together with the easy availability of alcohol – led to his becoming an alcoholic and subsequently to his developing cirrhosis of the liver. While the foregoing conception of alcoholism as an 'occupational disease' has not as yet achieved legal recognition, there is a growing trend, based on decisions in Workmen's Compensation Law in North America, for employers to take more and more responsibility for the mental health of workers. Alcoholism is beginning to be seen in this context (Jenkins and Shain, 1982).

Discrimination against homosexuals in the area of employment provides another area of majority/minority relations where employer decisions frequently are clouded by ingrained prejudice against stigmatized minorities, in this case by deeply rooted homophobic myths and fears.

We have argued earlier that institutionalized forms of discrimination rest on invalidation myths that provide majority authorities with prejudicial rationalizations for continuing violations of the fundamental human rights of stigmatized minorities. At this juncture, it may be useful to examine the stereotypical nature of some of these mythologies in order to aid the reader in understanding the way in which they are used to justify institutionalized discrimination.

Homophobic myths of invalidation
Among the most commonly held myths underscoring discrimination against homosexuals in the area of employment are the following:

[As a group] ...
1. homosexual men are effeminate and homosexual women are masculine
2. homosexuals are obsessed with sex
3. homosexuals recruit other people to homosexuality
4. homosexuals are child molesters (CHRC, 1979: 24)

While unsupported by any kind of scientific evidence, these myths continue to influence public opinion against homosexuals. The seemingly widespread homophobic fears of parents and school staff members that homosexual teachers will turn their pupils into homosexuals or will sexually attack young students, or will do both, rests on the erroneous assumptions of the last two myths (3 and 4).[4]

Despite the fact that none of these invalidation myths is substantiated by scientific evidence, the fears and the hatred they generate are deeply imbedded in the homophobic psyche of a great many members of the heterosexual majority. Not surprisingly, such highly charged feelings of prejudice provide potent ammunition for institutional discrimination against homosexuals, especially in work environments involving direct contact with children.

In November 1977, John Argue, an instructor in swimming at Glenview Senior Public School in Toronto, was threatened with dismissal by the principal when his homosexual orientation became known. After lengthy discussions with the students, their parents, and the principal, he was guardedly allowed to retain his job as lifeguard, provided that he observed strict limitations on his movements and on his associations with students both in and out of class.

Specifically, Mr Argue was required to observe the following job 'criteria': that he wear, on duty, clearly distinguishable bathing gear, to visibly set him apart from the students; that he not shower or swim with the students; that he leave his office door open into the boys' dressing-room while supervising students there; that he not eat lunch with the students or meet them in the ravine during lunch hour; that he not discuss his life-style – social or political – with students outside of school hours (CGRO, 1978: 12 and Appendices A–D).

Another area of employment where homophobic myths clearly underscore policies that exclude known homosexuals is in the Canadian Armed Forces. In May 1977, Barbara Thornborrow, stationed at the Canadian Forces Base in Ottawa, was expelled from the Armed Forces, after eighteen months of service, when it was discovered that she was a lesbian (CGRO, 1978: 12). In July 1977, Gloria Cameron, stationed at the Canadian Forces Base in Argentia, Nfld, was expelled from the Armed Forces, after eight years of service, when her superior discovered that she was a

---

4 Research evidence suggests the contrary. Children of homosexual fathers, for example, have not been found to be victims of sexual molestation, nor have they been found to harbour homosexual tendencies in disproportionate numbers. Most sexual offences against children are found to be perpetrated by heterosexual males, often relatives of the victim (CHRC, 1979: 24–5).

lesbian (CGRO, 1978: 12). The latter example highlights the fact that the stigma attached to homosexuality can wipe out the achievements of a long career in the service, in one fell swoop.

The reader may ask: How can the Canadian Forces Admiralty justify such discrimination? In a letter to Gordon Fairweather, then chairman of the Canadian Human Rights Commission, dated 26 July 1979, Admiral R.H. Falls of the Department of National Defence provided an 'official' rationalization for the discriminatory policy of the Canadian Forces. At the outset, he admitted that 'homosexual conduct is not condoned and, therefore, that homosexual persons are not knowingly enrolled or retained in the Forces' (CHRC, 1979: Appendix II, 74–5). In defence of this policy, he argued that because the Canadian Armed Forces provides a combined working and social milieu – frequently at isolated posts, at sea, or in barracks where there is little personal privacy – persons having 'unusual' behavioural traits may attempt to 'inflict them' on others. Moreover, he contended that the presence of known homosexuals can be disruptive, because there have been physical attacks against such persons in the past. As well, he said, a further risk posed by homosexuals in positions involving security clearance is that of blackmail because of the 'involvement of a partner.' Finally, Admiral Falls raised the 'serious question' of the public image of the Canadian Forces, in the eyes of nationals, foreign nationals, and allied military forces. The inclusion of known homosexuals in Canada's Armed Forces, he claimed, would mar the public image of the Armed Forces and, concomitantly, would lower morale and destroy group cohesiveness in the service. It would seriously dampen the 'military spirit' and the collective self-image of the Forces, both of which are of supreme importance in crisis situations (CHRC, 1979: Appendix II, 74–5).

The homophobic myths underlying the foregoing allegations are virtually self-evident. Most important, what should be clear to the reader is that the basic assumptions behind Admiral Falls's interpretation of the Canadian Forces' policy of exclusion of known homosexuals relate largely to invalidation myths about homosexuals, rather than to empirically documented evidence. To wit: it is feared that homosexuals will try to recruit; that they will be uniquely subject to physical attack; that they will be blackmailed; and that they will tarnish the image of the Armed Forces both at home and abroad.

In direct contrast to the discriminatory practices of the Armed Forces, the findings of a public-opinion survey carried out by the CHRC in 1976 revealed that 68 per cent of Canadians sampled were found to be in favour of a non-discriminatory hiring policy, even in the sensitive area of national security (CHRC, 1979: 41).

In March 1986, the federal government of Canada issued a policy report entitled *Toward Equality*. This report represented the government's response to the report of the Parliamentary Committee on Equality Rights (*Equality for All*) that recommended changes to federal laws and regulations to make them conform to the equality-rights provisions under Section 15 (1) and (2) of the CRF. In *Toward Equality*, the government made a commitment to abolish discrimination against homosexuals in all areas of federal jurisdiction, including the Armed Forces and the Royal Canadian Mounted Police (RCMP). The government also promised that the minister of justice would give careful consideration to the recommendation in *Equality for All* that the Criminal Code be amended to ensure that the minimum age or ages at which private consensual sexual activity is lawful be made uniform without distinction based on sexual orientation (*Toward Equality*, 1986: 13–14).

Should these policy recommendations have been implemented through appropriate legislative changes and through concomitant changes in federal-service employment practices, the federal government of Canada would have taken a giant step towards the recognition and protection of the human rights of homosexual (gay and lesbian) minorities.

However, the policy position on sexual orientation in *Toward Equality* sparked immediate opposition from politicians, from federal-service representatives, and from the public at large. Upon public release of the policy paper, an article in the *Toronto Star* (5 March 1986) indicated that more than half of the 211-member Progressive Conservative caucus were opposed to the proposals allowing homosexuals to serve in the Armed Forces and in the RCMP. According to this news source, Alex Kindy (PC–Calgary East) had expressed the opinion that 50 per cent of the Tory caucus would oppose 'special rights' for homosexuals because it would 'condone a third sex – somebody who is not exactly normal' (*Toronto Star*, 6 March 1986). Similar sentiments were expressed in a rural Ontario newspaper by reporter John Palmer who commented that 'homosexuals and butch-women are going to be let loose on our armed forces. Sanity, common sense and reasonableness are out the window . . . The fact is . . . that homosexuals in a military unit – and especially aboard a ship – are a third sex' (*Orillia Packet and Times*, 6 March 1986).

Vociferous opposition to the government's promise to include sexual orientation in the list of non-discriminatory grounds of the Canadian

Human Rights Act eventually led to the Conservative cabinet decision, in 1987, to block the introduction of all amendments to the act promised in *Toward Equality* (CHRA, III 10, November 1987). Pivotal for this retrogressive decision was the adamant refusal of commanders in the Canadian Armed Forces (CAF) to comply with the government promise to prohibit discrimination in all areas of federal jurisdication on the basis of sexual orientation. The position of the CAF clearly reflects the continuing, widespread embracement within military ranks of homophobic invalidation myths alleging that the presence of homosexuals in the Armed Forces poses a threat to national security (ibid).

The impact of the government's refusal to move ahead with the human-rights amendments promised in *Toward Equality* is ominous, not only for homosexuals, but also for other minorities affected. Disabled minorities, for example, have eagerly awaited implementation of a promised amendment that would require reasonable accommodation of their needs. Women, like homosexuals, have hoped that the military would, at long last, accept them simply as human beings, some of whom are fully capable of active combat duty in defence of their country. At the time of writing, however, these minorities must cope with a serious set-back to such human-rights aspirations at the level of federal jurisdiction.

Denial of educational opportunities
Denial of equal educational opportunities is another institutionalized form of economic neglect, a violation of the economic rights of stigmatized minorities. Because knowledge and skills acquired through formal education and training are keys to effective participation in the economic sphere of modern societies, denial of educational opportunities sets off a self-perpetuating cycle of economic deprivation – one of the most devastating manifestations of the self-fulfilling prophecy of stigmatization.

Non-existent or segregated and unequal educational opportunities historically have been responsible in large part for the systemic condition of unemployment and underemployment among physically and mentally disabled minorities in Canada.

In the case of the mentally retarded (developmentally delayed) minority, a pervasive invalidation myth underlying long-term denial of appropriate educational opportunities has been the 'myth of the menace of the feeble-minded' (Simmons, 1982). At the beginning of the twentieth century, existing Canadian laws (for example, in the province of Ontario) permitted the institutionalization of persons defined as idiots (irre-sponsible in their actions) or as lunatics (dangerous to the community). Social reformers of the time conceived of the 'feeble-minded' as a minority category different from, and more intelligent than idiots (the profoundly mentally retarded, for whom total institutional care and protection were deemed essential). Nevertheless, early social reformers considered the feeble-minded to be 'dangerous' to the community, on 'evidence' such as the high rate of illegitimacy among (alleged) feeble-minded women. By linking the feeble-minded minority with major social problems such as delinquency, prostitution, and other crimes, social reformers sought to demonstrate that the appropriate placement for this minority, as for 'idiots,' was in custodial institutions, segregated by sex.

While they argued for incarceration and sexual segregation of the feeble-minded as a means of social control, the early social reformers essentially presented a *paternalistic* case. They saw the feeble-minded as a class of permanent, irresponsible children who needed some form of permanent care and supervision under majority authorities. Simmons (1982: 108–9) contends, however, that it was never argued that all mentally retarded persons should be totally institutionalized. Rather, he says, the lines between that category of feeble-minded deemed unable to cope in society at large or who posed a social 'menace' (those who needed total institutional care) and those who presumably could be educated and trained to live in the community were constantly being drawn and redrawn according to changing majority definitions of feeble-mindedness and according to changing social conditions.

These *definitional* (and policy) distinctions notwithstanding, Simmons demonstrates that before the Second World War mentally retarded persons in *general* were regarded and treated as a pariah group: a class of non-persons, inherently inferior to and set apart from the rest of society. Moreover, as the myth of the menace of the feeble-minded gathered steam, in the pre–Second World War period, it gave rise to social policies that increasingly violated the human rights of 'non-persons,' labelled feeble-minded. Incarceration policies not only precluded educational opportunities, but also came to favour the sterilization of inmates. For the non-incarcerated (presumably more or less 'educable') members of the mentally retarded population, the provision of appropriate educational programs, from the beginning, was a policy goal marked by non-implementation or sporadic *paternalistic* implementation, at best. In both instances, the educational needs and capabilities of the 'educable' feeble-minded minority were not met.

In recent years, the educational placement of children with mental, physical, or emotional disabilities in Canada has been the subject of numerous studies, among the most extensive of which was the 1970 report of the Commission on Emotional and Learning Disorders in Children (CELDIC). The findings of the CELDIC report revealed widespread unfulfilment on the part of federal, provincial, and local officials of their educational obligations and responsibilities to children with special needs. Mentally and physically disabled children frequently were found to be deprived of access to public schools, and where access was achieved these children tended to be streamed off into separate classes and programs, usually with inadequate support services. Those children unable to participate in the regular school system typically were provided with minimum facilities, staff, and educational resources outside of the public school. Indeed, alternative school settings for disabled children far too often reportedly consisted of a kind of 'holding operation' inside or outside the regular school facilities.

While the last decade or so has seen considerable improvement in the education of disabled children throughout Canada, the pervasive effects of systemic discrimination leave much yet to be done. For example, a great many schools (especially older ones) are physically inaccessible to non-ambulatory disabled children, and/or do not have elevators or toilet facilities that accommodate wheelchairs (Brown, 1977: 197–254). As a result, many disabled children must be bussed long distances to adapted schools, which, concomitantly, end up with a disproportionate number of disabled students. Other obstacles to the right to education of disabled children include the unwillingness of some school-boards to devote resources to disabled children, a continuing lack of special teacher training, and difficulties in ensuring the education of disabled children at home or in hospitals (ibid). One of the many cases involving complaints based on barriers to educational integration of disabled youngsters within the Canadian public school system is detailed in chapter 7.

Discrimination in law and in law-enforcement agencies
Legal discrimination, and discrimination in the policies and practices of law-enforcement agencies, seriously undermine minority rights in those areas where violations occur (economic, political, social, or cultural spheres). At the same time, these 'legitimate' forms of discrimination provide majorities with their most effective techniques of domination and control of stigmatized minorities.

In the political sphere, legal discrimination against institutionalized minorities (criminal prisoners and mentally disabled inmates) through denial of franchise has been discussed previously. In the following section, I will briefly consider some of the provisions of the Canadian Criminal Code that have discriminatory implications in the sphere of law and justice for mentally disabled minorities (mentally retarded and mentally ill).

The Criminal Code (as well as other federal statutes, such as the Land Titles Act and the National Defence Act) at present employs such antiquated, stigmatizing labels as 'idiot,' 'imbecile,' 'lunatic,' and 'feeble-minded' in its description of various types of mental disability. Such labels act as a catalyst for the discriminatory practices institutionalized through the Code's provisions. Broadly speaking, a mentally disabled person currently accused within the criminal-justice system of Canada is denied the rights of legal protection and due process of law that other citizens enjoy (Canada, House of Commons, 1981: 25). For example, a mentally retarded person may be declared unfit to stand trial for the crime. Moreover, where mentally disabled persons are found to be guilty, the law does not clearly provide for appropriate treatment predicated upon a proper assessment of the mental condition of the offender, when determining the penalty for the crime.

As of April 1980 there were 834 persons in Canada being detained indefinitely under strict supervision or in psychiatric institutions on the grounds of 'criminal insanity.' The latter term covers persons deemed 'unfit to stand trial' (assumed mentally retarded) as well as persons deemed legally 'insane' (assumed mentally ill). Some of these detainees reportedly had been held for many years. Because the detentions were ordered under lieutenant-governor's warrants, in all of these cases the particular provincial government involved has the authority to determine the length of the period of detainment (Canada, House of Commons, 1981: 26). Moreover, the provincial government is not obliged to provide detainees with any form of treatment for their mental disability. Detainees will be allowed to leave the institution only on the recommendation of a government-appointed review board of psychiatrists and lawyers. However, the composition of such boards, to date, reportedly does not favour the detainee, especially if the person is a member of the mentally retarded minority. One obstacle in the latter case is that the recommendation must state that the person has 'recovered' from the mental disability. Insofar as mental retardation is a permanent disability, such a recommendation realistically cannot be made. How any of the detainees are expected to 'recover' without treatment is another critical question to be raised.

Finally, even where such a recommendation has been made, the provincial government has the authority to reject it and to continue to detain the mentally disabled person indefinitely (ibid).

Outside the federal jurisidiction of the Criminal Code provisions, the practice of involuntary detainment in psychiatric institutions of persons who are being treated for emotional/mental illnesses is a matter that comes under provincial jurisdiction, through various mental health acts. These acts differ markedly from province to province – for example, in the length of time they allow for involuntary confinement and in the degree to which they are regularly reviewed and updated. Accordingly, the legal protections as well as the violations of the rights of the mentally ill in Canada vary significantly from one province to another (Canada, House of Commons, 1981: 26–7).

In March 1985, a group of parents informed the Quebec minister of social affairs of numerous abuses against their sons and daughters at l'Hôpital-Rivière-des-Prairies, a Montreal psychiatric hospital (CHRA, I/8, July 1985). They pointed out that the vast majority of the residents in the psychiatric hospital are not persons with psychiatric disabilities, but persons who have been labelled mentally retarded. A psychiatric institution, they argued, is clearly neither an appropriate nor a humane 'home' for children to grow up in. Any child who spent his or her childhood years, from age ten to age sixteen, shut away in a large, barren institution, as these children have, would certainly have 'psychiatric troubles' at the end of it, even if he or she did not have any on entering. Residents, they alleged, spend their entire days without interest, without privacy, without respect, without individuality, without stimulation. The frustration, the boredom, and the despair give rise to non-normative behaviours, for which the residents are cruelly punished. Punitive measures, such as being tied to chairs and beds for hours and being locked in isolation cells for hours or days, it was alleged, are a 'major industry' at l'Hôpital-Rivière-des-Prairies.

Parents demanded that the minister take action and that he hold an inquiry into the institutional abuses within the hospital (CHRA, I/8, July 1985). In response, a one-year, government-appointed commission of inquiry was put into place. During the year of the inquiry, dozens of provincial and national disability-rights groups took a stong public stand, demanding respect for the human rights of residents in the psychiatric hospital. At the end of the year, the commission of inquiry released its report, which documented widespread, serious human-rights abuses at the Montreal psychiatric hospital (CHRA, II/5, May 1986). On the basis of the recommendations put forward in the report, the Quebec minister of health and social services ordered sweeping reforms. The hospital was instructed to act immediately to implement the reforms and was advised that a representative of the ministry would be appointed as an observer to monitor the process of implementation of the required changes (ibid).

The foregoing case highlights the vulnerability of institutionalized mentally disabled minorities to human-rights abuses under the legal practice of involuntary psychiatric confinement. Legal provisions and practices also violate the human rights of other minorities. The reader is reminded, here, of the various criminal-law provisions pertaining to prohibited sexual activities (detailed in chapter 2) which discriminate against homosexuals. An equally pernicious, legal form of discrimination against the homosexual minority lies in the sphere of law-enforcement practices. Harassment and entrapment by police officers constitute 'favourite' patterns of discrimination against homosexuals throughout North America. Such practices reflect deeply rooted homophobic attitudes found to be prevalent in police organizations (Niederhoffer, 1967).

Herbert Sutcliffe, a major in the Canadian Armed Forces, was exposed as a homosexual in 1962. A member of the Canadian Intelligence Corps, he had just been posted to the Pentagon in Washington, DC. Unknown to him, a CIA agent had been assigned to assess him as a security risk and entrapped him in a bar by posing as a homosexual, thus putting to an abrupt end his brilliant career marked by numerous medals for gallantry in wartime service (*Toronto Star*, 15 March 1986).

In 1979, in reaction against open support by the mayor of Toronto for Gay Rights, a number of articles written by police officers and openly denigrating homosexuals appeared in the Metro Toronto Police Association's magazine *News and Views*. One especially pernicious article, 'The Homosexual Fad,' written by Sgt Tom Moclair, 14th Division, warned Canadians of the serious state of 'corruption' in today's society, allegedly caused by homosexuals. 'Recruitment' of children, he says, is the key to survival for homosexuals, a 'depraved' category of persons who foist their acts of 'perversion' on the Canadian public. The underlying question behind the police officer's allegations was: how can (assumed) 'moral,' heterosexual Canadians allow these 'misfits' and 'weirdos' to turn their 'aberration' into a right? (CGRO, 1981: 12).

That this kind of police homophobia can lead to inhumane, discriminatory acts against (assumed) homosexuals may be illustrated by the following example (one of many, many more). In October 1979, Derek Grant was entrapped by two Metro Toronto police officers of the Morality

Squad while allegedly engaging in prohibited sexual acts in the wash-room of a Toronto bar. While in custody, the terror-stricken, accused man choked to death on his own vomit. At the coroner's inquest that followed, the testimony of the two arresting officers revealed that they were in disagreement as to whether or not the alleged sexual activities could be deemed in violation of the Criminal Code (CGRO, 1981: 12). Unfortunately, the victim of their 'entrapment' died before a decision was reached.

Notwithstanding the fact that surveillance of homosexuals by police officers may (at least in part) constitute 'legitimate' patrolling for potential (sexual) criminal offences, it is important for the reader to note that heterosexuals as well as homosexuals may be perpetrators of crimes as well as criminal victims. Accordingly, the *singling-out* of homosexuals for *special* surveillance and entrapment activities not carried out among parallel heterosexual populations constitutes a discriminatory practice on the part of police authorities.

While both heterosexuals and homosexuals may be perpetrators of criminal offences, homosexuals are particularly vulnerable as criminal victims (Sepejak, 1977: 22–3). A tradition of strained relations with the police heightened by continuing instances of police discrimination against homosexuals provides strong deterrents, preventing many homo-sexual victims from seeking protection of the law. Further, insofar as the vast majority of homosexuals remain in the closet, the possibility of disclosure of their homosexuality to family members, relatives, and friends through police identification in the reporting of a crime deters them from reporting criminal victimization to the police.

Results of a recent Canadian study of homosexual victims indicate that homosexual respondents were less willing to report sexual assault than other crimes and were less willing to report any crime in an identifying situation than in a non-identifying one (Sepejak, 1977: 49–51). These findings strongly suggest that the deep vulnerability of homosexual persons as criminal victims undermines their trust in the processes of law and law enforcement in Canada. The consequent unwillingness of many homosexual victims to seek the protection of the law is one of the most serious psycho-social ramifications of their stigmatized status as members of the homosexual minority.

Selective surveillance by the police also constitutes an endemic form of legal discrimination against 'skid-row drunks' (Giffen, 1966). In theory, the law forbids rich and poor citizens alike to be drunk in a public place. But, in practice, the police exercise considerable discretion in the use they make of public-intoxication laws, for the offence is a very common one.

As a direct result of the discretion allowed police officers, the sample of arrestees for public drunkenness is far from random, for it reflects the particular biases of the arresting officers.

The findings of sociological research on the alcoholic minority in Canada conducted by Giffen (1966) reveal that police arrests tend to be predicated upon quick judgments based on easily visible, stigmatizing criteria such as dress, companionship, and location as well as upon recognition of the inebriate as a 'regular customer' (chronic-drunkenness offenders). This class of offender typically is found lining the sleazy doorways and sidewalks of 'skid row.' Hence, frequent surveillance of these downtrodden, lower-class areas provides an almost foolproof method of finding likely candidates for arrest, that is, 'skid-row drunks.'

The cycle of public intoxication, arrest, trial, incarceration, and release that dominates the life of the skid-row alcoholic has been termed the 'revolving-door syndrome.' Since the overriding consequence of the syndrome is the perpetuation of the proscribed behaviour, the 'revolving door' provides a classic example of the self-fulfilling prophecy of stigmatization. Through the legal process of criminalization, the original stigma of alcoholism becomes compounded by the alienating effects of criminal stigmatization. The revolving-door syndrome begins with public intoxication and what follows is a cyclic series of degradation ceremonies – police harassment, arrest, court trials, and jail terms. The self-fulfilling prophecy ensues as the chronic alcoholic offender becomes more and more deeply involved with fellow alcoholic offenders and eventually becomes integrated into the minority subculture of the skid-row alcoholic.

Interviews conducted with chronic alcoholic offenders clearly indicate that these minority members perceive the police as prejudiced agents who are determined to convict them. They report that police discriminate on a class basis, particularly against chronic offenders, and that they insult and physically abuse known 'drunks.' Whether or not these allegations are wholly valid, the strong, emotional component in such beliefs reinforces the alienation of their bearers, the chronic alcoholic offenders. The result is that they come to embrace the minority subculture of skid-row alcoholics and to identify strongly with its members' self-image as a persecuted minority within a minority (Giffen, 1966).

FORMS OF DISCRIMINATION: CONCLUDING COMMENTS

In the foregoing pages, I have attempted to draw attention to some of the institutionalized techiques of discrimination and the systemic violations of human rights that have characterized majority treatment of stigmatized minorities in Canadian society. I also have attempted to demonstrate the way in which negative prejudice and stereotypes operating through deeply ingrained invalidation myths serve to underscore and to legitimate majority techniques of domination and control of stigmatized minorities.

From time to time, in this chapter, my analysis has alluded to the dehumanizing psycho-social consequences of minority stigmatization. In the next chapter I will elaborate on this phenomenon by examining in some detail the personal and social experience of stigma, and by unveiling its often overlooked human-rights implications for stigmatized-minority members.

4

Into the closet: the experience
of stigma

Probably the least well-understood aspect of stigmatization is its frequently shattering psycho-social consequences for the individual bearer of a stigma. Social-scientific research in this area is particularly difficult to carry out because one of the manifestations of the phenomenon is that it may be deliberately cloaked in a closet of secrecy and thus hidden from public view.

For purposes of analysis, we can distinguish between two types of closet: the involuntary and the voluntary. The involuntary closet is one that is forced upon the bearer of a stigma by majority authorities. This model is best exemplified by the involuntary placement of the stigmatized-minority member in a 'total institution' (Goffman, 1961) where residents live a formally administered and controlled existence in virtual isolation from majority society. The voluntary closet represents a self-imposed form of social seclusion. It is an invisible closet that rests on a fragile façade of deception and secrecy designed to fend off debasement and discrimination by an intolerant (if not hostile) majority.

THE INVOLUNTARY CLOSET

In the cases of the physically and mentally disabled minorities, 'going into the closet' has typically been an involuntary process rather than one based on personal choice. Because majority social attitudes and policies towards the disabled have long been predicated on invalidation myths of handicapism, the social placement of disabled minorities in Canada characteristically has been within the confines of a total institution.

Goffman (1961: 3) defines a total institution as 'a place of residence and work where a large number of like-situated individuals, cut off from the wider society for an appreciable period of time, together lead an enclosed, formally-administered round of life.' For disabled persons deemed by majority authorities to be too incompetent and/or too dangerous to be allowed to live freely in society at large, involuntary confinement within a total institution has been regarded as the most appropriate social placement. Only too frequently, however, the life of minority residents within the institutional closet has been characterized by ongoing experiences of oppression, diminution, and neglect at the hands of majority administrators (institutional caretakers): 'Life must now follow a time-table. This hospital-like atmosphere can cause stress, anxiety, depression and feeling of lost dignity and self-worth' (H. McMichael and B. Waechter, quoted in Canada, House of Commons, 1981: 110).

The involuntary nature of 'going into the closet' strips the institutional-ized, disabled person of the human right of self-determination. Thus begins the 'total closet' scenario: the round of degradation ceremonies/ human-rights violations through which the disabled resident comes to internalize the negative definitions imposed by majority caretakers and to develop a stigmatized-minority self-image and self-identity: 'About six months after I arrived in [the home for the physically disabled] a fellow patient ... casually remarked, "They got you by the hump. No matter which way you turn, they got you." ... In my ignorance, I did not understand that my fellow patient had simply unfolded what would ultimately seem a truism ... No matter which way I turned, they would decide, in their collective wisdom, how my fate was to be carved out ... The cripple, then, is a social fugitive, molded by a society that he makes uncomfortable by his very presence' (Kriegel, in Sagarin, 1971: 414–16).

In a gripping account of his visit to the Orillia Hospital School for the Mentally Retarded, in 1959, Pierre Berton brought to public attention the routine violations of the human rights of minority residents within this total institution. He documented the lack of privacy and the assault to human dignity in the endless rows of beds, sometimes only inches apart, in wards, on verandas, in class-rooms, and in virtually every conceivable space. He exposed the blatant neglect of residents by reporting the innumerable fire hazards and the appalling stench of urine and faeces that 'no amount of scrubbing could remove from 70 year old floors.' Berton also focused public concern on the lack of programming, the monotony, and the cold impersonality of closeted life within the walls of Orillia and other Canadian institutions for the disabled, where, he

alleged, residents' parents rarely visited, and where the shocking violations of human rights had long been hidden from public view (*Toronto
Star*, 4 January 1983).

While important policy changes designed to improve the life conditions
of disabled minorities have been put into effect since that time, even
today media reports continue to chronicle case after case of human-rights
violations within closeted institutional confines.

The public inquiry, in 1985, into the grave abuse of the human rights of
six hundred residents confined to a Montreal psychiatric hospital
(previously addressed in chapter 3) documented an exemplary case in
point (CHRA, 1 8, July 1985). The institution in question was alleged to
have been run on the 'medical model.' Oppression of minority residents,
accordingly, was built into hospital policy, which blatantly abrogated
their right to self-determination. Residents who disobeyed institutional
rules were routinely forcibly restrained: they were tied to their beds, to
toilets, or to chairs nailed to floors. They also were forced to take excessive
quantities of strong drugs and tranquillizers. Neglect of minority residents was rampant. Because of the utter lack of programming, residents
spent their days doing nothing and learning nothing. Diminution was an
everyday occurrence, for life within the psychiatric closet consisted of an
endless series of degradation ceremonies. To wit: in the mornings, naked
residents of both sexes were lined up in a public corridor to await their
turn for a shower (what the workers in the hospital called 'a true car
wash'). Not surprisingly, residents frequently 'acted out' by running
away from the institution. When they were caught, they were brutally
punished by being locked up in isolation cells for the length of time that
they were away. Within the confines of this psychiatric institution, as
within the involuntary closet of countless other total institutions, the
long-term result of oppression, neglect, and diminution was a self-
fulfilling prophecy of created dependency and desolation among minority residents.

THE VOLUNTARY CLOSET

For stigmatized minorities living within the community at large, continuing experiences of public degradation may be compounded by personal
experiences of rejection by family and peers. Over time, social repudiation may lead members of stigmatized minorities to develop deeply held
inner feelings of guilt, fear, and self-hatred. Such feelings, in turn, may

reverberate, affecting behaviour and resulting in increased withdrawal from society at large and the creation of an invisible closet.

In the closet, the minority member tends to become increasingly immersed in the secretive mechanisms designed to hide the stigmatized attribute(s) from public view. The protective cloak of deception afforded by the closet shields the bearer of a stigma from the anticipated pain and humiliation associated with social repudiation. However, as the closeted-minority member builds deception upon deception, the machinations involved in 'guarding the secret' become a major preoccupation. Thus, the closeted-minority member may become trapped within his/her own web of duplicity, ever more fearful of exposure, and increasingly filled with feelings of guilt and self-hatred for the deception upon which his/her closeted existence is predicated.

For members of the alcohol-disabled minority, the psycho-social reverberations of a stigma can be so harrowing that they lead to a preoccupation with thoughts (and sometimes, to the act) of suicide. For, in the case of alcohol-disabled persons, personal guilt, self-blame, and self-hatred tend to run high (Alcoholics Anonymous, 1976). Until they 'hit bottom' – when all the coping mechanisms designed to guard the 'secret' have broken down – members of this stigmatized minority generally do not understand the compulsive nature of their drinking patterns. They tend to see themselves as 'voluntary' minority members who can, if they so choose, control their intake of alcohol and their drinking behaviour. The blatant fact that their endless attempts to do so invariably result in failure only serves to reinforce their negative self-image as weak-minded persons, lacking in will-power, defective in character, and undeserving of respect. Unable to face themselves, they become increasingly unable to face the world outside themselves. Consequently, drinking becomes a private matter, increasingly veiled by the lies of hidden bottles, excuses for absences from work, weekend binges in lonely hotel rooms, and myriad similar closet mechanisms designed to guard the secret. Yet, despite all of the elaborate, protective mechanisms erected to hide the drinking problem, the closeted alcohol-disabled person lives in constant fear of the devastating consequences of public exposure.

The following examples, excerpted from the personal histories of members of the alcoholic minority (Alcoholics Anonymous, 1976), may serve to illustrate some of the key points raised in the foregoing analysis.

I should have realized that alcohol was getting hold of me when I started to become secretive in my drinking. I began to have to have supplies on hand for the people who 'might come in.' (336)

If my wife was planning to go out in the afternoon, I would get a large supply of liquor and smuggle it home and hide it in the coal bin, the clothes chute, over door jambs, over beams in the cellar and in cracks in the cellar tile . . . even the ash container. (176-7)

Many women who have reached the stage that I had reached in my drinking have lost husbands, children, everything . . . The important thing I lost was my own self-respect. I couldn't face people. I couldn't look them straight in the eyes . . . I got so that I hid quite a bit of the time, wouldn't answer the phone, and stayed by myself. (323–4)

The mental state of the sick alcoholic is beyond description. For the last two years of my drinking I prayed on every drunk that I wouldn't wake up again . . . [then] I made my second feeble try at suicide. (244-5)

While the homosexual closet tends to be somewhat different in its deceptive façade from that of the alcoholic closet, it nevertheless epitomizes a strikingly similar fear-filled and shame-filled response to public stigmatization and social rejection:

My upbringing, says Mary Meigs, prevented me from accepting my sexual nature by making me ashamed of it, doubly ashamed, because I belonged to a despised sexual minority. (Meigs, 1982)

A person cannot live in an atmosphere of universal rejection, of widespread pretence, of a society that outlaws and banishes his activities and desires, or a social world that jokes and sneers at every turn without a fundamental influence on his personality. (A homosexual spokesman, quoted in Plummer, 1975: 142)

The condemnation and degradation of homosexuality by the heterosexual majority renders the homosexual experience one that tends to arouse feelings of anxiety and guilt in the participants (Plummer, 1975). Surrounded by stereotypes of sin, sickness, and sadness, when not veiled in silence, the negative imagery of homosexuality increasingly impinges upon and debases the homosexual person's self-image and self-identity. Whether at the level of the 'queer joke' or the sex-education lesson that teaches about 'perversions,' the homosexual experience typically is presented as immoral, abnormal, or, at the very least, 'odd' (ibid, 143). Each source of societal reaction reinforces the 'abnormality' of homosexuality and the 'normality' of heterosexuality; thus a firm basis is laid for the casting of guilt, shame, and even hatred onto the self.

The next vital consequence of social degradation is the transformation of homosexuality into a secret: it is not spoken about openly, and it is not immediately visible; thus it becomes a 'problem' that can be kept to oneself, debated inwardly, and defended from public gaze (Plummer, 1975: 144). Secrecy leads to solitude; and the closet homosexual, like the closet alcoholic, may come to privatize his/her life to the point of utter social isolation.

THE DOUBLE CLOSET: THE EXPERIENCE OF MULTIPLE STIGMATA

'Maybe it's our dogged insistence on our essential health as gay people, on our persistent view of ourselves in our own media as whole, active, healthy, bright and beautiful. Maybe that's it. But I feel that somehow, way at the back of our own closets we have built another one, and into it we have shoved our gay deaf and our gay blind and our gay wheelchair cases, and we've gone on with the already difficult enough problems of living as gay people' (Hannon, in *The Body Politic*, 1980: 19).

In a report on the gay disabled in Canada, Hannon sensitively documents the fear-filled and shame-filled experiences of members of this multiply stigmatized minority in their attempts to come to terms with their sexual orientation and to fulfil their human needs for companionship and moral support (Hannon, 1980).

Richard, a blind homosexual, had no access to written information on homosexuality. The Canadian National Institute for the Blind (CNIB), through their Braille and talking-book library, was his only source of information on sexuality for blind Canadians. But the single title he found there was *The Gay Theology*. Because he could not see, and because he had no access to blind-adapted materials on gayness, Richard utilized highly stereotyped auditory indicators in order to identify fellow gays: he listened for 'queenly,' that is, lisping, mannered male voices. This strategy proved to be a most unsuccessful means of introducing him to the gay community, where 'queens' represent a minuscule minority.

Another major obstacle for the gay disabled population is the widespread myth that disabled people, in general, are or should be asexual in orientation. Institutions for the disabled tend to operate on this assumption, hence (reportedly) they teach repression of sexuality. In his research for the report on the gay disabled, Hannon found that residential institutions were generally 'cautious' in their approach to sexuality, and where gay sexuality was concerned, a kind of 'benign neglect' seemed to be the rule (Hannon, 1980: 22).

For members of the gay disabled minority, many of the obstacles to life in 'straight' (heterosexual) society have their parallels in gay society. In a survey of Toronto's gay establishments, Hannon found that despite the highly positive attitudes verbalized by their managers or owners, most gay 'watering holes' (bars, baths, discos) have a great many stairs, and none has wash-rooms adapted for wheelchairs. Moreover, in the cases of two gay taverns whose managerial staff professed to welcome disabled persons, service was reportedly refused on two different occasions to cerebral palsy–disabled gays in wheelchairs (Hannon, 1980).

Another form of the double closet occurs in the case of gay parents who are both openly gay and open about their desire for parenting. Because the parenting role in heterosexual society traditionally rests with the mother, the stigma attached to gay parents is much greater for a gay father than it is for a gay (lesbian) mother. As a result, the gay father lives in a 'double closet' (Fadiman, 1983). Isolated from 'straights' because he is gay; isolated from gays because he is an open father (one who has assumed a parenting role) he finds himself in a 'Catch 22' situation. This dilemma can be psychologically devastating: it can induce a paralysing sense of psycho-social marginality (incongruence of identities/roles). Put in the words of one gay father, the syndrome is experienced as 'fragmentation from the root of my body to the root of my soul' (ibid: 82).

Leading a double life: the chimera of passing

Unlike the involuntary closet of the total institution, where stigmatized-minority residents live an enclosed existence virtually divorced from public life, the voluntary closet not infrequently encompasses only the private sphere of social interaction. In order to cope in public life, minority members whose stigmata are 'discreditable' rather than 'discredited' may adopt the strategy of 'passing' (masquerading as majority members) in public life. Insofar as the stigmatized attribute is invisible or can be disguised, passing may be seen as a viable coping mechanism by closeted minority members. In this case, the 'double life' syndrome may emerge. The minority member may compartmentalize his or her social existence into two distinct life spheres, that is, private and public roles.

Passing in public life necessitates the creation of a normative front, the adoption of a normative life-style, and the assumption of a normative (majority) pseudo-identity. In private life, however, under the protective cloak of the closet of secrecy, the public mask may be dropped, a minority life-style pursued, and a minority identity expressed. Insofar as the minority member's private role is carefully kept secret (closeted) he or she may live in constant fear of public exposure. The public role, accordingly, may be a fragile façade, which rests on a host of deceptive mechanisms designed to guard the secret private life from public view.

Research studies on lesbian identity (Moses, 1978: Ponse, 1978) indicate that once a woman identifies herself as a lesbian, she begins to participate in the private, closeted life of the lesbian minority. She begins to go to lesbian bars where heterosexual persons are excluded. Because of fear of stigmatization, she wears a heterosexual mask and engages in passing in the presence of 'straights,' but among other lesbians she seeks relief from the stress of subterfuge in expressing her lesbian identity. Her need to express her 'real' self thus leads her to develop bonds with other closeted lesbians and to become involved in the private subcultural world of the lesbian minority.

According to Ponse (1978), for the closeted lesbian, passing refers to the successful accomplishment of presenting a virtual 'straight' (heterosexual) identity in public life. Because the majority community operates on the erroneous assumption that everyone (unless publicly labelled otherwise) is heterosexual, the self-acknowledged lesbian must develop a heightened consciousness of identity management in order to pass for 'straight' in public life. The strategy of passing involves the construction of a 'straight front' in terms of details of dress, speech, affect, and demeanour. The heterosexual mask necessitates the use of both verbal and non-verbal identity cues. Non-verbal cues include dress management to construct an overtly feminine front. Because the lesbian stereotype is that of a 'butch' or 'diesel dyke,' dressed in manly attire, passing requires the fabrication of an unmistakable feminine façade. Verbal cues may be overt or covert. Overt cues may include the deliberate reference to a boy-friend in conversations with majority members or bringing a male friend to a social gathering for (assumed heterosexual) couples. Covert cues may involve maintaining an indifferent front in the face of homophobic remarks or laughing at jokes about 'queers' or 'dykes.' For the closeted lesbian, then, passing demands a continuous process of identity management in order to maintain a public heterosexual front.

As in the previously discussed case of gay fathers (Fadiman, 1983), leading a double life can eventuate in a 'Catch 22' situation for lesbians – as homosexuals and as women. The lesbian closet, designed to provide an antidote to social rejection and personal alienation, can lead to a condition of psycho-social marginality, with heightened problems of identity conflict and confusion. Unable to resolve the dilemma posed by their homosexual orientation and their desire to maintain close relationships with heterosexual women friends, lesbians may experience increasing alienation from heterosexual friends. For example, Ponse (1978) reports that respondents in her research did not want to isolate themselves from their heterosexual women friends. Thus, when 'straight' friends would discuss their love affairs, lesbian respondents felt constrained to remain silent, to neither lie nor disclose lesbian relationships. However, their inability to express their need for sharing personal, loving experiences with heterosexual intimates generated feelings of meaninglessness and estrangement in these interactions. Such feelings were not diffused by the double-life strategy, because lesbian respondents did not give up their 'straight' friends.

Over time, leading a double life can become psychologically intolerable. Accordingly, the minority member may be propelled out of the closet, at least situationally, in order to find new coping mechanisms. The minority member may seek professional guidance through psychiatric, psychological, and/or spiritual counselling, or he or she may 'come out' in varying degrees through disclosure to selected others of his or her stigmata (sharing the secret).

When questioned about his past, double-life existence, a prominent gay leader had this to say:

Basically, I lived in anguish, and lived a dual role. I would occasionally have these [homosexual] experiences. I felt extremely guilty about it. I still continued to date women and to lead a very heterosexual social life ... I spent several years in psychoanalysis, trying [unsuccessfully] to become heterosexual ... then I moved to New York City and [here] it was easy to develop a gay niche of social activity. I continued a heterosexual façade when it came to my business life ... however, there was great ambivalence in having this heterosexual identity at business and having gay identity elsewhere ... [At work] I was always cryptic over the phone to gay friends and generally would discourage calls at work from gay friends ... I had to pretend I had a girlfriend ... I would always play the role with clients ... I would have a girl on my arm for these social occasions ... I was even engaged to be married, three times. (Excerpted from personal interview with gay leader from New York City)

Jeri Wine, writing about lesbian academics in Canada, expresses strikingly similar sentiments about the double-life syndrome:

Some of us have spent time attempting to protect ourselves by keeping separate our private lives and our public academic lives, in order to keep our lesbian identities secret. We are all aware of the immense personal toll taken by the secretiveness and deception involved in leading a closeted existence. The woman among us who is most nearly closeted in her academic position described her precarious existence as 'one foot in the closet, the other on a banana peel.' As well as involving a continuously high level of anxiety, and fracturing one's sense of self, leading such an existence grants tremendous power to anyone who might discover the truth. 'I feel that the more people are secretive, the more you seal your own self into those box cars for them to take you away.' (1983: 10)

The closeted community: minority support systems/minority subcultures

Whether or not closeted minority members attempt to pass in the outside (majority) society, in their private lives they tend to seek companionship, solace, and moral support among fellow minority members. For minority members with invisible stigmata, access to others who share the stigmata is undoubtedly impeded by the cloak of secrecy surrounding the closet. Accordingly, the lonely, closeted minority member in search of the support and companionship of similarly stigmatized others may be drawn towards known minority organizations and subcultural enclaves. Through participation in these collective aspects of minority life, the minority member may come to embrace a new and distinct minority identity and life-style. Insofar as the minority member remains closeted, such activities become part of the privatized, secret life of the bearer of stigma.

MINORITY SELF-HELP: THE ROLE OF SYMPATHETIC OTHERS

In order to cope with their stigmatized status and identity, minority members typically turn to sympathetic insiders, others who share the stigma, for support. They may form self-help groups, which provide minority members with a mutually supportive forum for airing and sharing their common experiences, problems, and hopes. Minority organizations such as Alchoholics Anonymous (AA), Blind Organization of Ontario with Self-Help Tactics (BOOST), On Our Own (ex-psychiatric inmates), People First (developmentally delayed), and associations of gay parents represent some of the many successful minority self-help groups currently operating across Canada. These self-help groups provide members with critical sources of mutual caring, sharing, and support.

Don Weitz, a founding member of On Our Own, points out that 'people who have experienced a particular problem, illness, institutionalization or invalidating label such as "mental patient" know what it's like, they've "been there" too. Such people have an almost instinctive or instant grasp of each other's problem(s).' It is this intuitive understanding and acceptance, together with mutual support, says Weitz, that are the real sources of a self-help group's strength and solidarity (cited in Lumsden, 1984: 312).

In addition to their mutual-support function, self-help groups also may take on public-information functions. They may produce their own literature designed to present a factual picture of the minority in order to combat public prejudices and stereotypes. They also may develop a rostrum of public speakers who volunteer to go out into the community at large in order to increase public awareness of and sensitivity to the violations of minority rights that have resulted from long-term stigmatization. These public-education activities represent attempts by minority self-help organizations to combat both public prejudice and categorical discrimination against minority members.

The importance of public education notwithstanding, the crux of a minority self-help group, Weitz (1984) asserts, lies in its mutual acceptance and support functions. This point is clearly illustrated in the following comments drawn from case-study materials:

Mentally handicapped people don't feel comfortable talking to 'normal' people . . . we are afraid someone will put us down . . . I got involved in People First . . . [and] it's certainly helped me to speak out. Before, I didn't want to tell how difficult it was for me to concentrate. Now I come right out and tell them (Barb Goode, in Canada, House of Commons, 1981: 117)

I went to [an AA] meeting to see for myself this group of freaks or bums . . . I went trembling into a house . . . filled with strangers . . . and I found I had come home, at last, to my own kind . . . I wasn't alone any more . . . I had found friends . . . who often knew what I was thinking and feeling better than I knew myself . . . Talking things over with them . . . I felt a new inner comfort. (Alcoholics Anonymous, 1976: 228–9)

The fastest route to reconciling identities [for gay fathers] is through local chapters of the Gay Fathers Coalition . . . some men are divorced, some still married, some still so closeted they introduce themselves by first names only. Here, diapers and PTA meetings are acceptable topics of conversation. So are such questions as how do you tell your wife? . . . your children? . . . The sense of commonality that arises from such discussions has proved a powerful healing force. (Fadiman, 1983: 82–3)

Another source of support solicited by stigmatized-minority members is that of sympathetic outsiders – majority members with whom they are involved through family ties, professional interests, or (more rarely) special friendships. Goffman (1963) refers to such sympathetic outsiders as 'the wise,' in contradistinction to 'the own' (sympathetic insiders).

Because of its contagion effect a stigma can lead to stigma by association – the coincident discrediting of those in close contact with stigmatized-minority members – and majority associates may come to acquire a 'courtesy stigma' (Goffman, 1963). Fear of stigma by association tends to impede the formation of close personal relations between stigmatized-minority members and outsiders other than family or professional caretakers. Consequently, the 'wise,' the few outsiders with a courtesy stigma, provide a crucial source of majority support for the stigmatized and can play a vital role as advocates for minority rights.

The role of sympathetic outsiders may be even more critical in cases where the family and close friends of stigmatized-minority members have become deeply involved in the secretive mechanisms of the closet syndrome. In such cases, those intimately associated with the stigmatized may not understand the benefits to be gained by minority members through involvement in self-help groups. Even more important, they may fear negative consequences for the minority member and for themselves of breaking with the closeted pattern of non-disclosure of stigmata beyond a closed circle of intimates.

Because the moral support of family and close friends can be pivotal for the growth of self-confidence and positive identity among the stigmatized, minority self-help organizations may assume the added task of developing affiliated self-help groups for families and friends. Minority-affiliated groups are designed to provide parallel programs for those closely associated with minority members, in order to help them cope with stigma by association (e.g., AA affiliates: Al-Anon [families and friends of alcoholics] and Alateen [children of alcoholics]; organizations of relatives and friends of the mentally ill and the mentally retarded; and parents of gays and lesbians).

For members of minority-affiliated self-help groups, the support of others in the same situation plays a significant role in attenuating feelings of guilt and shame related to stigma by association: 'I believe that just finding out that I was not alone, was the greatest gift Alateen gave me. I learned, too, that my mother was suffering from a disease [alcoholism] and I felt less ashamed. This is ... the first year I can smile at my fellow students ... I feel that I belong and am accepted' (a high-school student, quoted in Al-Anon Family Groups, n.d.: pamphlet No. 7).

Self-help in the closet: the role of anonymity

Minority self-help groups may themselves comprise part of the hidden life of closeted members. Fear of the social consequences of open disclosure of stigmatized-minority status may lead to the formation of highly closeted self-help groups where the minority identity of participants is cloaked beneath a veil of anonymity. Humphreys (1972) suggests that when fear of stigmatization makes anonymity rewarding and disclosure punitive, the membership list of a minority self-help group (in Humphreys's example, a homosexual organization) may be carefully guarded from public view. Even in cases where members are allowed to join under assumed names and mailings are made only to box numbers, associations of 'discreditable persons' are compelled to erect further safeguards for anonymity, such as limiting access to the membership list to a few, trusted, and highly committed old-timers (Humphreys, 1972: 95).

Probably the archetypical case of anonymity in minority self-help groups is that of Alcoholics Anonymous: 'Anonymity is the spiritual foundation of all our Traditions, ever reminding us to place principles before personalities' ('Tradition no. 12,' Alcoholics Anonymous, 1976: 564). The key role of anonymity in the Alcoholics Anonymous enterprise is attributed to decisions reached through the early experiences of members, as illustrated in the following example: 'One morning, I found myself crying and saying, "I've got to get out of this hell, some way". That promise of privacy, that pledge – implied in the name of Alcoholics Anonymous – to keep my shameful record absolutely confidential made it possible for me to show up at the local AA office' (AA Grapevine, March 1981: 26).

BEYOND MINORITY SELF-HELP: TOWARDS POSITIVE MINORITY
IDENTITIES AND LIFE-STYLES

Beyond the peer-therapy aspect of minority self-help organizations such groups typically offer a specialized system of teachings that members are expected to follow (Antze, 1976). The group ideologies underlying these teachings provide the positive life principles towards which the group is oriented. The teachings, in turn, provide the tools that are designed to equip members with the means to shed their stigmata, to develop positive new minority identities, and to embrace positive new minority life-styles.

On the basis of his perusal of minority self-help–group literature together with his observations of the ceremonies of induction of newcomers to such organizations, Antze (1976: 324) points out that 'a group's teachings are its very essence.' Slogans, such as 'get with the program' or 'just follow these simple steps,' are the group command-ments heard first, and most frequently, by the initiate.

Antze carried out a comparative analysis of three of the oldest and most prominent North American minority self-help organizations – Alcoholics Anonymous (alcohol-disabled), Recovery Inc. (mentally ill), and Synan-on (drug-addicted). His study findings reveal that there is a close correspondence between the distinctive and highly specialized teachings of each group and the peculiar dynamics of the stigmata that those who join share and that the self-help organization attempts to ameliorate. Put another way, each minority self-help group develops its own world-view, its own traditional wisdom, which infuses its particular teachings and gives a distinctive shape to the alternate life-style it offers.

Notwithstanding the distinctive ideological bases of minority self-help groups, these organizations share a fundamental destigmatizing, rehu-manizing function. Thus, even closeted in anonymity, they can provide members with a firm beginning for life-style renewal. By bolstering self-confidence and self-worth at a collective level, they also can provide an important first step in the long and difficult process of 'coming out.'

Subculture in the closet: stigma and solace

For deeply closeted minority members, participation in some aspects of the hidden subcultural life may heighten feelings of shame and guilt: 'Many [homosexual] people feel driven to these underground places . . . washrooms, parks, etc. This is their secret life. A high percentage, and this has been statistically noted, are married men with a double secret. They have to bury their true sexuality' (George Hislop, quoted in Foster and Murray, 1972: 227). For those who lead a double life, however, the pains of passing may be compensated for, at least in part, by the genuinely experienced satisfactions obtained through participation in the alternate, subcultural activities and by the adoption of one of the alternate life-styles found within the minority milieu.

Karla Jay (1983: 18) writes of the lesbian bar as one of the key institutions of the lesbian subculture:

It is probable that the first bars began operating at the end of the 19th century, a time when lesbianism itself (and homosexuality in general) was emerging as a lifestyle, not merely a sexual act . . . Far from being obliterated by gay liberation, the subculture of the bars has proliferated in the years since the 1969 Stonewall rebellion. There are bars, bars everywhere . . . For some people the lesbian bar is a world within our world replete with its own cast of characters, governed by its own rules, maintaining its own rites and rituals, and even comprising its own special geography. As for the last, I remember once being given a tour of a bar and shown exactly where to stand if I were part of a couple or looking for some action and also the pose I should take if I were butch or femme . . . In any case, like Edward Albee's Tiny Alice, the bar represents a world within a world.

A CASE STUDY: HOMOSEXUALITIES/ALTERNATE LIFE-STYLES

In a major study of the homosexual community in the San Francisco Bay area, Bell and Weinberg (1978) sought to explore the multifaceted dimensions of the homosexual experience and subculture. The study findings, in general, provide strong, empirical evidence that contravenes virtually every homophobic invalidation myth tested in the survey. Probably the most important myth exploded is that which underlies the stereotype of the homosexual as a sex-crazed and sex-tortured maniac, preoccupied with sex and prone to attack heterosexuals, especially the young, in order to satisfy unnatural cravings of lust. Not only was the homosexual stereotype disproved, but what was revealed in its place was that homosexuals are not 'all alike'; like heterosexuals, they were found to be involved in a wide variety of life-styles. Moreover, survey findings demonstrated that the sexual and affectional life-styles among homosex- uals had their direct parallels in prevailing heterosexual life-styles. On the basis of these findings, the authors concluded that if they had carried out a similar study among heterosexuals, they likely would have found that the chief difference between the two groups lay only in the nature of their sexual preference (ibid: 218).

Bell and Weinberg's study findings revealed five major affectional/ sexual life-styles among homosexual respondents, each with its hetero- sexual parallel: 1 / 'close-coupled' (partnerships involving enduring, mutual, affectional and sexual commitments); 2 / 'open-coupled' (part- nerships involving enduring, mutual, affectional commitments while allowing outside sexual encounters); 3 / 'functionals' (swinging singles, without commitment to special partners, who patronize the gay establishments in search of temporary affectional and sexual liaisons); 4 / 'dysfunctionals' (individuals experiencing problems in their affectional/sexual relationships and/or problems in coming to terms with their sexual orientation); and 5 / 'asexuals' (individuals living a 'solitary' life-style with little or no involvement with friends, either within the gay community or without).

The first three patterns of affectional/sexual relationships cited were found to be the predominant ones; and each of these can be seen to have its current parallel in heterosexual life-styles: close-coupled/lasting marriages; open-coupled/open marriages; swinging singles/the same. The last two patterns cited (dysfunctional and asexual) were found to be far less common, and the problems inherent in each – contrary to the media-fed stereotype of the tortured and/or lonely, brooding homosexual – were not found to be in any way unique to homosexuals. They were found to be essentially the same kind of problems that have been revealed among a similar subclass of heterosexuals.

The importance of the foregoing findings can be summed up as follows: first, they demonstrate clearly that the prevailing sexual/affectional life-styles found among homosexuals are strikingly similar to those found among parallel populations of heterosexuals (except in their sexual preference); second, they demonstrate that homosexuals, like heterosexuals, may find affectional and sexual satisfaction through a *variety* of life-styles; and finally, they demonstrate that the psycho-social problems in the area of sexual and affectional relationships found among a small minority of homosexuals are *not unique* to this population, but have their direct parallels among similarly troubled heterosexuals.

Bell and Weinberg's findings, based on their researches among homosexual men and women in the Bay area of San Francisco, California, are strongly supported by the comparable results of a sociological study of male homosexuals carried out in a large Canadian city (Lee, 1978). On the basis of several years of participant observation, openly gay sociologist John Lee uncovered a range of homosexual life-styles, strikingly similar to those revealed by the findings of Bell and Weinberg. Moreover, like the American researches, the Canadian data clearly demonstrated that homosexual life-styles strongly parallel their prevailing heterosexual counterparts.

In evaluating his own research findings (admittedly from the point of view of a gay sociologist), Lee contends that 'the lives of gay men are made better, not worse, by the opportunities of their ecosystem [gay subculture]' (1978: 299). Most of the psychological damage suffered by homosexuals in their efforts to satisfy their affectional and sexual needs, Lee suggests, comes from harassment by homophobic heterosexuals – police, religious bigots, moralisits. Yet, Lee goes on to argue, the existence of the gay 'ecosystem' does not in any way undermine heterosexual society. Indeed, Lee contends, the existence of equivalent/alternate sexual and affectional life-styles, whether adopted by homosexuals or heterosexuals, represents a legitimate, healthy expression of cultural diversity in Canadian society (ibid: 299–300).

CONCLUDING COMMENTS

Throughout this chapter, I have focused my analysis on the experience of stigmatization. I have detailed the social processes involved in becoming closeted, in creating a stigmatized identity, in establishing personal networks and self-help groups among stigmatized minority members, and in embracing an alternate minority subculture and life-style. I have attempted to show that the minority closet, whether voluntary or involuntary, is a function of human-rights violations: it is an institutional-ized response to majority degradation and exclusion of stigmatized minorities.

The closet is not only generated but also sustained through minority-rights violations for it provides majority authorities with a powerful technique of domination and control of stigmatized minorities. Alterna-tively, for the minority members in the closet, it nourishes the self-fulfilling prophecy of self-doubt, self-hatred, and alienation consequent upon stigmatization.

In the following chapter, I will turn my attention to the social processes involved in 'coming out' of the stigmatized-minority closet. I will focus my discussion on the phenomena of delabelling and relabelling at both the individual and group levels. I will then examine the social mechan-isms through which minority organizations attempt to develop new and positive minority group identities and life-styles. Finally, I will analyse the strategies adopted by minority organizations in order to raise group consciousness of minority-rights violations.

5

The process of destigmatization: 'coming out'

Coming out of the closet is a phenomenon that has been variously interpreted both by social-scientific researchers and by members of stigmatized minorities.

Altman (1971: 3) suggests that, in the case of the homosexual minority, the term 'coming out' refers to the process whereby a person comes to identify himself or herself as a [homosexual] and recognize thereby his or her position as part of a stigmatized and semi-hidden minority.

Plummer (1975: 147) argues that self-identification and recognition is only the first stage in the coming-out process. Beyond this stage, the bearer of a stigma seeks to resolve the problems of solitariness, guilt, and negative identity associated with closeted (homosexual) minority life. The solution of coming out, he says, represents the path of taking on the minority experience (homosexuality) as a legitimate, alternate life-style. In Plummer's view, 'coming out,' in its fullest conception, refers to the successive social processes through which individuals pass out of the 'moratorium' (of the closet); come to identify themselves more and more positively (as homosexuals), and are 'reborn' into the organized aspects of the (homosexual) minority community (ibid: 147–8).

Plummer (1975: 135–53) puts forward a social-interactionist model for understanding the psycho-social processes involved in 'coming out,' in the case of the homosexual minority. In the following pages, I will attempt to 'stretch' Plummer's model of 'career stages and the homo-sexual role' and to apply the adapted scheme to an understanding of processes of coming out among other stigmatized minorities focused on in this book.

Plummer traces the processes of coming out through four central stages: sensitization, signification, coming out, and stabilization. These four stages, he suggests, can be seen as gradations in the process of adult socialization leading from consciousness of stigmatized-minority identity towards positive re-identification with the minority category as a worthy human group.

SENSITIZATION

In Plummer's view, the initial concern of the social scientist investigating the coming-out process should be in analysing those societal reactions that create the potentiality for the individual to build up a stigmatized-minority identity (1975: 135). In each of these stigmatizing social experiences, he argues, a potential base is created for the subsequent internalization of derogatory labels by the bearer of a stigma.

Negative labelling by parents, teachers, and/or peers may have serious consequences for the individual's self-conception. When a child is continually told that he or she is 'different' (in some socially disapproved way) from other children (e.g., a boy caught in a sexually suggestive encounter with another boy; a pugnacious girl scornfully labelled as a 'tomboy'; an obese child scolded by parents/taunted by peers as a 'fatty'; a mentally retarded child, closeted by parents/ostracized by peers as a 'retard') these hostile societal reactions are experienced as degradation ceremonies. Such invalidating experiences, in turn, may become internalized by the bearer, resulting in a stigmatized self-image and a tendency to withdraw into a closet of privacy. The following examples may serve to illustrate this phenomenon:

If the society has a horror of fat people and sees them as basically antisocial characters who are isolated, secretive, greedy, and if fat people are excluded as early as childhood from the ranks of the normal society, so does the fat person naturally come to feel more comfortable being alone, set apart from others, privately gratifying [himself or] herself by eating. If the world treats the fat person with hostility, so does he [or she] come to feel embattled with the environment. Hence, a correspondence is constructed between the image and the reality. (Millman, in Wolman, 1982: 85)

When a person is not accepted as a whole, it is difficult for him [or her] to accept himself [or herself], particularly if feelings of inferiority and shame are associated with the handicap. Self-depreciation interferes with the desire to enter into relations with others. (Office des Personnes Handicappées du Québec, 1981: Report 5, 15)

The rest of the evening was like a nightmare. We were taken to police headquarters ... and then ... to the offices of the Morality Squad. Then ... photographed and fingerprinted. I was struck by the matter-of-factness of the policemen. We were simply two of the night's quota of faggots. (Jackson and Persky, 1982: 7)

NEUTRALIZATION: BLOCKING THE PROCESS

Plummer (1975: 140–1) argues that a critical variable in the process of coming out is that of identification with 'significant others.' Should stigmatized individuals develop strong attachments to non-stigmatized majority reference groups, the potentiality for labelling themselves as minority members may be neutralized. Alternatively, should such social supports be lacking (unavailable or not perceived as viable/desirable) minority sensitivity is highly likely to occur. In those instances where minority identification is successfully neutralized, the minority member may continue to engage in behaviours associated with minority stigmata and yet avoid minority self-identification, by employing rationalizations that link him or her to another (non-stigmatized) reference group. For example, a male homosexual may project the self-image of a 'Don Juan' – a highly sexed heterosexual who enjoys all kinds of sexual experiences and for whom sexual experimentation (including homosexual acts) presents an exciting challenge. Similarly, an active alcoholic may project the 'macho' self-image of a 'hard drinker' presumably able to 'hold his liquor.' The employment of rationalizations such as these may lead the minority member to form attachments to outside reference groups for social support (in the above examples, heterosexual swingers and social drinkers, respectively). By so doing, the potential sensitivity of the individual to the fact that he or she belongs to a stigmatized-minority group is neutralized, and the individual may be able to accommodate stigmatized (minority) behaviours that are insulated from self-labelling implications (Plummer, 1975).

SIGNIFICATION AND DISORIENTATION

Plummer (1975: 142) contends that signification begins where sensitization ends. It entails all of the psycho-social processes that lead to a heightened minority identity – from the subjective sense of being different to a developed minority identity; and from minor [closeted] minority-related behaviours and attachments to the stage of coming out.

For some individuals, the awakening sense of minority identity is accompanied by a feeling of positive relief; for others, it is fraught with anxiety and ambiguity. Where the process generates heightened self-awareness and meaningfulness in the minority experience the phase may be termed 'signification.' Where the process brings on confusion and tension in coping with one's life situation, the phase may be termed 'disorientation.'

Disorientation and signification represent differential responses to the bearer's awareness of the stigmatizing condition. Disorientation may lead to the closet syndrome, with its associated problems of secrecy, guilt, and access. Yet, secrecy itself, through the self-isolation process, can lead to signification. Lack of social support from significant others – both insiders and outsiders – can lead to the individual's self-perception as 'the only one in the world' and to the related feelings of pain, frustration, and fear that accompany the utter loneliness of feeling like an exile from humankind. Yet, despite the agonies of isolation, the fear-filled minority member may be unwilling to broach 'the subject' with family, peers, or 'officials' in order to obtain help in coping with his or her life situation. Consequently, he or she may become preoccupied with the question of core identity; and 'who am I' may, in turn, become a key problem that leads to signification. Plummer argues that such problems, if unresolved, serve to heighten disorientation and to amplify signification. In some cases, they may linger on even for a lifetime; but in an equally large number of instances, individuals confronted with such problems may seek to resolve them in various ways (Plummer, 1975: 147).

In the case of physically disabled minorities, the initial experiences involved in coming out are likely to lead to disorientation. Because disabled-minority members for so long have been closeted within isolated total institutions and thereby hidden from public view, majority members tend to define and treat disabled persons in terms of their visible stigmata and not in terms of their human personalities and capabilities. Stigmatizing stereotypes of disabled minorities are indirectly reinforced through media images that glorify cultural norms of physical strength, able-bodiedness, health, and beauty. As a result, when majority members are confronted with a person perceived to possess a deformed body, a disfigured face, a mobility impairment, a visual or auditory impairment, or other physical disabilities, their initial reaction tends to be one of unease or embarrassment, if not revulsion. Psychological unease may be manifested in behaviours such as staring, laughing, pity, or ridicule of the disabled minority member. All of these negative, societal reactions on the part of majority members can precipitate a psychological condition of disorientation on the part of the disabled-minority member (Office des Personnes Handicappées du Québec, 1981: Report 5, 12). Disorientation, in turn, can lead the disabled person to retreat from public view and to re-create a protective closet of privacy. Whether or not invalidating experiences precipitate a return to the closet, they serve to reinforce minority stigmata and to impact negatively upon the disabled person's self-image and minority identity.

The following quotes may serve to illustrate:

I was born with cerebral palsy . . . but it is only society's reaction to my condition that makes me think about it . . . People rarely say the insults they are thinking, but I can sense what's going through their minds. I find this very uncomfortable and embarrassing to deal with. (Serge Leblanc, in Canada, House of Commons, 1981: 84)

Except for the fear that sighted people have in my presence, I would forget that I am blind. (Denise Beaudry, ibid: 16)

I consider people's attitudes towards the disabled as one of the most difficult obstacles that I face. It expresses itself as, 'we'll take care of you' . . . In other words, our status as dependent people is always guaranteed . . . they are always doing things for you, but never with you . . . When people prevent you from making decisions, as is done with the disabled, they are depriving you of a key activity of being human. (Shaun McCormick, ibid: 114)

COMING OUT

"To come out [of the closet] . . . means bucking the most basic and deep-seated norms of a society' (Altman, 1971: 8). Altman points out that the neophyte, warily emerging from the closet, is highly conscious of the fact that, in openly declaring a stigmatized-minority identity through disclosures to others, he or she is repudiating deeply ingrained and cherished (majority) social norms. It is far from surprising, therefore, that the initial phase of coming out is one that typically is fraught with tension and fear. Nevertheless, once the neophyte takes the first steps, through disclosures to other similarly stigmatized minority members, he or she soon comes to discover the existence of a whole new world (minority subculture) and his or her attempts to deal with it, to integrate into it, can become a major preoccupation.

Within any minority subculture there is a range of possibilities for identification and involvement, and the neophyte's choices among the various options to be pursued will generally reflect the extent to which he or she is prepared to come out openly. Altman (1975: 13) suggests that in the case of homosexuals it would be possible to graph individuals according to their degree of openness or 'outness' at any given time. At one extreme, he points out, there are those who seek to maintain a self-image of heterosexuality and who pursue homosexual contacts furtively, and often only when drunk; at the other extreme are those who are open to both themselves and others about their homosexuality. At present, says Altman, there are very few homosexuals who do not feel the need, at least in part, to live a double life. For, all of evidence suggests that a majority of those who identify as homosexuals (self-disclosure) fear disclosure to others, and especially to heterosexuals (ibid: 29).

Elliott (1983) conducted a study of the coming-out process among a sample of 305 lesbians, 171 from Canada and 134 from the United States, and representing all income and educational levels. Research data for the study were gathered by means of questionnaires distributed through the researcher's contacts in friendship networks, gay churches, feminist organizations, women's bookstores, and a university women's centre. While Elliott's study sample cannot be taken as representative, her research findings may be indicative of the kinds of coming-out patterns that are emerging among positively identified lesbian women.

Study findings revealed that most lesbians, (13 per cent) had achieved a positive sense of lesbian identity. Some (13 per cent) further reported 'pride' in their lesbianism and saw lesbianism as the most important part of their personality. The latter category of respondents tended to be more politically active in feminist, lesbian, and/or Gay Liberation movements than were others, and tended to be more 'out' (in terms of disclosures) to a variety of people.

A number of factors were found to be important predictors of the extent of 'outness,' that is, the extent to which lesbians had disclosed their sexual orientation to others. Political awareness and involvement were strongly associated with a high degree of outness, while reported 'fears' were strongly associated with a low degree of outness. A high degree of social interaction and involvement with lesbians and gay men was found to be associated with outness, and appeared to be especially important for those lesbians who came out to the media.

The most unexpected finding was that lesbians who reported the greatest number of 'problems' (stigmatizing experiences) tended to be those with the highest degree of outness. A possible explanation for this finding, Elliott (1983: 512) suggests, is that it represents the outcome of a two-way process: negative experiences generated anger; anger triggered the coming-out process, and, once out, negative experiences increased.

In her (1982) doctoral dissertation, Eisener developed a model of the coming-out process, based on personal interviews with a small, Canadian-based sample of thirty lesbians. In this model, the process of coming out is divided into four (interrelated) steps: 1 / recognition and development of a positive homosexual identity, 2 / contact with a homosexual community, 3 / interpersonal events, and 4 / disclosures.

Eisener's model may be fruitfully addressed in light of Plummer's conceptualization of the coming-out process. Eisener divides the first step of her model into three stages: i / recognition of feeling different, same-sex attraction (sensitization); ii / recognition of possible identification with homosexual label, followed by denial, confusion, rationalization (e.g., label oneself bisexual) (disorientation and neutralization); iii / label oneself homosexual, integrate homosexuality into positive self-identity (signification). In step two of the model, Eisener focuses on the initial phase of coming out. She describes the various means of establishing contact with the minority community: seeking information, attending meetings, patronizing minority clubs and events, and joining minority organizations. In step three, Eisener describes the different (affectional/ sexual) relationships and life-styles that may be pursued by minority members at different points of the coming-out process. In the fourth and last step of the model, Eisener outlines the general pattern of disclosures in the process of coming out found among her limited sample of Canadian-based lesbians.

With specific regard to Eisener's fourth step, it may be instructive to examine the sequence of disclosures revealed in her study findings. In this connection, a reasonable hypothesis may be that the choice of relevant others to whom disclosures voluntarily are made would begin with one's most trusted associates, whose support was virtually certain, and would move cautiously from this base of assured support towards those whose trust and support were deemed to be less certain. It should be noted, here, that at any point along this process, others may find out about the stigmatized attribute without explicit disclosure by the minority member.

In Eisener's scheme (1982: table 20) the sequence of voluntary disclosures begins with lesbian lover and moves through therapist, homosexual community, close heterosexual friends, (some) siblings and peers among relatives, other relatives, parents and employer, until the final stage of public disclosure. While this pattern of disclosures may be useful as a starting-point for the analysis of the coming-out process among other stigmatized minorities, the reader should note that, in some specific respects, it reflects problems peculiar to the homosexual minority. Altman argues, for example, that it is in relationships with one's family that the peculiar nature of the stigma of homosexuality cuts most deeply (1971: 28). Unlike those stigmatized by colour or caste, Altman contends, the homosexual bears a stigma that is not shared by his or her family, and unlike those stigmatized by physical disabilities, for the homosexual the nagging suspicion remains that the stigma could be got rid of if the desire was strong enough. In other words, Altman's argument is that homosexuality tends to be defined in terms of behaviour, and homosexual behaviours or acts are assumed to be a matter of voluntary choice on the part of the actor.

Deeply held majority assumptions about the voluntariness of homosexuality create an 'insoluble dilemma' for homosexual persons: if their homosexuality is disclosed to parents or other family members, they risk anger and pain (if not total rejection), and yet, if they hide their stigmatized identity (keep it in the closet), they risk becoming alienated from their families, drifting away from them, and living in perpetual fear of any contact that might uncover their stigma. Insofar as homosexual partnerships do not in themselves create families, the estrangement of homosexual persons from their families of origin can be psychologically devastating; thus they tend to keep the secret from families, and especially from parents, even longer than from others. The latter observation is particularly applicable to gay men, for lesbians more often come out of the closet only after they have been married and after they have borne children.

With regard to the question of differential patterns of coming out, Valverde (1983: 66) suggests that the degree to which individual lesbians come out is, to some extent, a function of privilege. The 'rich and famous,' she argues, can come out with relative impunity. In such cases, moreover, even individual acts can have an important public impact. The ordinary office-worker, however, is far more likely to jeopardize her position, without generating much political impact, by her act of courage. This argument is in keeping with my earlier discussion of the concepts of multiple majority and minority status, where, following Prus, I pointed to the moderating effects on minority stigmata of socially valued attributes deriving from majority-status criteria.

Another factor affecting the rate and degree to which lesbians come out, says Valverde (1983), is that of coming out together with friends. By way of example, Valverde points to her own experience; she claims that she came out relatively quickly, not so much because of her own courage, but because of the solicitous support of her lover and of friends who came out with her.

There also are various support systems designed to help lesbians during the various stages of the coming-out process. Some are open groups based on gay pride while others are part of the complex, hidden lesbian subculture that has developed out of the stigmatization of gay women.

According to Ponse (1978: 92) minority support groups in the lesbian world are important in neutralizing and overcoming the stigmatizing effects of the negative judgment of the heterosexual world. Ponse distinguishes between two types of minority support groups: secretive groups and activist groups.

Secretive groups provide an opportunity for lesbians to socialize with one another in an atmosphere where closeted gay women can relax and possibly develop relationships with other gay women. Women joining the group usually must be acknowledged as being gay by personal knowledge of existing members or by passing an interview. Secretive groups often emphasize the need for gays to accommodate to their minority status, not to change the status. These groups stress the need for gays to harmonize with the 'straight' world, and they emphasize the similarities between the two worlds. Lesbianism is seen as a sexual preference only rather than as a distinct sexual orientation expressed in an alternative life-style. While secretive groups often do not directly address lesbian identity as an issue, they must make sure members identify themselves as lesbian in order to ensure and protect the secret status of the group. Occasionally, bisexual women or sympathetic heterosexual women (in Goffman's parlance, the 'wise') may be admitted to the group by virtue of their trustworthiness (Ponse, 1978: 90).

Activist groups, committed to gay liberation and/or feminism, reject the minority status of lesbians by challenging heterosexism. Changing the lesbian identity to a positive identity choice is the primary issue. Activist groups help women coming to terms with their lebianism by starting with the assumption that being a lesbian is a natural alternative life-style. Most gay women in the initial stages of coming out tend to have a negative view of their gayness. Activist groups therefore make a concerted attempt to instil feelings of lesbian pride. They use proud gays as role models, and they discuss sensitive identity and life-style issues in a supportive environment.

Activist groups may accept bisexual women, but they tend to regard bisexuality only as a preliminary stage in the process of coming out. Accordingly, they try to influence women towards acceptance of their lesbianism by pressuring them to conform to the identity norms of the minority subculture. While activist groups encourage their members to come out and to label themselves proudly as lesbians, they will protect the identity of their members wishing to remain secret (Ponse, 1978: 91).

Minority support groups, whether secretive or activist, can play a vital role in the long and difficult process of coming out by providing a supportive context of similarly stigmatized others to whom disclosures about minority identity can be made without fear of hostile societal reactions.

In the case of the alcoholic minority, awareness of the stigmatizing condition on the part of family members tends to develop over extended periods of direct exposure to the 'problem,' rather than through the voluntary disclosures of the alcoholic member. Indeed, the alcoholic member may continue to deny the problem and to engage in rationalizations for alcohol-related behaviours (neutralization) for a long time after other family members have recognized and accepted the alcohol-related disability as such (Al-Anon Family Groups, n.d.: Pamphlet no. 19). For members of the alcoholic minority, such self-help groups as AA may come to provide the requisite protected environment of social support, through anonymity, that enables the alcohol-disabled person to take the first step in the process of coming out. In established AA practice, this critical first step (disclosure) consists of openly declaring among AA members: 'My name is [*first name only*] and I am an alcoholic' (Antze, 1976: 329).

GROUP-LEVEL STIGMA CONVERSION: THE ROLE OF SELF-HELP GROUPS

In addition to their therapeutic value in offering members a knowledgeable and supportive community of relevant others, minority self-help groups may develop a complete program for life-style renewal designed to effect the transformation from a stigmatized self-identity to a positive minority identity and life-style. Central to such a program are the group's teachings, which contain the ideological legitimation for the alternative life-style promoted by the self-help group.

In the following pages, in order to demonstrate to the reader the way in which minority self-help programs work, I shall present a case-study of a very successful program, the one afforded members by Alcoholics Anonymous.

ALCOHOLICS ANONYMOUS (AA): A CASE STUDY[1]

The key to the program of life-style renewal offered to alcohol-disabled persons by AA can be found in the first of the twelve suggested steps that provide the foundation for the entire program: 'We admitted that we were powerless over alcohol – that our lives had become unmanageable' (Alcoholics Anonymous, 1952).

Before arriving at the doorstep of AA, the alcohol-disabled person has typically reached 'rock bottom' – having fought a long–drawn-out and repeatedly unsuccessful battle to 'control' his or her consumption of alcohol and related behaviours. He or she has (at least temporarily) virtually run out of the many rationalizations used in the futile attempts to control drinking – to limit the number of drinks, to confine the time period of drinking, to change from hard liquor to beer or wine, to refrain from bringing liquor into the home, to refrain from bringing liquor into the office, and so on. Finally, (perhaps) grudgingly, admitting that his or her life has become 'unmanageable,' the alcohol-disabled person may seek help. However, it should be noted here that the initial motivation behind coming to AA may not be (indeed, usually is not) a conscious desire to stop drinking. Rather, what is sought by the alcoholic person is the 'secret' of drinking with impunity. Accordingly, the neophyte exposed to the first step in the program of AA may admit with relative ease that his or her life has 'become unmanageable' but he or she may continue to block the more important tenet, that is, that he or she is 'powerless over alcohol.'

It is this central notion of *powerlessness over alcohol*[2] that constitutes the key to AA's program for life-style renewal. For AA teaches that alcoholism is a permanent disease for which there is no cure (Antze, 1976).

1 Materials for this section and for later sections of the book dealing with AA have been drawn from a wide variety of primary and secondary sources. The Conference Approved Literature produced by AA and used by AA, Al-Anon, and Alateen groups has afforded the main set of primary sources. Secondary sources most heavily drawn upon and cited throughout the book are listed in References.
2 AA acknowledges the tendency for newcomers to resist acceptance of this central tenet. Accordingly, AA teaches that 'recovery' begins only after the alcohol-disabled person has 'reached bottom' – the personal experience of utter hopelessness and despair that persuades the individual that, for him or her, self-control is impossible and that finally compels the self-confession of 'illness' (Antze, 1976: 329).

According to AA, the alcohol-disabled person is constitutionally different from other persons.[3] In AA's teachings, alcoholism is equated with an allergy that renders the bearer constitutionally incapable of tolerating alcohol in any amount and in any form. Like an allergy, alcoholism is seen as a permanent condition, which can be arrested but not cured.

With regard to the process of coming out of the alcoholic closet, the foregoing belief is critical, for it removes the whole issue of drinking from the voluntary sphere of behaviour (Antze, 1976: 332). The member of AA who accepts this view acknowledges that, for him or her, 'controlled drinking' is impossible. This realization, in turn, may bring much-needed relief from the feelings of guilt and self-hatred that have accompanied long-term patterns of secret drinking, failed attempts at controlled drinking, and all of the anti-social behaviours associated with abusive drinking in general. Thus, important psychological support is afforded by the AA rationale, namely, that if the alcoholic person is a victim of a disease, then he or she cannot be held accountable for his or her past actions when 'under the influence.' The reader should note, however, that the AA rationale provides solace only for those behaviours unwittingly engaged in while drinking in the past. For the life-style–renewal goal of the AA program is to provide a positive, alternative life-style for alcohol-disabled persons, based upon total abstinence. AA defines alcoholism as a physical, mental, and spiritual disease; concomitantly, its program of life-style renewal aims to bring about physical, mental, and spiritual growth and health.

The spiritual aspect of the AA program is tied in with the group's core belief in a 'higher power,' a source of spiritual strength and support outside the individual, but the exact nature of this power remains deliberately undefined. AA thus grants to each member the right and the freedom to interpret this notion in his or her own way.[4]

Within the program of life-style renewal, the goal of spiritual growth represents one vital ingredient within a holistic conception of psychosocial well-being. This aspect of the AA program has been known to evoke a certain wariness among some potential AA members because of its religious (and especially, Christian) overtones. AA teachings, however,

3 This belief has its current parallel among homosexuals. Here, it provides a counter-rationale (especially for openly gay persons) against homophobic myths based on unproven notions of 'contagion,' role-modelling, and learning theory.
4 For the wary newcomer, AA teachings suggest that the AA group itself (or the local chapter) may be adopted as the member's 'higher power,' or that GOD may be taken to mean 'Good Orderly Direction.'

emphasize the fact that the program is a broadly spiritual one, rather than a formally religious one (Gellman, 1964: 159). Indeed, one of the key principles behind AA is that the group has no affiliations with outside organizations, religious or otherwise, and that it is open to all, regardless of their religious (or non-religious) background. Further, AA teachings strongly discourage any discussion of religion or political opinions at meetings.

The program's 'twelve steps' contain the AA strategy for psycho-social growth and well-being. Viewed from the vantage point of the coming-out process, these steps can be seen to provide a blueprint for destigmatization and for positive, minority identification within the fellowship and subcommunity of AA. From the initial point of accepting alcoholism as an incurable disease (allergy), the member moves on towards a positive self-identification with the role-models provided by 'recovering' and 'recovered' (arrested or inactive) alcoholics. He or she discards the 'garbage' of alibis, denial, and deceptions used in guarding the secret of alcohol abuse and seeks to come out of the alcoholic closet and to make amends (where possible) to those persons known to have been harmed by alcohol-related behaviours. Most important, the neophyte makes a personal commitment to practise the AA program and to 'carry the message' to others. Commitment to AA is expressed through staying sober ("one day at a time'), following the life-style guidelines contained in the twelve steps, attending meetings, helping newcomers, helping to set up meetings, volunteering to assume a (rotating) position in AA, speaking at meetings, and becoming involved in public-information activities. The last named involves 'carrying the message' not only to active alcoholics, but also to members of the public at large (Csicsai, 1983: 21).

Stabilization: the not-so-final stage of coming out

'Coming out,' says Plummer (1975: 150), 'is by no means a simple, automatic, or immediate process.' Nevertheless, Plummer goes on to say, as the neophyte moves from a world characterized by secrecy, solitude, self-hatred, and guilt to a subculture where positive role-models are available, where a belief system is provided to legitimize the minority experience, and where a community of peers is on hand to lend continuing support and guidance, a positive minority role and identity become crystallized. Gradually, the neophyte's identification with and commitment to the minority community reach a stage of stabilization.

Stabilization of minority identity does not imply that the coming-out process has reached completion nor does it preclude further psycho-social growth or further changes in subcultural priorities and life-styles. It does, however, represent a critical stage in the process of coming to terms with one's core identity and of establishing oneself as a person of worth, within the minority milieu.

Within the ideological framework of AA, the program of twelve steps is projected as a 'lifetime' program. Neophytes are frequently reminded that it is a program from which no one graduates. Rather, the program is one that provides a 'blueprint for [continual] progress' towards psycho-social growth and health. According to AA teachings, as the AA member 'grows' within the program, he or she may have occasional 'slips' along the way, but once having made an active commitment to the program, a member rarely slips back to 'rock bottom.' He or she may slip back a rung or two (say the old-timers) but won't fall off the ladder as help from fellow AA members is always as close as the nearest telephone, the nearest AA member, or the nearest AA meeting.

Csicsai (1983: 18) views the process of participating in the AA program as a resocialization process, whereby the member is stripped of his or her (negative) old identity as a practising alcoholic and moves through a series of status passages from 'newcomer,' through temporary 'relapse' (slipping back), to 'social integration' and 'AA as a career' (stabilization and carrying the message to others).

Stabilization of the member's new identity as a 'recovered' or inactive alcoholic is formally recognized by the membership group through the periodic, ritual awarding of tokens (e.g., variously coloured poker chips) that symbolize the length of the period of sobriety achieved (e.g., three months or six months) by the individual AA member. Additionally, 'birthday' and 'anniversary' celebrations are held by local AA groups to mark the achievement of yearly periods of sobriety (e.g., one year or twenty years) by individual members (Gellman, 1964). In AA argot, a 'birthday' means the date upon which an enduring period of sobriety was first achieved in AA, and an 'anniversary' means the annual date of first achieving sobriety in AA (ibid: 175).

'Birthday' parties and 'anniversary' celebrations constitute regularly held ritual events in local AA groups, events that lend continuing strength and salience to the collective AA ideal of sobriety. At the same time, these highly emotionally charged events serve to reinforce bonds of friendship, trust, and commitment to the AA fellowship among minority-group members.

The secret of AA's *'success': self-help in spirituality, camaraderie, and anonymity*

From a social-scientific perspective, the widely reputed 'success' of AA's program for life-style renewal can be seen to derive from the organization's peculiar constellation of ideological, interpersonal, and organizational features.

The fundamental, initial 'message' of AA to its members is that they are not 'all powerful,' not God (Kurtz, 1979: 3). Insofar as the alcohol-disabled person's problem is rooted in the fact that he or she is not in control, even of himself or herself, the first step towards recovery from the 'disease' of alcoholism, AA teaches, must be admittance and acceptance of this fact. But, as Kurtz points out, AA is a fellowship as well as a program, and this represents the second side to the group's message of 'not-God–ness,' that is, acceptance of one's personal limitations. Within AA, such acceptance implies also affirmation of one's connectedness with other alcoholics. Gellman (1964: 152) suggests that the fact that the members of AA are all 'social deviants' whose basic purpose is to serve themselves provides the critical underpinnings of social support behind AA's program and activities. Within the AA enterprise, Gellman continues, social control rests upon members' motivation to gain and to maintain sobriety and to grow spiritually, mentally, and physically, and upon the collective belief that these goals can be accomplished through minority-group support and participation. In this connection, even the core AA belief in a 'higher power' translates into the power of the AA collectivity itself. Moreover, says Gellman, this central self-help aspect of AA facilitates effective proselytization efforts. When an alcohol-disabled member grows, within the program, from a practising (active) alcoholic to a 'recovered' (inactive) alcoholic his or her own status and identity are enhanced by ample opportunities to 'carry the message' to AA newcomers and to practising alcoholics. With regard to the latter, AA members make regular visits to jails, hospitals, psychiatric institutions, and so on in order to carry the message to alcohol-disabled–minority members.

The AA model of minority self-help represents a radical departure from the paternalistic model of alcohol treatment characteristic of majority-controlled, institutional settings. In a comparative evaluation of the two models, Gellman throws light upon some critical distinctions that clearly serve to reveal the underlying 'secret' of AA's success (relative to the abject failure of its institutional counterparts) (1964: 153–8).

In chapter 1 of this book I presented the main points of Gellman's comparative analysis. At this juncture, with specific application to the alcohol-disabled minority, I will highlight those aspects of the argument that can be seen to account for AA's success.

Unlike institutionalized alcoholics, AA members are not cut off from contact with the community at large; they participate in their regular familial, occupational, and other social roles. AA members also maintain their personal identities; they are not subject to 'identity-stripping.' AA practice identifies members by their first names only, in order to protect anonymity. However, individual members are free to reveal their full names, should they choose to do so.

Membership in AA is voluntary; members are free to join or not join a group, to attend or not attend meetings. Their individual right to self-determination is respected. Unlike (voluntary or involuntary) institutionalized alcoholics, they are not coerced into any form of 'treatment.' Rather than being stigmatized through institutionalization the AA member acquires a positive new group identity, as a 'recovered' alcoholic. Yet, anonymity is provided, as a protection against stigmatization by outsiders.

In stark contrast to the formally administered total institution, with its authoritarian hierarchy of 'treatment and control,' AA is egalitarian in ideology and in organization. Members share the common status of the alcoholic minority, and leadership positions are carefully rotated and open to all. Decision-making is democratic, and each member is given the opportunity to express his or her opinion on all issues.

Finally, AA offers a positive, new life-style for members through participation in a minority subculture whose norms are congruent with those of society at large. This is a critical point of contrast with the nonconformist counter-culture, divorced from society at large, of the 'skid-row' alcoholic. AA provides a program of life-style renewal that enables and assists members to fulfil their outside social roles in a meaningful and effective fashion.

As Gellman points out, in practice local groups differ in the degree to which they rigorously follow or deviate from AA's ideological design for living. The most successful groups, however, are those that closely adhere to AA teachings. From a human-rights perspective, the AA model, as a blueprint for life-style renewal, provides alcoholics with a humane alternative to the paternalistic institutional model. AA protects, while the total institution violates, the fundamental human rights of freedom, equality, and dignity of the minority it is designed to serve.

The AA *model: replication by other minorities*

AA's reputation for 'success' has spawned a variety of minority self-help organizations – Gamblers Anonymous, Smokers Anonymous, Fattys Anonymous – whose programs for life-style renewal are closely patterned on the AA model (Antze, 1976). The successful operation of these and other minority self-help groups has gone hand in hand with a growing critique among a broad spectrum of minorities of majority-controlled, institutional settings whose paternalistic policies and practices are seen to create and sustain the very stigmata that AA and other self-help groups are designed to ameliorate. Where possible or feasible, minority members increasingly are choosing the destigmatizing and rehumanizing self-help option.

Minority dissatisfaction with the total institution model is clearly revealed in the following comments of a member of Canada's disabled (blind) minority: 'Having your life run by the CNIB [Canadian National Institute for the Blind] is like having your life run by a church group . . . they're arbitrary, they provide "services", they have a custodial attitude' (Richard [a gay, blind respondent], quoted in Hannon, 1980: 20).

In direct contrast to the paternalistic approach of the CNIB, Richard, (the respondent quoted above) contends that BOOST (Blind Organization of Ontario with Self-Help Tactics) fosters independence among members of the blind minority. BOOST, a minority self-help group, has criticized the CNIB on the grounds that fewer than one-third of the members of CNIB's board are blind – a fact that ensures that the blind cannot control the organization. Like everyone else, Richard contends, the disabled (blind) want to control their own lives. If they must live in institutional settings, they want to control these institutions and make them responsive to what they (disabled-minority members) perceive to be their real needs. Richard, who has spent most of his life in institutions for the blind, currently has a job with BOOST. He sees his present involvement in this minority self-help organization as the key to his personal independence (Hannon, 1980).

The limits of anonymity

Insofar as minority self-help groups cope with stigma(ta) by remaining closeted (secret/anonymous) they can provide individual members with important support for the development of a positive minority identity and life-style, but they cannot actively promote social reforms designed to protect the human rights of minority members at the group level.

In the case of the secretive, anonymous minority organizations, such as AA, 'carrying the message' to outsiders, beyond the confines of the closed sessions of the minority self-help group, entails the risk of public exposure of one's stigmatized status. Even if pseudonyms are employed to protect anonymity, minority members who volunteer to 'carry the message' at open (public) AA meetings and/or through public-speaking engagements risk identification by members of the audience, since self-help groups, by and large, operate at the local level, the level of the community in which minority members reside and work. While some minority members may be willing to risk exposure and a few may even be willing to come out publicly, most members of anonymous self-help groups fear disclosure of their stigmatized status to outsiders. It is, indeed, the very guarantee of anonymity that enables them to participate in self-help groups and to make disclosures to insiders. It is here that the limits of anonymity are revealed.

While anonymous self-help groups can aid in the process of destigmatization of individual members at the level of personal identity, I will argue that they fail to destigmatize the minority at the group level. For masked identities remain inherently suspicious in the eyes of wary majority audiences.

It is only through 'coming out' to the public of substantial numbers of minority member from all walks of life that the process of *group-level* destigmatization can be set in motion. For it is through public disclosures that the human similarities between majority and minority members – similarities long masked by distorted stigmatizing stereotypes – can be revealed to majority audiences.

It is a sorry comment on the extent of homophobia in North American society that it took the untimely death (in 1985) of the 'all-American male' movie star, Rock Hudson, a victim of AIDS, to reveal to the public the fact of his hidden, fear-filled, and guilt-laden homosexual life-style. How many more Rock Hudsons will it take before the heterosexual majority realizes the human commonalities between homosexuals and heterosexuals?[5] These comments are not meant to suggest that stigmatized-

5 At the time of writing, Svend Robinson, the Burnaby-Kingsway New Democrat MP, had just publicly proclaimed his homosexuality. Robinson's courageous decision to come out to the public was precipitated by the federal government's lack of action on the recommendation of its (1986) *Toward Equality* report that sexual orientation should be included among the enumerated, non-discriminatory grounds of the (federal) Cana-

minority members have a societal obligation to 'come out' at any cost. The closet exists because it protects vulnerable minority members from everyday experiences marked by human-rights violations. The ultimate societal obligation rests with majority members who must ensure that the human rights of all citizens are respected and protected. But, until such time as majority members take up these societal obligations with some seriousness, the onus for raising minority rights claims will lie with those members of stigmatized minorities who have the resources and the courage that enable them to come out of the closet. By participating in open, activist minority organizations, those who have come out can begin to lobby for the rights of others.

CONCLUDING COMMENTS

This chapter has focused on the analysis of the steps or stages involved in the processes of destigmatization of minority identity and coming out of the closet. This analysis has revealed the importance of minority systems of social support in the coming-out process and has shown the critical role played by anonymous or secretive self-help groups in the early stages of destigmatization of minority identity. I have drawn the reader's attention to the limits of anonymity, the obstacle it imposes upon the pursuit of minority-rights protections. I have suggested that, in order for destigmatization to occur at the group level, more and more minority members must come out to the public. Finally, I have argued that in order for minorities to become engaged in the process of putting forward minority rights claims, minority organizations must assume open, activist, human-rights platforms.

In the following chapter, I will turn my attention to the processes involved in raising collective minority consciousness of human-rights violations and in generating activist minority organizations and protest movements. I will assess the factors leading to a response of contention and compare this response with that of revitalization. Finally, I will assess the nature of the minority rights claims that can be put forward by stigmatized minorities through open, activist groups.

---

dian Human Rights Act. While the public impact of Robinson's endeavour is yet to be demonstrated, New Democratic party leader Ed Broadbent has acknowledged that homosexual rights could become an issue in the next federal election (*Toronto Star*, 7 March 1988).

6

From secretism to activism: the evolution of minority protest

In the last chapter, I argued that for destigmatization to occur at the group level, substantial numbers of minority members would have to reject majority-imposed stigmata, to re-identify collectively in positive terms, and to come out of the closet. Once this happens, the stage is set for the development of activist minority organizations designed to put forward minority-rights claims.

FROM NEGATIVE TO POSITIVE MINORITY IDENTITY

In the initial stage of minority-protest organization, a significant rite of passage involves the rejection of stigmatizing labels and their replacement with affirmative, minority-chosen group designations: from 'queer' to 'gay,' 'nigger' to 'black,' 'cripple' to 'disabled.' Minority members may also create group symbols (diacritica) expressed in nomenclature, logos, emblems, and so on, which can play an important part in the creation of a new collective identity. As visible indicators of positive group identification, symbols can become the rallying points for repeated occasions of collective mobilization and group affirmation.

Symbols typically are drawn from a stigmatized minority's distinctive group history, a history that is likely to include continuing experiences of personal and group degradation and harassment at the hands of majority authorities. Like many other stigmatized populations, the gay/lesbian minority has a group history marked by persecution. Indeed, gays and lesbians have been singled out as targets for the most extreme, collective form of human-rights violation, namely, genocide. Just as Jews, marked for extermination in Nazi concentration camps, were compelled to wear the yellow Star of David as a symbol of their stigmatized ethnicity, so gays and lesbians were compelled to wear the pink triangle as a symbol of their stigmatized sexual orientation. For gays and lesbians, as for Jews, the symbols of their collective defamation and persecution have become hallowed emblems, central to minority members' self-identification with their group history. Like the Jewish Star of David, the pink triangle is worn openly, displayed in parades and marches, and commemorated in collective ceremonies.

A news report (Gays of Ottawa, 1983) on 'Pink Triangle Week' in Ottawa reveals the symbolic importance of this emblem for the contemporary gay/lesbian community in Canada:

"Pink Triangle Week – A Gay Community Appeal'. The first gay community appeal in Ottawa was held during Pink Triangle Week, February 11 to 19 [1983]. The Pink Triangle is the symbol which lesbians and gay men were forced to wear in the Nazi concentration camps. Gay people worldwide have adopted this symbol as a reminder of anti gay oppression and as a symbol of the determination of gay people to live full lives in spite of the oppression. Gays of Ottawa (GO) organized the community appeal as part of its campaign to raise funds for its community and social services.

From 'faggot' to 'gay'/from 'dyke' to 'lesbian'

For homosexuals, stigmatized on the basis of sexual orientation, current group symbols such as the pink triangle represent overt manifestations of the minority's long and dramatic struggle for human recognition and human-rights protections. As a minority protest movement, this struggle is alleged to have begun in 1869, with Benkert's designation of the term 'homosexuality' to refer to sexual acts between persons of the same sex (Lauristen and Thorstad, 1974: 6).

In the latter part of the nineteenth century, the European legal climate towards 'homosexual acts' was in a state of constant flux, responding variously to the growing spirit of social reform emanating from France and to the reactionary trend setting in against it. Benkert, a Hungarian doctor on the side of reform, coined the term 'homosexual' to refer to specific sexual acts previously defined as unnatural, perverse, and sinful, and, accordingly, condemned by law. As Benkert conceptualized it, the new term 'homosexuality' symbolized a 'natural' human condition. He argued that homosexuality, like heterosexuality, is inborn, not acquired; hence it cannot be held to pose any threat to heterosexual society and it should not be regarded as a punishable offence by 'rational persons' (Lauristen and Thorstad, 1974: 7). The presence of homosexuality in all known human cultures, Benkert contended, is proof that it deserves the same recognition as a natural human phenomenon as does heterosexuality. Benkert also was among the first social critics to openly point out the sociological fact that persecution of homosexuals by heterosexuals constituted the discriminatory practice of 'scapegoating.' This practice is predicated upon a 'double standard' whereby innocent persons are categorically singled out for debasement and punishment by others who often commit the same acts (albeit with persons of the opposite sex) with legal and social impunity (ibid: 8).

By the end of the nineteenth century, the term 'homosexual' had become widely adopted by majority authorities, particularly doctors and psychiatrists. But, as employed by these majority 'experts,' the term soon acquired modified connotations that accorded with their generally agreed-upon view that homosexuality was a less acceptable form of sexual behaviour than was heterosexuality (Altman, 1982: 4).

In the decades to follow, majority authorities increasingly came to employ a medical model of 'deviance' that conceptualized homosexuality as an 'illness' or a 'maladjustment.' As medicine and psychiatry became increasingly important institutions of power in the early twentieth century, the medical stereotype of the 'sick homosexual' gained prominence. This medical reconceptualization of the term 'homosexual' virtually reversed the connotation of the term as Benkert used it, for it returned the definition of homosexuality to the stigmatizing realm of the unnatural or abnormal. Moreover, in contrast to Benkert's definition of homosexuality as an inborn aspect of human nature, which implied an involuntary, immutable characteristic, the medical definition of homosexuality as an 'illness' implied a mutable condition with a strong assumption of voluntariness, that is, an illness that could and should be cured (Altman, 1982).

As a popular belief, the concept of homosexuality as a sickness that should be cured remains widely held in North America, even in the 1980s, despite increasing scientific challenges, over the last two decades, which have persuaded professional medical, psychological, and psychiatric associations to abandon this definition and to *delist* homosexuality as an illness.

Among social scientists, with the rise to prominence of social-deviance theory, the medical model of homosexuality as an illness gradually became replaced by the model of sexual deviance (behavioural non-conformity). But, from the view of the homosexual minority, this redefinition does not remove the stigma from the label. Homosexual spokespersons have argued – despite the protestations of such labelling theorists as Goffman and Becker – that the idea of deviance cannot be value-free; hence, the 'sexual deviant' label suggests that homosexuals are not just different, they are 'bizarre.' And, because they are 'strange,' homosexuals clearly are less socially acceptable than their heterosexual counterparts.

From the late 1960s, prevailing majority approaches to homosexuality – which, despite their differences, agreed that it was a condition less preferable than heterosexuality – have come to be challenged by homosexuals themselves (Altman, 1982: 6). Two quite new and related conceptions of homosexuality were put forward by minority spokespersons in the 1970s – the concept of a legitimate, alternate life-style (gay subculture) and that of a gay minority group. Altman points out that the increasing adoption by homosexuals of the concepts of alternate life-style and gay minority reveals a fundamental reappraisal of the meaning of homosexuality and a tendency to see it as a legitimate form of sexual and cultural expression rather than as a bio-psycho-social aberration.

Over the last decade, homosexual organizations have put forth enormous efforts to shift the minority definition farther, from behaviour to identity. The prime symbol of this shift lies in the replacement of the majority-contaminated term 'homosexual' by the positive self-designation of 'gay' men and women.

Positive affirmation of gay identity is clearly expressed in the minority's redefinition of gayness as sexual and affectional preference. This definition departs radically from previous majority-imposed labels, first, in that it refers only to one's sexual orientation or predisposition, not to sexual acts or behaviours and, second, in that it provides a legitimate alternative to heterosexual 'love' for it includes *affectional* as well as sexual preference. What is implied in this definition is that it is 'natural' for persons whose sexual and affectional preference is for members of their own sex to pursue a legitimate life-style as gays (homosexuals), just as it is 'natural' for persons whose sexual and affectional preference is for members of the opposite sex to pursue a legitimate life-style as 'straights' (heterosexuals). In both cases, gay and straight, one's natural 'orientation' would lead one to pursue and to form sexual and affectional relationships with partners of the same (gay or straight) sexual orientation. Hence, neither orientation can justifiably be held to pose any kind of 'threat' to the other.

While this redefinition of homosexuality as 'gayness' has become generally acceptable to both gay men and gay women, the label 'gay' tends to connote male homosexuals. Thus it is seen as problematic for their self-identification by increasing numbers of gay women. Accordingly, more and more organizations of gay women are adopting the self-designation 'lesbians.' The latter term of reference not only distinguishes female from male members of the gay minority, but it also symbolizes the *double-minority status* of lesbians – as gays and as women.

Adam (1987: 92) argues that, from the beginning of Gay Liberation, the number of lesbians in the movement was far smaller than the number of gay men. Moreover, gay men tended to be preoccupied with their own issues (police entrapment, sodomy laws) and unaware of the special concerns of lesbians as women (equal opportunity, violence against women). Whereas gay men generally had financial independence, many gay women did not. Gay women, accordingly, found themselves in a minority position, without an equal voice, within male-dominated gay organizations. Their self-perception as a double minority (within gay organizations, as within society at large) led to the development of independent lesbian organizations.

The positive affirmation of the collective identities of gay men and lesbian women is symbolized in current organizational logos that have been adapted from traditional anthropological/biological emblems for sexual identification, as shown in the scheme below:

Sexual status	*Sexual orientation*	
male	♂ (straight man)	♂ ♂ (gay man)
female	♀ (straight woman)	♀ ♀ (gay/lesbian woman)
minority-group symbol		♂ ♂ ♀ ♀ (gay/lesbian community)

The replacement of stigmatizing majority labels with minority-chosen self-designations and group symbols represents an important initial step in the processes of destigmatization and positive minority-group affirmation. With specific reference to minorities stigmatized on the basis of sexual orientation, we may chart the development of positive group redefinition in 'Two Acts,' as follows:

ACT I	ACT II
Majority label (focus on acts, 'unnatural' behaviours)	*Minority redefinition* (focus on natural human predisposition)
queen (unnatural [biological])	
faggot (sinful [religious])	homosexual (Benkert)
dyke (immoral [moral/legal])	(natural, biological alternative)
homosexual (sick [medical/ psychiatric])	gay and lesbian (legitimate alternative life-styles and identities based on sexual
homosexual (socially/sexually deviant [sociological])	orientation [i.e., natural sexual and affectional preference])

MINORITY ACTIVIST ORGANIZATION: MOBILIZATION FOR PROTEST

Mobilization of members of a stigmatized minority for a specific collective purpose (e.g., sit-in, march, or rally) to protest against group discrimination may be fairly easily attained even in the early stages of activist organization because of the catalyst to action provided by the external threat. But such precipitating events do not serve to guarantee any long-term commitment to the group on the part of participating members. An important variable in gaining such commitment is the valence (positive or negative direction) of minority identity among group members. The greater the proportion of members possessing and retaining a negative identity, the more difficult is the effective long-term organization of the minority collectivity. Minority organizations whose members lack positive group commitment may be held together only or mainly by outside pressures, such as continuing acts of collective discrimination (unity in defence). Such minorities lack *internal* unity based on shared values and commitment to group ideologies and goals. They tend, as a result, to become easily fragmented or factionalized within. In contrast, those minority organizations in which substantial numbers of members are strongly, positively identified are more likely to achieve ideological unity and collective commitment to organizational goals.

In addition to the degree of positive identification of minority members, there are a number of other variables that affect the ability of an activist minority organization to gain and sustain group solidarity and to mobilize members for active participation in endeavours designed to effect desired social change.

Drawing upon key concepts from the literature on social movements (addressed in chapter 1), one may posit five variables that affect the degree to which activist minority organizations are able to effectively mobilize members in pursuit of collective goals:

1 the development of a unifying ideology that identifies sources of discontent and formulates strategies and goals for group betterment
2 the emergence of able, willing, and representative leadership
3 the availability of channels of communication and networks of co-operative relationships among members
4 the development of an autonomous organizational base
5 the salience of lines of social segmentation within the society

The development of a unifying ideology is a critical variable in the creation of group solidarity for it serves to increase commitment to collective goals and to promote co-ordinated action among minority members. In the case of non-ethnic minorities lacking an existing organizational base of communal structures to draw upon, the potential bases for internal fragmentation of an activist minority organization are manifold. Accordingly the development of a unifying ideology may be the deciding factor in the ability of leaders to transform a loosely organized aggregate of minority members into a tightly knit pressure group.

In contradistinction to majority-created stereotypes, which typically depict minorities in terms of standardized, collective images (skid-row drunks, effeminate queers, helpless cripples, incompetent retards), the real-life picture of any minority is that of a population with internal cleavages parallel to those found in society at large. In the case of stigmatized, *non*-ethnic minorities, members may be drawn from many different ethnic communities. Thus, in addition to potentially divisive lines of sex, age, class, interest, ideological persuasion, and so forth, non-ethnic minorities may be internally fragmented along ethnic lines. These lines of division can pose some of the most serious identity conflicts for minority members, for ethnic communities tend to maintain communal (*Gemeinschaft*) structures that impose heavy constraints on members for expressed commitment to the minority community and its goals.

Within the gay community, for example, in addition to the primary, sex-based divisions between gays and lesbians, organizations such as gay synagogues, Asian gays, and black lesbians, clearly reflect the salience of lines of ethnic fragmentation within the minority community (Adam, 1987).

Compounding the problem of external bases of minority fragmentation is the fragmenting potential of minority status itself. Insofar as members of any minority may (and do) react in different ways to the life conditions attendant upon minority status, their various responses can give rise to serious lines of division within the minority community (e.g., between the closeted and the open members, and between those who aspire to assimilate to majority cultural norms and those who prefer to maintain alternate life-styles).

Moreover, lines of internal division within the minority community not infrequently give rise to conflict between different leaders and different minority organizations. Thus, a critical problem for the leaders of minority organizations lies in developing community- or population-wide strategies and goals that can override or accommodate internal factional interests.

Clearly, it can be seen that the greater and the more potentially conflicting the lines of division within a stigmatized minority population, the more formidable will be the task for leaders of minority organizations to achieve a modicum of consensus among group members on organizational strategies and goals. Divisiveness *within* minority organizations may, in turn, impede efforts of leaders to develop a spirit of co-operation between members of *different* organizations representing conflicting factional interests within the minority community.

LESBIANS AGAINST THE RIGHT (LAR): A CASE STUDY OF FRAGMENTATION[1]

Stone's (1983) analysis of the first year of operation of the LAR organization in Toronto well illustrates the way in which lines of fragmentation within a newly formed minority organization may impede the achievement of consensus on organizational strategies and goals.

When LAR was formed, its membership was drawn almost entirely from the ranks of political activists, that is, lesbians who had been active for some time in the gay and/or feminist movements. Over the first year, however, the composition of the membership both changed and diversified. Accordingly, what began as a fairly homogeneous group (in terms of ideological commitment) soon became fragmented along multiple lines, including age, education, occupation, political orientation, social identity, and personal interest. Beyond their collective identification as lesbians and as a persecuted minority, members of the organization remained divided on almost every important front. A major obstacle to the development of a definitive, unifying ideology for the group was the diversity of ideological conceptions among members. While all supported a general, abstract notion of LAR as a 'lesbian/feminist' organization, the group could not agree on a collective definition or a unifying theory of 'lesbian/feminism.' Accordingly, the fledgling minority organization was unable to formulate long-range collective strategies and goals. Critical lines of ideological fragmentation emerged between those who saw lesbian issues as a subset of women's issues, those who saw lesbian issues as a subset of gay (homosexual) issues, and those who saw lesbian issues as distinct from both of these other, related, yet fundamentally different issues. Because a unifying ideology was not developed, representative leadership did not emerge, and the general level of commitment to LAR diminished.

1 Data for this case study were drawn from Stone (1983).

Despite serious lines of group fragmentation, LAR members were able to mobilize politically during the first year, on a number of different occasions, because group consensus was achieved on the value of co-operative relationships between lesbians inside and outside of the organization. The group maintained open channels and networks of communication with other lesbian organizations. This meant that even in its first year of existence, LAR was able to corral support for its activities from the broader Toronto community of lesbians. Significant among the activities undertaken by the organization in its first year were the city's first lesbian march, participation in gay/lesbian and women's events, organization of workshops on lesbian issues, and organization of several cultural events for lesbians.

Yet, as has been argued earlier, mobilization of minority members for a specific, collective purpose (e.g., a march or cultural event) does not guarantee long-term commitment to the minority organization on the part of participating members. To ensure long-term commitment, the achievement of a solid consensus among members on group ideologies, strategies, and goals is essential. To the extent that LAR was unable to attain such consensus in its first year of existence, it experienced significant loss of members.

MOBILIZING THE DISABLED IN CANADA: THE CONSUMER MOVEMENT

Probably the most problematic minority with regard to internal lines of fragmentation, and the one posing the most formidable obstacles for attempts by leaders to achieve minority-wide organization, is the disabled population in Canada. Because of the wide range of types of mental and physical disabilities and because of the many variations in the degrees and spheres of handicap imposed by different disabilities, a sense of collective consciousness has been late in emerging. One important factor that has impeded the development of collective identification of the disabled has been the fact that a widely agreed-upon 'general purpose' definition did not emerge until very recently among professional caretakers or majority policy-makers in this country (Canada, House of Commons, 1981). The proliferation of 'special purpose' definitions, geared to particular policies (transportation, housing, income security) for particular classes of disabled persons (non-ambulatory, hearing-impaired, mentally ill), served to reinforce internal lines of division within the disabled minority. Accordingly, while uni-disability groups emerged, the cross-disability population as a whole constituted an unorganized minority category with a variety of subclasses, but not a minority group with the potential for concerted action.

As has been documented in earlier chapters of this book, social policies towards the disabled population in Canada traditionally have been highly paternalistic in thrust. Consequently, disabled persons as a minority (including a great number of members capable of independent living) have become over-dependent on public (government) funding. Both as individual recipients of 'care' under various government programs, and as members of uni-disabled organizations designed and controlled by majority caretakers, they have long been dependent on the 'goodwill' of more powerful outsiders. Because of their powerlessness and their many internal lines of division, as a minority, disabled persons in Canada have had monumental obstacles to overcome in their efforts to create a movement for advocacy as well as self-help. Yet, in the 1980s, such a movement has come into being.

The roots of the current consumer movement of the disabled can be traced back to the early 'begging guilds,' the first self-help groups organized by the disabled during the long, historical period when the customary role of disabled persons was that of begging in the streets (Derksen, 1985). While begging guilds proliferated for centuries throughout the urbanized areas of Europe, Africa, and Asia, they were fairly limited in pre-industrial Canada. Moreover, following the First World War, traditional patterns of disablement began to change as young adults (war veterans) with spinal-cord injuries and other acquired disabilities began to survive. Unlike the traditional membership of begging guilds, these new members of the disabled minority included many who were highly educated and who had high social status (for example, as military officers). These newly disabled young adults vehemently rejected the traditional beggar role, and they began to band together to make a place for disabled persons in Canadian society. They soon emerged as the new leadership of the disabled and they created the impetus among minority members to form new organizations that addressed human-rights concerns, such as discrimination in access to jobs and housing (ibid).

Until the late 1960s, organizations of the disabled had been uni-disability–oriented. There was no sense of collective identity among disabled persons as such. However, during the 1970s, the influence of burgeoning North American minority-rights movements, such as the civil-rights movement and the women's liberation movement, served to generate a sense of collective awareness among Canada's disabled as persons with disabilities who shared many common problems. The cross-disability movement emerged as a result. This movement, the precursor to the current consumer movement of the disabled, changed the focus of minority organization from a preoccupation with medical intervention (surgery and drugs) as means of life improvement to a goal of community integration of the disabled as a human need and a human right (Derksen, 1985).

Brown (1977: 29–44) traces the beginning of the current 'consumer movement' among Canada's disabled population to the organized reaction on the part of the National Advisory Council on Voluntary Action (NACOVA) to a 1977 speech by the Honourable Marc Lalonde (then minister of national health and welfare). In this address, Mr Lalonde told volunteers working with various organizations for the disabled that relationships in respect to disabled persons must change in their composition from two-way (government/service agencies) relationships to three-way (government/service agencies/advocacy representatives of the disabled 'consumers') relationships. In short, established majority control in decision-making must give way to a more democratic form in which minority representatives have an equal voice.

In response to the minister's speech, NACOVA presented a brief to the government, which revealed the growth of a critical consumer movement among Canada's disabled population. The brief, 'People in Action,' pointed out that a growing number of disabled persons, in reaction against the dominance of large, established (majority-controlled) 'total institutions' in Canada, were determined to control their own destinies. Further, they were banding together in an activist, self-advocacy movement not only to help each other, but also to make their voices heard by majority Canadians. Their voices were expressing their demand that disabled Canadians should be accorded their fundamental human right to full participation as equal citizens in Canadian society at large.

The Coalition of Provincial Organizations of the Handicapped (COPOH), headquartered in Winnipeg, Manitoba, currently represents a national coalition of a wide range of advocate consumer groups among the disabled. COPOH requires that its member groups include 50 per cent disabled persons in the membership, and more than 50 per cent on the board of directors. Moreover, it requires also that member groups be totally independent while carrying out consultation with service agencies.

Despite their insistence on working towards a common goal of self-determination and independence for the various constituencies among Canada's disabled population, consumer-advocate groups remain dependent on federal, provincial, and municipal governments for funds. Accordingly, the viability of the consumer movement among Canada's disabled minority remains dependent, because of financial needs, on the vagaries of majority-controlled government policy.

Our analysis of the LAR oganization among Toronto's lesbians and of the consumer-advocacy movement among Canada's disabled minorities highlights the difficulties involved, for minority organizations, in overcoming lines of internal fragmentation and achieving unity of purpose as well as in mobilizing economic resources and creating an independent organizational base.

In the following pages I will turn attention to the problems and tasks facing leaders of minority organizations in their efforts to mobilize members to participate in activities designed to bring about human-rights–oriented social changes.

IDENTIFYING SOURCES OF DISCONTENT:
CONTRAST CONCEPTIONS

When the stigmatized and disadvantaged status of the minority as a collectivity is perceived by more and more members as unjust and dehumanizing, *contrast conceptions* are likely to develop in which the majority group is perceived as the unjust persecutor and the monority group is perceived as the innocent victim of majority persecution. Such contrast conceptions serve to heighten 'consciousness of kind' among minority members, based on a shared sense of victimization.

The ethnic-relations literature is replete with examples: Jewish victims/ anti-Semitic Gentile persecutors; black victims/racist white persecutors; homosexual victims/homophobic heterosexual persecutors. With regard to the latter example, Ponse (1978: 93) points out that, among lesbians, repudiation of the importance of heterosexuals through derogatory names and jokes serves to diminish the status of the majority persecutor in the eyes of the minority victim. At the same time, the implicit employment of contrast conceptions bolsters the positive self-identity of the minority member.

The negative stereotype of the majority persecutor employed in contrast conceptions can also provide fear-filled and vulnerable minority members with a source of justification for minority demands. The employment of contrast conceptions can thus facilitate the process of coming out of the closet, and, by providing a rationale for minority-rights claims, it also may give minority members the confidence with which to make justifiable demands upon majority authorities for desired social changes.

TASKS OF MINORITY LEADERSHIP

In the initial stages of mobilization of minority members, leaders are faced with four main tasks: to formulate and promote acceptance of a legitimating ideology to justify the groups' demands and goals; to formally articulate corporate strategies and goals; to clearly communicate the design or program of action to minority members; and to organize and wield together the minority collectivity as an activist organization or pressure group (Kallen, 1982). Only when these tasks have been accomplished may leaders begin – with a sense of confidence in the outcome of their efforts – to 'lobby' majority authorities in order to persuade them of the legitimacy and the urgency of minority demands.

Insofar as a significant degree of politicization and unity of purpose has been achieved within the minority collectivity, important factors influencing the outcome of minority leaders' lobbying efforts will include the degree of credibility accorded minority leaders; the perceived legitimacy of their cause; and the degree of demonstrable political, economic, and social power of the minority as a collectivity. With regard to the latter factor, the degree to which minority demands are perceived by majority bodies as posing a *palpable threat* to their entrenched societal dominance and control will clearly affect the outcome of minority lobbying efforts (Clark et al, 1975; Kallen, 1982).

Majority bodies may perceive minority demands as both legitimate and threatening but they may, nevertheless, be unwilling and/or (realistically) unable to accede to these demands, at least in the short term. In response, majority bodies or authorities may attempt to appease and contain minority demands, through strategies designed to maintain their (majority) hegemony. They may, for example, accede to limited, expressive (subcultural) demands of minorities in order to contain more threatening instrumental (political/legal) demands (Kallen, 1982). An example of this strategy of appeasement and containment of minority claims is revealed in the nature of the federal government response to demands put forward by Gays of Ottawa, an activist gay/lesbian organization. The federal government provides (partial) funding for the Gay Cultural Centre, but 'sexual orientation' is not (as yet) listed among the prohibited (non-discriminatory) grounds of the Canadian Human Rights Act, the legislation that is applicable in all areas of federal jurisdiction.

In connection with the (above) reference to government funding, it should be pointed out that a major technique of 'management' of minority demands is through majority (government or private) funding of minority organizations. I have previously alluded to the relationship of dependency this creates in my discussion of the consumer movement of Canada's disabled. In elaboration of this point, I will argue that a majority fund-giving agency is a 'controlling' agency, for it sets the terms (conditions) under which funds are allotted, selects the recipients, and oversees and regulates the process through which the funds are distributed or expended. As a result, government as well as private majority funding of minority organizations subtly (and sometimes not so subtly) allows majority intervention in minority affairs. In this way, the minority is kept in a dependent position and collective minority demands are 'managed' and kept under majority control (see, especially, Ponting and Gibbins, 1980).

In order to gain control of their own affairs and life-destinies, minority members must seek to create an economically independent organizational base under politicallly astute and capable leadership. One example of how this can be done is provided in the case of Alcoholics Anonymous.

Mobilizing alcoholics: early leadership in Alcoholics Anonymous (AA)

The way in which leaders of minorities are able to mobilize and organize members, even in the face of lack of majority support, is well illustrated in the case of Alcoholics Anonymous. In AA tradition, the beginnings of the minority organization are traced back to a dramatic personal experience reported by the founder, Bill W. After a long series of hospitalizations for alcohol-related problems, in 1934, Bill W. had a 'spiritual revelation' that allegedly freed him from the alcoholic compulsion (Gellman, 1964: 21–2). This experience gave rise to a key belief at the core of AA ideology, that is, that the achievement of sobriety constitutes a 'spiritual awakening.'

Upon discharge from the hospital, Bill W. became affiliated with a religious revivalist organization, the Oxford Group. He hoped that by promoting this group's religious principles, he could help alcoholics to achieve sobriety. Through the Oxford Group he met another alcoholic, Dr Bob, who eventually became the co-founder of AA. Discussions between the two men proved beneficial in their mutual attempt to refrain from drinking, and both remained sober. From this early practice of one alcoholic sharing experiences, trust, and hope with another minority member emerged the fundamental self-help principle behind AA ideology.

Initial attempts by these two incipient leaders to broaden their efforts to help other alcoholics through following the religious principles of the Oxford Group met with failure. What became increasingly apparent to the two men was the incompatibility of their principal goals with those of the Oxford Group. The Oxford Group, designed to 'save the world,' was open to all; but, by way of contrast, Bill W. and Dr Bob wanted only to help fellow alcoholics. Moreover, the Oxford Group relied heavily on the use of prominent names in order to attract members. The co-founders of AA realized that because of the stigma attached to being an alcoholic it was disadvantageous for members of this minority to publicize the fact of their stigmatized status. Thus another key principle of AA ideology came into being, the principle of anonymity.

In 1937, the two co-founders of AA dissociated themselves from the Oxford Group movement, although they borrowed heavily from the group's spiritual teachings. They sought followers in New York and in Akron, Ohio, the cities where each of the co-founders resided, and soon a solid nucleus of over thirty recovering alcoholics was attained (Gellman, 1964: 23). Encouraged by this initial recruitment success, the early leaders resolved to embark on a campaign to publicize the activities of the new movement. The embryonic membership agreed and they decided also that the ideologies, strategies, and goals of the movement should be formally recorded so as to be more readily available to larger numbers of alcoholics. After some debate, it was agreed that a book should be published that would set forth the movement's original ideologies and goals, as well as the details (steps) of its program of recovery from alcoholism through life-style renewal. Such formal codification, it was believed, would not only facilitate communication of the movement's message, but also prevent distortion of the underlying group ideologies (ibid).

The task of attaining financial backing for the publication of the book and for the promotion of the program of the movement now loomed large for the two co-founders. Initial lobbying of wealthy (majority) persons and private bodies met with unexpected failure. Potential sponsors apparently had doubts about the success of the movement for they rejected the idea, in some cases on the grounds that there were many far better known 'respectable and established' causes appealing for their funds. Clearly, fear of stigma by association also played a part in the negative reaction to the movement by would-be sponsors. In a last desperate attempt, the co-founders turned to the Rockefeller Foundation for private charities, but their request for funds again was turned down. At the time, this rejection was thought to be the 'final blow.' Ironically, however, it turned out to be a significant turning-point for future AA policy, for, in rejecting the request for financial sponsorship of the fledgling minority organization, Rockefeller argued that the movement should become financially independent so that it would not be subject to pressure (majority intervention) from outside sources (Gellman, 1964: 25). Financial independence became a basic ideological principle of AA and continues to be strongly adhered to today. Not only did the principle of economic self-sufficiency prove to be sound financial policy, but it also became an effective rehabilitation strategy for previously irresponsible (begging, borrowing, and stealing) alcoholics who now had to be self-reliant.

Yet, there remained a dire need for immediate funding in order to get the movement off the ground. Moreover, there was a general feeling among the membership that some kind of formal umbrella organization was needed to unify the fragmented local groups of the movement. To resolve these problems it was decided that the movement, insofar as it was dedicated to a socially valued goal – the recovery of alcoholics – should establish a tax-free foundation to which voluntary contributions could be made, anonymously, if so desired, by majority sympathizers.

The Alcoholic Foundation (since renamed the General Service Board of AA) was formed in May 1938, with a board of trustees consisting of three non-alcoholics and two alcoholics. The minority status of alcoholics on the board of their own foundation was rationalized, at this time, as a necessary 'safeguard' given the previous socially discreditable behaviours of many of the alcoholics behind the movement. But, by 1959, the self-image of members of the movement had become sufficiently destigmatized, and the principle of mutual trust within the membership sufficiently well established, that equal representation of minority and majority on the board was instituted.

In 1939, the book *Alcoholics Anonymous* was published and the same name was officially adopted by the monority organization. In 1940, the stock of Works Publishing Inc. (a body that had been established by the early membership so that minority members themselves would be responsible for publishing the 'Big Book') was taken over by the Alcoholic Foundation. Increasing sales of the Big Book provided a more solid financial base for the growth of the minority organization, and by early

1941, the membership had reached an estimated two thousand (Gellman, 1964: 29).

The assumption by AA of responsibility for the publication of the group's teachings (first the Big Book, and later all of the foundation's conference-approved literature) came to provide a crucial source of unity among the membership. The standardized format and literature used exclusively at meetings in the various chapters or local groups ensured that a member of AA would feel 'at home' in any of the local groups. As the umbrella minority organization expanded, the membership's insistence on the use of conference-approved literature at meetings became a principle of the utmost importance in maintaining the spirit of AA unity and in preventing fragmentation along ideological lines among local chapters.

The biggest single impetus to AA's growth in the early years of the minority organization reportedly occurred in March 1941, with the publication of a laudatory and highly informative article about the group in the *Saturday Evening Post*, a magazine with national circulation in the United States. When the article came out, the AA office was immediately deluged with requests for personal help, for information, and for orders for the Big Book. By the end of 1941, membership in AA had mushroomed from around two thousand to an estimated eight thousand.

From this time, the AA umbrella organization has expanded internationally, with chapters continuously being formed not only in North America, but virtually throughout the globe. By the time of publication of the third edition of the Big Book in 1976, the world-wide membership of the minority organization, in some forty thousand chapters, was estimated conservatively at one million (AA World Services Inc., 1976). Current (1980s) figures for Canada indicate an AA membership in this country of close to fifty-seven thousand, in more than three thousand local chapters (Csicsai, 1983: 2).

Mobilizing and organizing alcoholics: analysis

The foregoing account of the early organizational efforts of the co-founders of AA, their attempts to recruit followers, to achieve organizational unity of purpose, and to lobby majority funding bodies, can be seen to illustrate the conceptualization of the problems and task facing leaders of minority organizations, presented above. In light of this conceptual framework, the development of AA may be analysed as follows:

1 Formulation of legitimating ideology: Sobriety was conceptualized by the founders as a 'spiritual awakening' or rebirth – the beginning of a new life-style dedicated to spiritual, mental, and physical growth and well-being.

2 Articulation of strategies and goals: The early leaders articulated and promulgated the key principles of self-help and anonymity. The early membership adopted the strategies of creating a tax-free foundation and of minority organizational control of the publications of the membership. These early principles and strategies were designed to promote the independence of the organization, in ideological, political (policy-making), and financial spheres.

3 Communication of program and teachings: Role-models of success were provided by each of the two co-founders; intense efforts were made by the co-founders to 'carry the message' through personal contacts with known alcoholics; promotional activities were undertaken through the news media; and the membership undertook publication of the Big Book, *Alcoholics Anonymous*. (Later, the membership assumed control of continuing publication of the group's teachings through conference-approved literature.)

4 Organization and unification of membership: The AA program encouraged self-reliance and interdependence among members; standardization of conference-approved literature for use at meetings created and sustained ideological unity within and across local chapters of the minority organization. (Later, the world-wide conference [foundation] co-ordinated the activities of all AA branches and provided a stable mechanism for intercommunication between local groups through leadership meetings, conferences, newsletters,etc.)

In light of the postulates of the conceptual scheme discussed above, an analysis of the early lobbying efforts of the co-founders of AA for financial support of the movement suggests that the *lack of credibility* of alcoholics was largely responsible for the failure to elicit support. While the two leaders, one a physician and the other a stockbroker, may *themselves* have been accorded a modicum of credibility, their fledgling organization was perceived as highly discreditable. The movement was virtually unknown, and the membership of alcoholics was decidedly suspect. The powerlessness of the destitute membership, together with their stigma of alcoholism, created extreme wariness among potential majority funding bodies lobbied by the co-founders, and resulted in their failure to elicit financial support.

Ironically, however, it was this early failure to gain majority backing that was indirectly responsible for the eventual successful development of the movement into a financially independent minority organization. The early rejection of backing by potential majority sponsors led to the growth of the Alcoholic Foundation (later, the World Conference of AA) built upon, and carrying out in practice, the minority organizations' central ideals of self-help, self-reliance, interdependence (of members and chapters), and anonymity.

As is the case for the current consumer movement of Canada's disabled minority, in the early stages of AA the minority organization – despite its goals of self-reliance and independence – remained financially dependent for its continuance upon monetary contributions (in this case, donations) from powerful majority supporters. However, with the growth of the World Conference and especially with its intensive and extensive publication mandate, the AA organization has become virtually self-sufficient and independent.

AA and the limits of anonymity

While the success of AA as a minority self-help group is laudable, as suggested earlier the fact that the organization is founded on the principle of anonymity sets limits upon its ability to move beyond self-help and to promote social reforms designed to protect the fundamental human rights of members of the alcoholic minority. AA is not an activist minority organization; its members do not engage in political lobbying for policy and legal changes designed to protect their rights, for (by and large) members remain in the closet.[2]

In order to comprehend the processes that enable minorities to come out of the closet and to begin to make human-rights claims upon majority bodies, in the following pages I shall examine some of the conceptual underpinnings of activist minority organization derived from the literature on ethnic minority protest movements.

BEYOND SELF-HELP: THE EVOLUTION OF MINORITY ACTIVISM
AND PROTEST

Activist minority organization takes place when collective minority consciousness of human-rights violations reaches a boiling point. Activ-

2 In my research for the present book, not a single organization of alcoholics with an activist human-rights mandate was found to exist in Canada.

ism represents the second stage in the development of minority organization, the stage at which the cumulative experience of long-term human-
rights violations, together with the agonies of a secretive existence, makes
the closet insufferable. With the stark realization that minority rights will
never be recognized unless minorities themselves fight to have them
recognized, more and more members of stigmatized minorities are finally
propelled out of the closet.

Activist minority organizations seek social changes designed to eradicate institutionalized forms of prejudice and discrimination against the
minority and to ensure recognition and protection for the human rights of
minority members. Collective claims put forward by minority organizations seek redress against past discrimination and 'justice now.' However, before such claims can be made with any degree of confidence in their
successful outcome, leaders of activist organizations must be able to
persuade majority authorities of their legitimacy. Accordingly, minority
members must be mobilized to undertake activities in support of minority
claims.

In order to substantiate claims, evidence for long-term human-rights
violations must be documented. Thus, considerable research must be
undertaken by minority members to compile reliable data files for claims.
Effective lobbying efforts may involve the mobilization of members to
develop briefs to governments and to circulate petitions for support of
human-rights claims among concerned citizens' groups and other majority sympathizers. In order to broaden their basis of support, minority
organizations may also carry out public-education campaigns through
the use of media channels. All of these organized activities represent a
necessary prelude to the making of a claim that can be seen as justifiable
or 'legitimate' by majority authorities.

Forms of organized protest among stigmatized minorities

Organized minority protest may take the form of contention through
reform movements predicated on goals of empowerment, or it may take
the form of revitalization through movements bent on gaining legitimacy
for alternative subcultures and life-styles.

In *contention*, the minority protests against its subordinate political,
economic, and social status and demands policy and legal changes geared
to the collective goal of positional equality (proportionate representation
throughout the ranks) within the societal order. In order to bring about
concrete changes towards equality in the immediate future the minority

may put forward group claims for redress against past systemic discrimination based on categorical human rights (see Introduction).

In *revitalization*, the minority protests against its subordinate ideological/cultural status and demands group equality as a subcultural collectivity within the societal order. In order to bring about concrete changes towards cultural equality the minority may put forward group claims based on collective cultural rights.

Insofar as the movement encompasses both instrumental/empowerment and expressive/cultural goals, minority representatives may make a variety of individual, categorical, and collective human-rights claims in order to gain recognition of and protection for the individual and collective rights of the minority membership.

Minority protest movements: from contention to revitalization

Minority discontent in the intitial stages of protest tends to be mobilized in terms of reform movements under leaders seen as credible by majority audiences because they support the ideological status quo. That is to say, social-reformist leaders support established societal ideals. What they criticize are the inequities consequent upon non-fulfilment of these ideals. Accordingly, reformist leaders can often rally support for their claims from both majority and minority audiences, through mass appeals to the public conscience.

More radical leaders, who reject the ideological status quo in pursuit of more revolutionary goals necessitating structural changes in the societal order, do not usually emerge or come to the forefront of a minority protest movement until the movement for more limited reform has run its course, that is, until it is widely perceived by members to have failed, or until it has clearly achieved the goals articulated by early reformist leaders.

In a 'liberal-democratic' ideological environment – a social context, such as Canada's – where the prevailing view of social justice focuses on *individual* rights and freedoms, the politico-legal climate clearly is more hospitable to minority demands for individual human-rights protections than it is for demands for protection of rights of minority subcultures. One of the most persistent criticisms of Canada's current multicultural policy, in this connection, is that it so clearly reflects the liberal-democratic ideology of its drafters. Through its stated policy objectives, it reduces the whole complex matter of cultural transmission through time to a question of voluntary ethnic identification on the part of individual minority members, while it offers no formal guarantees for the equal recognition and protection throughout this country of the legitimate cultures and subcultures of the nation's various minority collectivities (Kallen, 1982b). Like the policy statement itself, multicultural programs of implementation have been criticized for their focus on negative individual freedoms (non-discrimination) at the expense of positive collective rights (e.g., guarantees of equal/equivalent funding for all minority religious or language schools throughout the country).

Given this ideological bias in Canadian public policy, it is not surprising to find that minority demands for social reforms couched in assimilation- ist terms, such as demands for 'normalization' (integration into main- stream society) put forward by some reformist groups among disabled minorities, meet with a more understanding response from majority authorities than do pluralist demands for cultural group equality. Accordingly, claims for recognition and protection of legitimate life-style alternatives or subcultures, put forward by some 'liberation' groups among gay and lesbian minorities, continue to meet with formidable majority opposition.

In the following pages, I will sketch the course of the normalization movement among Canada's disabled and the Gay/Lesbian Liberation move- ment among Canada's homosexuals, and I will compare their platforms and their prospects as minority protest movements.

THE NORMALIZATION MOVEMENT AND CANADA'S
DISABLED MINORITY

The principle of normalization was first introduced in 1959 by N.E. Bank-Mikkelson, then head of mental-retardation services for Denmark. In reaction against the dehumanizing life conditions characterizing 'total institutions' for the mentally retarded minority, Bank-Mikkelson argued that mentally retarded people should be allowed to live in as 'normal' a fashion as possible within the parameters of 'mainstream' society. This idea was soon embraced by other Scandinavians working with the mentally retarded and, a decade later, the principle of normalization was formally articulated by Bengt Nirje of Sweden. Nirje described normaliza- tion as 'making available to the mentally retarded patterns and conditions of everyday life which are as close as possible to the norms and patterns of the mainstream of society' (quoted in Biklen, 1979: 49).

According to Biklen, the normalization principle as articulated by its Scandinavian originators gained immediate favour in the United States, where it was popularized by Dr Burton Blatt, author of *Christmas in*

Purgatory (1966) – a major exposé of American institutions for the mentally retarded. The introduction of the principle of normalization in the United States generated a wave of shockingly documented critiques of existing institutions including, most importantly, Goffman's seminal work *Asylums* (1961). These revelations by leading researchers of the routinized dehumanization of inmates within the confines of the 'total institution' sparked the North American movement towards 'deinstitutionalization' and 'normalization.'

The seminal work on normalization, in the opinion of a great many scholars today, is Wolfensberger's *Normalization* (1972). Indeed, Wolfensberger has been cast in the prophet role in the North American normalization movement (Tanaka, 1982). His broad visionary perspective extends well beyond the original Scandinavian conceptions of normalization, which were tied specifically to the mentally retarded minority, and is designed to encompass all stigmatized minorities labelled as 'deviant.' For, Wolfensberger has declared: 'deviancy is of our own making; it is in the eye of the beholder' (1972: 13).

Wolfensberger reformulates the principle of normalization as the 'utilization of means which are as culturally normative as possible in order to establish and/or maintain personal behaviours and characteristics which are as culturally normative as possible' (1972: 28). This reformulation of the normalization principle employs the term 'normative' (as opposed to 'normal') to indicate that there is no absolute standard (of normality or normalcy) to which disabled persons must aspire. Instead, disabled persons should be helped to adapt to the culturally specific norms governing the particular communities in which they will reside.

The implications of this reformulation for social policy are that wherever appropriate and wherever possible a process of 'conversion' from segregated total institution towards integration into the mainstream community should be undertaken. This position, favouring a policy of residential, educational, and occupational 'mainstreaming' of disabled minority members, has been strongly and consistently supported by research data on the comparative effects of segregated institutional life and community placement and programs (see, especially, Edgerton, 1967; Edgerton and Bercovici, 1976; Zigler and Balla, 1977).

Two of the earliest studies of deinstitutionalization programs that involved moving mentally retarded inmates from large institutions to group homes or community residential facilities attributed their success in large part to 'benefactors' or supportive networks within the community at large (Biklen, 1979: 52). These findings point to the crucial role of majority sympathizers and supporters ('the wise,' in Goffman's parlance) in normalization movements among minorities with authentic (as opposed to arbitrary) disabilities. Where authentic disabilities impede the efforts of members of stigmatized minorities to integrate into the mainstream of society and to become self-determining there, entirely on their own, then the help of majority supporters is not only appropriate, but necessary. From this view, citizen advocacy groups and satellite support programs can be seen as compensatory mechanisms that serve to ensure that a goal of equivalence of opportunity can be realistically pursued by the minority. The role of community advocacy in securing protection for minority rights will be elaborated in my discussion of strategies for change in chapter 7.

While programs based on the principles of deinstitutionalization and normalization have met with varying degrees of success from the researchers' point(s) of view, their perception by minority clients, whatever the measures used, has been found to be overwhelmingly positive (Edgerton and Bercovici, 1976). By far the largest proportion of formerly institutionalized minority members (sometimes, almost 100 per cent) do not want to return to the institution.

The findings of a research study on the meaning of life as experienced by mentally retarded adults living in a group home revealed that the theme of independence was a major preoccupation for respondents (Heshusius, 1981). Study subjects had been transferred from the setting of a total institution to that of a community-based group home, supervised by professional counsellors ('houseparents').

Two patterns of responses predominated: the first was a desire for independence, and the second was pride in independence. The desire to live 'on one's own' represented respondents' ultimate 'dream,' as revealed in the following comments: '[Max] said that he wanted to go home ... ' "where I can be by myself, you know"' (1981: 26); '[Don] said that he wanted to get his own apartment because "no one bothers me ... no hassles ... I don't like to be pushed around"' (1981: 29); '[Pam] said that she hoped to be living alone in three or four years because she would be "better off alone than with all the others"' (1981: 29).

The general findings of the study revealed that mentally retarded respondents wanted very much to be more independent than was possible in a supervised group-home situation. They wanted to be able to stay home alone, to go out by themselves, to spend money in the way they chose. They wanted to be able to drive a car, own a car, hold a job, but above all 'to get out of here' and 'to be on our own' (Heshusius, 1981:

136). Respondents complained about having to listen to others, some-times much younger than themselves. Their ultimate dream was to live alone or with a room-mate or to marry and be on their own.

If the research data are unequivocal in their support for deinstitutional-ization, Biklen (1979: 53) asks, why do so many large institutions continue to operate? Why has there been so much controversy and public opposition over the release of formerly institutionalized (mentally and physically) disabled persons and the establishment of group homes and other residential facilities within the mainstream community?

Biklen's own response is most instructive. In part, he says, the difficulty lies in the ideological (paternalistic) bias of the majority professionals who work with the disabled. Trained to work in the segregated and majority-controlled setting of a total institution they find it exceedingly difficult to adopt and to put into practice the diametrically opposed model of normalization, which favours community integration and minority independence. Further, Biklen points out, there has been a widespread failure to develop an orderly transition from institutions to community.[3] Most important, he says, there is the problem of 'recalci-trant, unwilling, prejudiced communities' (1979: 53).

Recent Canadian documentation supports Biklen's position on both counts. First, with regard to the problem of failure to develop a support structure for the transition from institution to community, numerous news reports have documented the current state of homelessness among Toronto's discharged mentally ill, many of whom find themselves literally out in the cold on Metro's streets. Two recent cases, one of a mentally disabled 'bag lady' who froze to death in a car, and another of an ex-psychiatric patient who drowned in the bathtub of an unsupervised rooming-house, represent only the 'tip of the iceberg,' according to Metro Police (*Toronto Star*, 9 March 1986). Hostel supervisors and police officers reportedly are familiar with a large number of mentally ill persons involved in a 'revolving-door game that moves disturbed people back and forth from hostels, to psychiatric wards, to jails, and back to the streets.' According to this report, an estimated 1,800 people in Metro Toronto are chronically mentally ill, moving in and out of institutions (ibid).

---

3 The 'orderly transition' conceived by Biklen and other supporters of the normalization movement necessitates a complex and multifaceted process of change. Conceptual-ized in terms of a 'conversion plan,' the transition has been put succinctly, as follows: 'By conversion, we mean an orderly transition from an institutional to a community-based system of services with concomitant plans to transform existing facilities, staff resources, institutional ideologies, community attitudes and agency policies to alter-native, more humanizing uses and postures' (Blatt et al, 1977: 243).

Because Toronto has housed some of the largest total institutions for mentally disabled minorities, the problems involved in providing adequate services for community living there are probably more acute than in other locales. Nevertheless, a recent report, *Deinstitutionalization: Costs and Effects* (Canadian Council on Social Development, 1984), indicates that problems in the transition from total institution to community have been experienced across the nation.

With regard to Biklen's second point, concerning the problem of 'recalcitrant, unwilling, prejudiced communities' whose members oppose the establishment of group homes in their neighbourhoods, media reports provide continuing documentation. In 1984, there were 157 group homes in Metro Toronto (*Globe and Mail*, 5 March 1984). The uneven distribution of these community placements suggests that opposition to group homes is much stronger in some communities than in others. One (unsubstantiated) theme running through many instances of community opposition is that group homes will result in a decline in property values in a neighbourhood. Not suprisingly, in light of this prevailing prejudice, opposition appears to be strongest in the wealthiest and most socially exclusive areas of Metro.

In 1984, a group of Rosedale physicians reportedly drafted a brief to the Ontario minister of health that labelled the *future residents* of Craigleigh House, a group home for psychiatric patients, as chronic psychotics, capable of 'bizarre and frightening behaviour' such as removing their clothes, urinating and defecating openly, making terrifying noises, and even becoming violent. In rebuttal, the executive director of the group home in question stated that the final selections for residents had been made so recently that it was impossible for neighbourhood doctors to have known the characteristics of the residents selected when they wrote the brief. Clearly, the opposition of the physicians and that of others in the exclusive Rosedale neighbourhood was based on a host of untested preconceptions, not the least of which was the notion that group-home residents would tarnish the community's reputation of 'civility and old money' and would bring down the property value of homes in the exclusive, upper-crust neighbourhood (*Globe and Mail*, 5 March 1984).

The foregoing examples, and many more that could be cited, highlight the relationship between community prejudice against mentally ill and mentally retarded minorities and community opposition to group homes for minority residents. Even in neighbourhoods where most residents express no formal opposition, among those who do oppose the establishment of such facilities concern is focused on the behavioural characteristics of facility users (Dear and Taylor, 1982: 167).

The results of a survey of 1,090 Toronto households in five different neighbourhoods revealed a relatively high degree of community tolerance; only 25 per cent of respondents anticipated a negative impact following the opening of a group home for mentally disabled persons (Dear and Taylor, 1982: 166). Among those who expressed fears of negative impact, concern focused on anticipated behaviour of facility users, property-value decline, and increased traffic volumes. Negative attitudes were found to be strongest within one block of a facility, and to move towards neutrality beyond six blocks (ibid: 167). Appropriately, the book based upon this research study is entitled *Not on Our Street*.

The results of this research study, together with parallel newspaper documentation on community reaction to group homes, demonstrate a continuing need to improve public awareness and education regarding mentally disabled minorities. Particularly important, in this regard, is to put in place a community-education program well before a group home is located in a given neighbourhood and to familiarize neighbours and residents with the facility and its users when the group home is established.

Another problem that has emerged with regard to the movement towards deinstitutionalization and normalization for disabled minorities is that the principle of normalization itself has long been widely misunderstood both by many of its advocates and by many of its critics. Perrin (1982: 39) contends that it has been so misinterpreted as to produce programs directly opposite to what is meant by the principle.

Among the many misconceptions about the concept, the most commonly held is that normalization requires physical and behavioural conformity to 'abled' majority norms on the part of disabled minority members. Disabled persons must be expected, indeed forced, to present a normative façade and to behave in a normative fashion, insofar as possible, given the limitations of their authentic disabilities.

From the human-rights perspective adopted in this book, this misconception can be seen to reflect an assimilationist ideology in which the goal of equality is predicated upon *sameness*. Perrin (1982) argues, by way of contrast, that normalization means accepting persons with their disabilities within mainstream society and according them rights and opportunities equivalent to those enjoyed by others. Seen from the perspective of this book, Perrin is arguing for *equivalence* of treatment that takes into account and attempts to compensate for the handicapping effects of authentic disabilities rather than for standard/equal treatment that allows the handicapping effects of disabilities to continue and to cumulate. The argument for equivalence of treatment also speaks to the second misconception about normalization, namely that the principle is inconsistent with the provision of special services geared to special needs. Alternatively, Perrin argues that, on the contrary, normalization insists upon the provision of whatever (special/compensatory) services, training, and support are necessary in order to meet the special needs of disabled minorities and in order to provide disabled persons with access to living conditions and routines equivalent to those of others in the community. At a minimum this would include appropriate (perhaps, specially adapted) forms of housing, work, education, and leisure (ibid: 40).

In the Canadian context, the principle of normalization has become increasingly adopted both by a variety of minority activist organizations run by disabled persons and by professionals offering services to the disabled. Some of the early results of the deinstitutionalization and normalization movement in this country are evident in the progressive integration of disabled children into the regular education system and a de-emphasis on segregated schooling (Brown, 1977: 456). It is reflected also in a number of reports and briefs to government that emphasize the responsibility of governments to include the special needs of the disabled in the planning of community recreation programs, to provide accessible public transportation or parallel transportation systems, and to institute regular housing programs (Canada, House of Commons, 1981).

Despite important policy changes towards deinstitutionalization and mainstreaming of disabled minority members, the continuing ideological hiatus between supporters of normalization and its opponents leaves much to be accomplished before the right of the disabled to live lives equivalent to those of mainstream Canadians will be firmly established. In the view of the disabled minority, it is deeply rooted public prejudice that presents the major impediment to community integration of the disabled:

Disabled persons each have particular obstacles to overcome which are mental or physical in origin. For many, these are the least of their problems. More serious are the obstacles they face which are caused by other people's attitudes. Disabled persons are deprived both of rights and opportunities because of the myth that they are 'strange', that they lead lives which 'normal' people cannot comprehend. This leads to the belief, widely held, that they are not motivated by the same needs for love, participation, opportunity, expertise, achievement, appreciation and self-esteem that govern the lives of other Canadians (Canada, House of Commons, 1981: 8)

The foregoing analysis of the normalization principle and of the movement for deinstitutionalization and mainstreaming of disabled minorities predicated upon it provides and example of a minority response of *contention* leading to a movement for social reform.

In the following pages I will discuss the Gay/Lesbian Liberation movement, a minority protest movement that provides an example of a minority response of *revitalization*. Through an analysis of the historical development of this movement I will attempt to reveal the factors responsible for changes in minority organizational ideologies, strategies, and goals from secretism to activism, and for a shift in emphasis from fundamental human rights to cultural liberation.

THE GAY/LESBIAN LIBERATION MOVEMENT

Altman (1982) traces the roots of the current Gay/Lesbian Liberation movement to the formation in the late 1940s of homosexual organizations in France, Switzerland, the Netherlands, the Scandinavian countries, and the United States. Within the North American context the first organization with a clearly articulated liberation ideology was the early Mattachine Society formed in Los Angeles in 1950 by a nucleus of five homosexual men.

The embryonic Mattachine group was a closeted organization, whose members were pledged to secrecy. Not only were all of the members homosexuals, dedicated to liberating the homosexual minority in the United States at time when openness about their sexual orientation guaranteed ostracization, but also the group's founders were communists or communist sympathizers, at a time (the infamous McCarthy era) when institutionalized anti-communist sentiment sparked trials and blacklisting of known sympathizers in the United States. Secrecy thus was deemed to be a vital strategy for the survival of the organization. The need for secrecy was symbolized by the name 'Mattachine,' taken from the mysterious masked figures who performed at festivals during the Middle Ages and who were thought to have been homosexuals (D'Emilio, 1982).

At first, the Mattachine Society functioned as a self-help organization. Members exchanged stories of loneliness and fear, of coming out, and of seeking out affectional and sexual relationships with other homosexuals. Out of these discussions, however, an analysis gradually emerged as to the structural sources of homosexual persecution. The group began to see the majority-created ideology of 'sexual deviance' as a primary agent of collective discrimination against homosexuals. Accordingly, they deemed the first task of a homosexual emancipation movement to be to challenge the internalization of this heterosexist ideology by homosexuals. In its place, they sought to develop among homosexuals a sense of group consciousness as an unjustly stigmatized and persecuted minority with a legitimate (alternative) subculture.

For almost three years, the Mattachine Society flourished, giving rise to more than a hundred discussion groups. The society attempted to fight discrimination against homosexuals (particularly police harassment and entrapment) by distributing leaflets and flyers that attempted to dispel derogatory homosexual stereotypes. Not suprisingly, however, given the paranoid atmosphere of the McCarthy era, an article by a Los Angeles newspaper columnist raising sinister questions about the potential subversive power of organized left-wing homosexuals provided sufficient negative provocation to arouse serious in-group tensions and suspicions. The bitter in-fighting that ensued seriously fragmented the organization.

In the tense political atmosphere of 'red-baiting' together with endemic homophobia, the founding members of the Mattachine Society lost credibility within the organization and the leadership of the society was taken over by a highly assimilationist opposition group emphasizing homosexual 'respectability.' The new leaders rejected the founders' notions of minority status and homosexual subculture (alternative life-style) and adopted a socially conventional or 'normative' strategy bent on proving to heterosexuals (the majority) that homosexuals were solid citizens and deserving of the same respect as other citizens. With this change in organizational strategy the early goal of homosexual liberation became a 'dream deferred' (D'Emilio, 1982). The conservative and highly assimilationist course pursued by the successive leadership of the society had little appeal among its larger constituency and, together with its serious lines of internal division, made the demise of the minority organization all but inevitable.

Since this time, Humphreys (1972: 96) points out, it would appear that as many homosexual organizations have fallen apart as have been created. Yet, given the homophobic constraints of the societal context in which the Gay Liberation movement has emerged, Humphreys observes that the wonder is not that so many of the groups failed, but that so many continued to survive and flourish. Besides the fragmentation of groups along ideological lines – for example, between closeted and out-of-the-closet members, and between the civil libertarians and the gay liberationists – there have emerged ever new tensions within the movement, revolving around lines of strategy and interest. There is, for example, a serious split between 'behind the scenes' organizations and political activist groups, and, most important, there is the increasingly salient dichotomy between gay men's and lesbian women's groups.

A number of minority spokespersons, reflecting on the development of the Gay/Lesbian Liberation movement in the United States and in Canada, divide the movement into stages, each (roughly) representing and occurring within a particular decade or decades following the Second World War (Altman, 1982; Jackson and Persky, 1982). In the 1950s, and throughout most of the 1960s, the (then) homophile movement remained, for the most part, in the closet. A major constraint operating against open gayness, both in Canada and in the United States, was that imposed by legal discrimination. In Canada, various prohibitions within the Criminal Code made a person's pursuit of a homosexual orientation a criminal offence.

The year 1969 is seen today as a watershed year for the Gay/Lesbian Liberation movement both in Canada and in the United States. South of the border, in New York City, street demonstrations (which the press referred to as 'riots') took place at the Stonewall Inn, a gay bar in Greenwich Village. Here, for the first time, gay customers fought back during a police raid. In the United States, this event is taken to mark the symbolic beginning of contemporary Gay Liberation.

In Canada, amendments to the Criminal Code came into effect in 1969, legalizing sexual acts between two consenting adults (over the age of twenty-one) in private. While the word 'homosexual' does not appear in the amendment, homosexuals and others soon began to deem the document the 'homosexual bill,' for it clearly opened the closet door for Canada's homosexual population. After the Criminal Code was changed, (then) homophile organizations sprang up across Canada and their membership grew rapidly (Foster and Murray, 1972: 29). *The Body Politic*, a national gay newspaper, in the forefront of the Gay Liberation movement in Canada, was published for the first time in 1971.

The 1970s are hailed as the decade of gay rights in North America. The name of the umbrella movement and of its many and varied organizations shifted perceptibly from 'Homophile' to 'Gay' and 'Lesbian.' This change in nomenclature clearly symbolized the politicization of the movement through its open affirmation of homosexuality and of gay and lesbian rights. Within the movement, there developed an increasing number of political action groups – gay and lesbian caucuses and lesbian- and gay-rights lobbying groups that sought to persuade politicians and governments to amend and/or to create legislation that would recognize and protect the fundamental human rights of gay and lesbian persons.

By the end of the 1970s, however, the backlash of the 'moral majority' against the new visibility of open (or out-of-the-closet) lesbians and gay men and had begun to take serious hold. Sparked by the highly propagandized anti-gay and anti-lesbian campaigns of 'Born-again Christian' Anita Bryant and others, attacks on minority members in the known gay and lesbian 'ghettoes' became more frequent and police harassment in these areas was stepped up (Jackson and Persky, 1982: 225).

The result of this majority backlash has been an increased gay and lesbian resistance, and this in turn has served to solidify the minority community. It has fortified minority members' determination to gain legitimacy both as individual citizens with fundamental human rights and as a minority collectivity with collective cultural rights.

The latter goal of the Gay/Lesbian Liberation movement has given a new dimension to their agenda in the 1980s. In Canada, the 1970s – the human-rights decade – was a decade marked by extensive lobbying efforts by gay and lesbian organizations to have 'sexual orientation' listed among the specified non-discriminatory grounds in human-rights legislation throughout the country. With the single exception of the Quebec Charter of Human Rights, this effort was unsuccessful.

An elaboration of the events leading up to the inclusion of sexual orientation among the enumerated non-discriminatory grounds of the Quebec Charter may affort some insights into the political context within which this unexpected endorsement for gay rights was achieved. Under the homophobic Drapeau administration, in the months preceding the opening of the 1976 Olympic Games, Montreal police launched a 'clean-up' campaign in the form of four raids on gay and lesbian institutions (seven bars and a bath house) (Adam, 1987). Under antiquated 'bawdy house' laws (to be resurrected again in the infamous Toronto raids in 1981) police seized membership lists and arrested 'found-ins.' The raids provided the catalyst for the formation of the Association pour les Droits des Gai(e) du Québec (ADGQ). When the Montreal police raided another gay bar, in 1977, arresting 145 'found-ins' and 8 persons for 'gross indecency,' the ADGQ mobilized demonstrations that effectively disrupted the city core and organized a defence committee, which fought every case through several years of litigation. The ADGQ was part of the Franco-Québécois nationalist movement, and, as such, the organization pressured the Parti Québécois, which had recently assumed power as the provincial government, to redress the Montreal persecution and to protect gay rights. In response, the new government, 'not averse to tweaking the noses of the old guard' (Adam, 1987: 118), added sexual orientation to the enumerated grounds of the Quebec Charter in December 1977.

The Quebec case, however, proved to be unique. During the constitutional debates of 1980–2, despite considerable support from civil-libertarian and other majority sympathizers, gay and lesbian lobbying efforts failed to have 'sexual orientation' included in the enumerated non-discriminatory grounds of Section 15 of the Charter of Rights and Freedoms. Accordingly, the minority rights of gay and lesbian Canadians were not afforded specified protection under Canada's amended (1982) Constitution Act.

The Gay/Lesbian Liberation movement in Canada today continues its struggle for legislative change designed to protect the fundamental, individual human rights of minority members throughout the country. In the last two years, the unflagging lobbying efforts of activist gay and lesbian organizations in Ontario and Manitoba have finally achieved success in obtaining protection for sexual orientation under the provisions of the human-rights codes of these two provinces. Most recently, sexual orientation has been included among the enumerated, non-discriminatory grounds in the Yukon Human Rights Act. In spite of these positive developments, however, police harassment, especially through selective surveillance of gay institutions and through traditional practices of entrapment, appears to be on the rise. Similarly, the number of reported instances of homophobic 'queer-bashing' has increased. Adam (1987) provides evidence to support his observation that an increase in anti-homosexual persecution, following the liberalization of legislation affecting this minority, is a pattern reproduced elsewhere 'with suspicious regularity' (132).

In the 1980s, heterosexist manifestations of discrimination against gays and lesbians (such as stepped-up police surveillance of gay/lesbian institutions) have increasingly been sparked by public condemnation of open (out-of-the-closet) gay and lesbian life-styles. This negative majority response to 'coming out' has generated a new form of minority protest, a protest against interference with the minority's social space (Jackson and Persky, 1982). Attacks on minority institutions (bars, baths, and discos) are now seen as attacks on the collective life of the community and as serious threats to the gay/lesbian subculture. Accordingly, activist gay and lesbian organizations currently are fighting back with a collective response of revitalization expressed in minority members' demands for recognition of the legitimacy of their distinctive gay and lesbian subculture. In the words of one Canadian researcher: 'One result of the gay liberation movement is that homosexuality as a way of life is now held up as a viable alternative for those whose sexual orientation is biased in that direction' (CHRC, 1979: 46).

Today, minority demands for subcultural legitimacy are expressed through minority claims for protection of the collective cultural rights of the gay and lesbian minority throughout Canada.

The case for Gay/Lesbian Liberation: a human-rights approach

In the Introduction to this book I suggested that the internationally recognized provisions of the *minority rights* article (s. 27, ICCPR) could be interpreted, from a social-scientific perspective, so as to provide a basis of justification, in principle, for the collective cultural claims of some *non*-ethnic minorities. I argued that those *non*-ethnic minorities that have developed legitimate and viable subcultures are entitled to the same legal protections as parallel ethnocultural minorities. In the following pages, I will elaborate upon this position, using the case of the gay/lesbian minority in Canada as an example.

Guided by Breton's seminal concept of 'institutional completeness' (elaborated in chapter 1), I posit three prerequisites for the development and maintenance of a distinctive minority ethnoculture or subculture: 1 / a living community of collectively identified members committed to the preservation of cultural distinctiveness, 2 / the development and maintenance of a viable institutional infrastructure for intra-ethnic communication and interaction and for transgenerational cultural transmission,[4] and 3 / sufficient political and economic resources (voting power and buying power) to defend the minority community against external discrimination and to lobby effectively for collectively desired social changes. I will argue that insofar as these three prerequisites are met by *non*-ethnic collectivities, such collectivities should be able to put forward claims for protection of their collective cultural rights, under the guidelines afforded by Sections 15 and 27 of the CRF, taken together. This position is bolstered by current legal opinion, which holds that the provisions of Sections 15 and 27 of the CRF are 'open' in their intent, that is, they are not *limited* in their applicability to enumerated social categories

---

4 My first two prerequisites have been subsumed by some authors under the concept of 'social vitality' (see Matthews, 1983; Gibbins and Ponting, 1986).

(Beckton, 1987). As was pointed out earlier, the list of enumerated, anti-discriminatory grounds of Section 15 of the CRF is *not* exhaustive. That is to say, identifiable groups *not* specified under Section 15 should also be able to make claims for 'freedom from discrimination.' With regard to Section 27, the vague notion of 'multicultural heritage' is nowhere defined, and it includes no reference to ethnicity or ethnic groups. Thus the concept of 'multicultural heritage' could be interpreted so as to support the collective cultural claims of *non*-ethnic as well as ethnic collectivities.

A second argument supported by some legal scholars is that, when the provisions of Section 15 and 27 of the Charter are read together, the equality-rights provisions reinforce the interpretation of the multicultural provision as affording an equal basis for collective cultural claims across diverse minority groups (Beckton, 1987).

In the following analysis, I will provide evidence in support of the collective cultural claims of the gay/lesbian minority in Canada. To begin, I will call into critical question the prejudicial assumptions built into traditional legal and social-scientific interpretations of 'culture' as 'ethnoculture.' I will demonstrate that it is these unsubstantiated assumptions that have underscored majority refusal to recognize alternative gay and lesbian life-styles as legitimate forms of minority subcultural expression.

The social-scientific model of transgenerational ethnoculture is rooted in the twin institutions of ethnic endogamy and family socialization. The family of procreation is conceptualized as the primary ethnic institution responsible for the function of biological reproduction and for cultural transmission through child socialization (enculturation). The greater ethnic community is conceptualized as an extended web of kinship and pseudo-kinship, with institutions providing activities and services beyond the family, but within the bounded infrastructure of the ethnic community.

Current international human-rights instruments and their Canadian counterparts (the CRF, as well as federal and provincial human-rights legislation) continue to be rooted in this traditional, family-oriented model of culture as ethnoculture. Accordingly, they tend to discriminate in various ways against non-ethnic (assumedly non-reproductive) subcultures.

The first prejudicial assumption to be called into question is that of the family as the primary (indeed, 'natural') unit of biological reproduction and cultural transmission. The 'father/mother/children' model of the nuclear family of procreation, whether based on biological parenthood or social adoption, continues to be held sacred, constitutionally protected, and institutionally legitimated throughout Canadian society, despite the incontrovertible evidence for the following social facts of contemporary life: high and ever increasing rates of divorce and desertion; the rise of the single-parent family; increasing numbers of couples living together who choose not to have or to raise children; increasing numbers of single females who choose to bear (or adopt) and to raise children on their own; and, finally, gay and lesbian individuals and couples who choose to bear or not to bear, to adopt or not to adopt, to raise or not to raise children.

With particular reference to the function of *biological reproduction*, for those individuals or couples who do not choose to form part of a traditional family unit, but who choose to have and to raise children, contemporary society affords a number of viable options: the artificial insemination of a woman with sperm from an anonymous or a chosen male donor, voluntary sexual intercourse with a selected partner for the purpose of child-bearing, and the adoption of children. All of these options can be pursued (and, indeed, currently are being pursued) outside of the nuclear-family framework, and all can lead to reproductive success.

With particular reference to the function of *cultural transmission*, the role of the family as primary agent of child socialization has increasingly been taken over by non-familial delegates within and outside the parameters of identifiable cultural groups.

In the case of school-age children, under the Canadian system of compulsory education, teachers have legally assumed the role of delegate parents (West, 1978: 5). Additionally, the growing trend towards full-time participation of women (50 per cent) and particularly of mothers of pre-school children (30 per cent) in the Canadian labour force has led to the proliferation of a wide range of child-care institutions – infant-care facilities, nursery schools, day-care centres, after-school facilities, and the like – where the socialization of children, from early infancy through childhood, is a task increasingly assumed by non-familial parent delegates (Barrie et al., 1982; Cook, 1976). What is brought into serious question by all of these social changes is the continuing assumption that the family constitutes (or should constitute) the primary unit of biological reproduction and cultural transmission.

The second prejudicial assumption built into the traditional concept of culture as ethnoculture is that of 'groupness.' Ethnic collectivities, it is assumed, constitute transgenerational cultural groups; non-ethnic collectivities do not. These contrasting assumptions fail to take into account the demonstrable social fact that both ethnic and non-ethnic collectivities exhibit a wide range of variation with regard to their members' commitment to group survival and with regard to the viability of their institutional infrastructures for cultural transmission.

In the following section, I will attempt to demonstrate, with specific reference to the gay/lesbian community, that *non*-ethnic institutional infrastructures can provide viable options to the family and to the ethnic group for purposes of development and perpetuation of distinctive subcultures and life-styles.

The primary question to be posed here is: to what extent does the gay/lesbian community have the requisite institutional infrastructure for cultural development and transmission through time? As in the case of ethnic collectivities, the degree of institutional completeness of particular gay/lesbian communities is highly variable and tends to be most comprehensive in large urban areas of high population concentration. The City of Toronto represents the area of highest population concentration of gays and lesbians in Canada.

A feature article in the *Toronto Star* (7 January 1979) described the 'world of Metro [Toronto's] 200,000 homosexuals' as follows:

There is a gay baseball league, a gay synagogue, a gay bookstore and a gay archivist in Toronto. There are gay grandmothers, gay youth clubs, and a club called Parents of Gays.

There is the Ontario Gay Teacher's Caucus, and a gay union for college professors. There is a gay travel agency and gay real estate company.

There is a gay business council and a gay newspaper.

There is a gay church, and two gay bowling teams. Both the Anglicans and the Catholics have gay organizations. Osgoode Hall law school has a gay group. [So does York University and the University of Toronto.]

The area bounded by Yonge St., the Don River, Bloor and Carlton St. is known as the 'gay ghetto'. Gay leaders estimate that in this area, one out of every three persons residing in and or frequenting the district is gay.

With regard to specific mechanisms for the maintenance of gay/lesbian cultural distinctiveness, it can be demonstrated that in all important institutional areas (political, economic, educational, membership retention, and defence against discrimination) the gay/lesbian collectivity has developed a solid institutional infrastructure. In the economic sphere there are a variety of flourishing gay businesses and professional firms, not to mention the large number of economically successful gays who choose to remain in the closet, yet who lend financial support to gay institutions and causes.

Politically speaking, the gay/lesbian community in Canada is highly sophisticated, with active lobbying organizations at the municipal, provincial, and federal levels. Gay/lesbian political organizations continue to lobby for the inclusion of 'sexual orientation' among the enumerated, non-discriminatory grounds of human-rights legislation. Recent success in Ontario (1986), in Manitoba (1987) and in the Yukon (1987) has given renewed impetus to lobbying efforts designed to gain parallel protections across Canada.

The gay/lesbian minority also is beginning to organize politically at the international level. At the seventh International Gay Association Conference in Toronto (1–7 July 1985) the gay/lesbian community voiced its condemnation of international human-rights organizations, including the United Nations, for refusing to recognize gay/lesbian rights (*Body Politic*, August 1985).

Turning to a consideration of educational mechanisms, the gay/lesbian community infrastructure includes a wide variety of formal and informal institutions – (gay churches and synagogues, counselling groups for gay parents and grandparents, gay youth and gay adult self-help and encounter groups, religious study groups, special-interest study groups, and organizations of gay teachers and professors). With regard to the larger (Canadian) educational system, gay and lesbian teachers and professors are seeking to attain cultural legitimacy for alternative gay life-styles through their representation on public and private school-boards and through their presentation of accurate, factual materials on gay/lesbian life-styles in the class-room context. The latter represents something of a 'dream deferred,' for heterosexist opposition here is still strong. These educational objectives are nevertheless deemed to be of critical importance for the development of a positive gay/lesbian identity among homosexual adolescents.[5]

A minority institutional infrastructure also must include group mechanisms for defence against external discrimination. For minorities, by definition, constitute populations whose collective stigmata are used by majorities to 'justify' violations of minority rights. Insofar as the gay/lesbian community is politically organized at all levels of its constituency

---

5 Insofar as gay and lesbian cultural distinctiveness is linked to same-sex orientation or preference, the adolescent age sector is the critical age cohort with regard to membership inclusion, for it is in this phase of the life cycle that sexual identity becomes salient.

it has the requisite political mechanisms with which to defend its members against the corrosive effects of external discrimination. Moreover, in situations of crisis, that is, discriminatory attacks perceived to threaten the community as a whole, the gay/lesbian collectivity is capable of spawning new organizations designed to deal specifically with the 'crisis' situation at hand.

As detailed earlier, in 1981 police in Metro Toronto organized and carried out a series of raids on gay bath houses in which private property was smashed, 'found-ins' were charged and exposed to public ridicule, and 'keepers' were dragged through the courts under antiquated and *rarely invoked* 'bawdy house' laws. This discriminatory attack upon gay institutions and persons spawned the formation of the Right to Privacy Committee, a very active committee that continues to protest against outside interference with the gay/lesbian community's 'social space' (Jackson and Persky, 1982).

Most recently, discriminatory attacks upon the gay/lesbian collectivity arising from sensational media coverage about the spread of AIDS (Acquired Immune Deficiency Syndrome), and linking this deadly disease with the gay male population, have spawned a variety of educational and anti-discriminatory defence mechanisms within the target community. Gay/lesbian organizations have raised funds for research into the sources of AIDS; they have developed public educational materials designed to refute the prejudicial assumption that AIDS is a 'gay disease,' and they have been in the forefront of the movement to combat the *fear* of AIDS and to protect its victims (homosexual and heterosexual alike) from the dehumanizing effects of social ostracization and isolation (*Body Politic*, passim).

CONCLUSION

This examination of the institutional infrastructure of the gay/lesbian community demonstrates clearly that this non-ethnic minority has developed the requisite institutional framework for the preservation and transmission of a distinctive subculture (alternative life-style) through time. Evidence based upon the case of the gay/lesbian minority thus lends strong support to my argument that, insofar as a non-ethnic collectivity constitutes a living community whose members express a desire to perpetuate their distinctive subculture and who have developed the requisite resources and institutional infrastructure for cultural transmission through time, such a collectivity can put forward justifiable minority

TABLE 4
The evolution of self-help and protest movements: stigmatized minorities

CLOSET	ALCOHOLIC	DISABLED	HOMOSEXUAL
	Alcoholics Anonymous	Recovery Inc. (mentally ill)	Mattachine Society (secret)
SELF-HELP	Al-Anon Alateen	People First (mentally retarded)	
CONTENTION: (reform) (individual/ categorical rights claims)		consumer movement Normalization movement (mentally and physically disabled)	homophile organizations gay and lesbian rights organizations
REVITALIZATION: (pluralism/multiculturalism) (collective cultural rights claims)			Gay/Lesbian Liberation movement (1980s)
OPEN			

claims. Under the guidelines of Sections 15 and 27 of the CRF, these non-ethnic minorities, like their ethnic counterparts, can put forward claims to governments for recognition and protection of their collective cultural rights. In my view, the gay/lesbian community can justifiably put forward such minority claims in Canada today.

From a human-rights approach, this chapter has analysed different forms of minority protest organization. The analysis has shown that protest movements developed by stigmatized minorities have different strategies and goals and that these have different implications for the development of minority rights claims (see table 4).

The following points of contrast are offered by way of summation:

1 Insofar as minority organizations cope with a stigma by remaining closeted (secret-anonymous) they may provide members with import-

ant support for the development of a positive minority identity, but they are not designed to promote society-wide recognition and protection for their members' human rights (AA and the early [gay] Mattachine Society are prime examples).

2 Insofar as minority organizations cope with a stigma by promoting assimilation (normalization/ integration) they may be designed to seek social reforms (through contention) in order to protect members' fundamental, individual human rights. (The later Mattachine Society was not so designed; the consumer and normalization movements among Canada's disabled minorities are involved in advocacy for minority rights.)

3 Insofar as minority organizations cope with a stigma by positively affirming the legitimacy of their (alternative) subculture/life-styles they may be designed (on a pluralistic model) to seek recognition and protection of their members' collective cultural rights. (Introverted religious communities such as the Hutterites are not so designed; the Gay/Lesbian Liberation movement of the 1980s incorporates the cultural dimension of minority protest.)

In the next and final chapter I will assess the current state of protections for the individual, categorical, and collective rights of non-ethnic minorities in Canada. I will examine a selected sample of cases that have been brought by stigmatized minorities before various human rights bodies in this country. In conclusion, drawing upon evidence presented throughout this book, I will speculate about the future prospects for stigmatized minorities in their pursuit of recognition and protection for their human rights in Canada.

7

Towards equality: human rights as minority rights

Throughout this book, I have employed a human-rights–oriented theoretical framework in the analysis of two sets of social processes: the processes through which stigmatized-minority status is created and perpetuated and those through which minority stigmata are shed and minorities attain human and cultural liberation. The conceptual scheme that informs the analysis has been divided into three sequential phases for heuristic purposes. In the first phase of the analysis, the focus has been on the processes through which majority authorities inflict stigmata on vulnerable minorities and manipulate prejudicial invalidation myths in order to rationalize violations of minority rights. This initial phase of the analysis has addressed the ways in which the adverse impact of disadvantaged minority status is augmented through discriminatory public policy, legislation, and public practice. Phase one has examined also the self-fulfilling prophecy of stigmatization through which minorities become psychologically entrapped and politically immobilized within the restrictive bounds of their voluntary or involuntary closets.

In the second phase of the analysis, the focus has been on the processes involved in coming out of the closet and in the creation of positive new minority identities and life-styles. This phase of the analysis has focused on the role of minority self-help groups and support networks in facilitating the process of coming out.

Phase three of the analysis has addressed the transition from secretism to activism and the development of minority protest movements. The culmination of the third and last phase of the analysis lies in the explication of human-rights–oriented social movements, designed to put forward minority-rights claims.

In this chapter I will focus analytic attention on the current state of legal and non-legal protections for minority rights in Canada. I will critically assess current constitutional and statutory provisions affecting minority rights, with particular attention to the rights of non-ethnic minorities. In light of this assessment, I will propose legal and non-legal strategies for change designed to improve the treatment and life conditions of stigmatized Canadian minorities in the future.

IMPLICIT VERSUS EXPLICIT LEGAL PROTECTIONS FOR MINORITY RIGHTS

In Canada, the 1970s will probably go down in history as the human-rights decade. For a wide variety of minority Canadians struggling to attain recognition and protection for their individual and collective rights, the focus of organized lobbying efforts was on desired changes in statutory and constitutional law. Such changes were directed towards the twin goals of *elimination* of existing discriminatory legal provisions and *specification* (of the minority condition) under the non-discriminatory provisions of human-rights legislation. In the latter connection, the advent of the Constitution Act (1982), with its newly introduced Charter of Rights and Freedoms (CRF), was an event that signalled a large measure of success for some minorities (notably women, and the mentally and physically disabled), but was marked by grave disappointment and bitterness for others (notably gays and lesbians).

All in all, from the perspective of minority rights, it can be said that some important breakthroughs were made throughout the 1970s at all jurisdictional levels. Further, in keeping with the constitutional mandate of the CRF, the process of bringing statutory law into line with CRF principles continues in the 1980s.

At this point, the reader may well ask: But what does it all mean? What good has all of this legal manoeuvring done for Ms and Mr *Minority Public*? Does it really make any difference to minority members if their status or condition is enumerated or is not enumerated in the non-discriminatory grounds of human-rights legislation? Do the provisions of human-rights legislation not apply equal/equivalent protection to the individual and collective rights of all Canadian minorities?

In order to answer these questions, in the following pages I will assess the nature and scope of protections for minority rights offered under various provisions of constitutional and statutory law in Canada. To begin, I will assess the provisions of the CRF that constitutionally guarantee minority rights. I will then look at the Charter's provisions in light of the Constitutional Amendment (Meech Lake Accord) of 1987.

The CRF and the constitutional debates (1980–2 and 1987–8)

Throughout the 1980–2 constitutional debate, legal scholars who voiced support for constitutional entrenchment of a CRF argued that an entrenched Charter would override existing legislation and would thus render all discriminatory laws throughout the country inoperative (Kallen, 1982: ch. 9). Moreover, it was argued, an entrenched Charter would serve to eliminate existing disparities in the provisions of federal and provincial human-rights legislation as it would provide the standard to which all legislation should conform (ibid).

It follows from this line of argument that a constitutionally entrenched CRF should provide all Canadian minorities with an equal/equivalent basis for making claims for redress against perceived human-rights violations. The question now arises: Is this in fact the case? Is the CRF truly an egalitarian human-rights instrument or is it informed by established ethnic and non-ethnic group priorities that serve to render some categories of Canadians *more equal* than others?

In order to assess the priorities behind the Charter's provisions, the relative strength or weakness of protections for the minority rights of different population categories must be taken into account. A central thesis informing my analysis is that the more explicit the provisions for minority rights, the stronger the protection afforded. In this connection, the pivotal distinction is between *specified* and *unspecified* protections for minority rights. Unspecified protections apply generally; they do not specify particular target populations. Specified protections, in contrast, apply specifically to particular, enumerated target populations.

When the differential strength of protections for minority rights is taken into account in assessing the provisions of the CRF, it becomes evident that the Charter is not a truly egalitarian human-rights instrument. Rather, the CRF, together with related (1982) constitutional provisions, can be seen to perpetuate a long-institutionalized hierarchy of ethnic and non-ethnic group inequalities. For purposes of the present book, our analysis will focus on differential protection for non-ethnic minorities.

EQUALITY RIGHTS AS MINORITY RIGHTS:
A CRITIQUE OF CRF SECTION 15

Equality rights
(1) Every individual is equal before and under law and has the right to the equal protection and equal benefit of the law without discrimination and, in particular

without discrimination based on race, national or ethnic origin, colour, religion, sex, age, or mental or physical disability.

(2) Subsection (1) does not preclude any law, program or activity that has as its object the amelioration of conditions of disadvantaged individuals or groups, including those that are disadvantaged because of race, national or ethnic origin, colour, religion, sex, age or mental or physical disability. (Minister of Supply and Services Canada, 1982: 15)

Section 15 of the CRF, Constitution Act (1982) affords Canadians the key constitutional provision for individual and categorical rights claims based on equality rights. While there is general agreement among legal scholars that the non-discriminatory grounds of Section 15 are 'open', that is, that claims can be put forward by minorities not enumerated in its provisions, enumerated minorities are afforded *specified* protection for their human rights, while non-enumerated minorities have only *unspecified* protection. Enumerated minorities, specified on the grounds of race, national or ethnic origin, colour, religion, sex, age, or mental or physical disability, thereby have a firmer basis for claims than non-specified minorities. Even among the different enumerated minorities, a covert status hierarchy can be discerned. Ethnic (aboriginal and multicultural) minorities and women have specified human-rights protections under other Charter provisions (Sections 25, 27, and 28, respectively), whereas other enumerated minorities do not. In light of the fact that the provisions of Section 15 of the CRF are subject to the possibility of provincial-government override under CRF Section 33, while Sections 25, 27, and 28 are not vulnerable in this respect, it becomes apparent that ethnic minorities and women enjoy greater Charter protections than do other minorities enumerated under Section 15.

The foregoing analysis suggests that the equality-rights provisions of Section 15 of the CRF can be seen to underscore a status hierarchy in which enumerated minorities with other constitutional protections (namely, ethnic minorities and women) rank highest; other enumerated minorities (namely, those specified on the basis of race, age, or physical or mental disability) rank second; and non-enumerated minorities (namely, un-specified populations whose minority status is based upon sexual orientation, political belief, criminal record, history of alcoholism, or other grounds) rank lowest. Given this interpretation, it would not be surprising if some version of the U.S. approach to equality rights, involving three levels of judicial scrutiny – strict, intermediate, and minimal – were to be adopted by Canadian courts in their assessment of the claims made by non-enumerated minorities, enumerated minorities without other constitutional protections, and enumerated minorities with other protections, respectively (see Tarnopolsky, 1982: ch. 1). Should this happen, the discriminatory implications of the inegalitarian nature of the Charter's differential protections for Canada's minorities could be profound. Tarnopolsky (ibid) suggests that it would follow that the lower the status of the minority the greater would be the burden of proof upon the victim of discrimination.

The Meech Lake Accord (MLA) and the CRF: a threat to minority rights?[1]

Notwithstanding the serious reservations of many minorities concerning the differential nature and extent of protections afforded under the equality-rights provisions of the CRF, these constitutional provisions tend to be regarded as sacrosanct by minority Canadians. For deeply stigmatized, non-ethnic minorities, they represent a truly memorable achievement in the arduous struggle to gain lawful recognition and protection for minority rights. The unambiguously negative response of Canada's non-ethnic minorities to the provisions of the currently proposed constitutional amendment (MLA) (1987) should, therefore, be viewed in light of the perceived threat to minority rights, secured under the CRF, posed by this constitutional amendment.

In the expressed view of representatives of Canada's non-ethnic minorities, the provisions of the 1987 MLA serve to undermine cherished Charter guarantees for minority rights. Minority spokespersons have pointed out, in this connection, that legal precedent supports the view that the corpus of the constitution, and presumably the MLA, supersedes the CRF.

Notwithstanding their particular constitutional concerns, Canada's minorities have been virtually unanimous in their declared opposition to the provisions of Section 2(1) a and b of the MLA. These provisions, respectively, recognize the existence of French-speaking and English-speaking Canadians as a 'fundamental characteristic' of Canada, and recognize that Quebec constitutes a 'distinct society' within Canada.

---

1 The analysis of the MLA in the section to follow is taken from my article 'The Meech Lake Accord: Entrenching a Pecking Order of Minority Rights' in *Canadian Public Policy*: The Meech Lake Accord, XIV Supplement, September 1988. This article analyses the potential effects of the accord on the constitutional rights of both ethnic and non-ethnic minorities in Canada. For a fuller discussion of the issues in the debate, together with a full listing of sources drawn upon, the reader is referred to my original work.

Minority spokespersons argue that this section of the MLA gives priority to the constitutionally entrenched, collective rights of Canada's 'founding' majorities over the individual and collective rights of minorities throughout this country. Among non-ethnic minorities, women's groups have been most resolute in articulating their strong opposition to these MLA provisions. Women's lobby groups have voiced concern that Section 2(1)a of the MLA could weaken women's equality rights by directing the courts to give priority to policies designed to promote French/English bilingualism (*Toronto Star*, 27 August 1987). Accordingly, women's organizations have pressed for an amendment to the MLA giving specified protections for women's rights so as to ensure that the courts would give more weight to CRF provisions guaranteeing sexual equality (Sections 15 and 28) than to Section 2(1)a of the MLA (*Toronto Star*, 21 August 1987). Some women's representatives have expressed fears about the potential, negative impact on women's rights in Quebec if the 'distinct society' provision of Section 2(1)b supersedes CRF provisions against sex discrimination. They suggest, for example, that Quebec could replace affirmative-action programs aimed at increasing the proportion of women employed in the civil service with programs that would be 'language-oriented' (*Toronto Star*, 17 August 1987).

Women's representatives have objected also to Section 16 of the Accord. This clause, they have argued, singles out multicultural and aboriginal groups as minorities whose constitutionally recognized rights are not affected by MLA amendments, implying (by omission) that the rights of other minorities not mentioned would thereby have less recognition and protection (*Toronto Star*, 22 August 1987).

Briefs to the Joint Commission from a number of national organizations representing other non-ethnic minorities have echoed the concern expressed by many women's groups that the MLA undermines Charter equality rights. There appears to be strong support for the recommendation that a provision be added to the MLA to ensure that the Constitution of Canada shall be interpreted in a manner consistent with the CRF (CHRA, III/8, September 1987). A brief from the Canadian Association for Community Living (formerly the National Institute on Mental Retardation) contended that the MLA served to legitimate an apparent hierarchy of minority groups by affording different and unequal protections for different groups (ibid). The March of Dimes, a major organization representing Canada's disabled minorities, voiced fears that the hard-won rights of mentally and physically disabled Canadians – the last minority category to be enumerated under Section 15 of the CRF – would be at risk under the provisions of the MLA (*Toronto Star*, 20 September 1987).

Organizations representing non-ethnic minorities also have expressed concern about the potential undermining of national, cost-shared programs by the provisions of Section 106A(1) of the MLA, which allow provinces to opt out of these programs and yet receive funding for a program or initiative that is compatible with the national objectives. The vague wording of this provision, it has been argued, could lead to a scenario where provinces accept federal funding but provide no alternative program by shifting the onus to the private sector through the provision of certain initiatives (CHRA, September 1987). A specific concern raised by spokespersons for the March of Dimes and by the Coalition of the Provincial Organizations of the Handicapped (COPOH) was that this provision would impede the efforts of the federal government to introduce a comprehensive disability-insurance program much needed by Canada's disabled minorities. In similar vein, women's organizations have objected to the provisions of this section of the Accord, arguing that they could impact negatively on efforts to establish national child-care programs (*Toronto Star*, 20 September 1987).

At the end of August 1987, an ad-hoc coalition of community organizations representing ethnic minorities, women, disabled minorities, unions, and human-rights groups sent an open letter to Canada's premiers calling on them to delay ratification of the MLA in order to allow for public analysis and debate (CHRA, September 1987). The coalition argued that once again, in 1987, as in 1982, the Canadian Constitution was being amended with virtually no direct participation or input from Canada's minorities. The letter pointed out that the Joint Committee on the Constitutional Amendment had allowed less than two months for briefs from the public and argued that this highly restrictive time frame had prevented many minority organizations from properly informing and consulting with their membership.

What this argument implies is that particular minority concerns have been unequally voiced and represented in the constitutional debate over the provisions of the MLA. Moreover, insofar as minority organizations have focused their reaction to the Accord on its potential threat to the minority rights of their own constituencies, what becomes apparent is that the most vulnerable and least powerful minorities are those least likely to have had their concerns articulated. Some women's groups, for example, have recommended only that recognition of women's equality rights be added to the provisions of the MLA. But would such an amendment to adequate to ensure the recognition and protection of the rights of disabled women? And what about the rights of immigrant women, black lesbians, and other members of multiple minorities?

Effects of the MLA on the CRF: entrenching a pecking order of minority rights[2]

The foregoing critique suggests that the MLA may serve to constitutional-ize a hierarchy of majority and minority Charter rights, within which the majority rights of Canada's two founding peoples/nations assume highest priority and rank first; the minority rights of ethnic (aboriginal and multicultural) minorities rank second; and the minority rights of non-ethnic minorities – nowhere alluded to in the amendment – have lowest priority and rank third. If this interpretation is correct, what it implies is *not* that the MLA simply reinforces the 1982 constitutional status quo. Rather, as explicitly articulated in the briefs presented to the Joint Committee by minority representatives, the provisions of the MLA can be seen to weaken the constitutionally recognized Charter rights of Canada's non-ethnic minorities. Accordingly, the MLA can best be understood as a retrogressive amendment, which may be interpreted by the courts in ways that undermine the constitutional guarantees for non-ethnic minority rights under Section 15 of the CRF. Probably the most telling comment on the MLA-endorsed minority 'pecking order' is that Canada's most vulnerable minorities – those disadvantaged by multiple minority status and those most clearly in need of specified human-rights protections – are those whose human rights are most seriously violated through omission.

Whether or not the MLA in its present form will gain the unanimous provincial support necessary for its legal enactment as part of Canada's constitution is an open question at the time of writing. If this amendment does succeed in gaining constitutional status, a second question remains as to the interpretation of its provisions by the courts. The expressed fears of representatives of non-ethnic minorities that the MLA will undermine CRF guarantees for equality rights may or may not be borne out by court decisions. In any case, the CRF will continue to provide the legal underpinnings for minority rights throughout Canada, for it represents the nation-wide, constitutional standard for human rights to which all statutory law should conform.

2 I have borrowed the term 'pecking order' from the headline of the September 1987 issue of the *Canadian Human Rights Advocate* (CHRA). The headline reads: 'Constitutional Amendment Opens Door to Pecking Order on Human Rights.'

In the following section of this chapter, I will examine statutory human-rights legislation, designed to regulate discriminatory actions of individuals against other individuals within specific (federal or provincial) jurisdictions. In order to provide documentation for the main points of my analysis, I will present relevant summary evidence, pertaining to the minorities focused upon in this book, drawn from the case files of human-rights jurisdictions across Canada. As in my previous analysis of constitutional CRF provisions, in this analysis of the provisions of statutory human-rights legislation, the central thesis that I will attempt to demonstrate is that the greater the *specificity* of legal provisions, the stronger and more reliable are the safeguards for minority rights.

STATUTORY LAW

Protections for sexual orientation

At present, the only jurisdictions that specify sexual orientation in the enumerated, non-discriminatory grounds of their human-rights legislation are Quebec (1977), Ontario (1986), Manitoba (1987) and the Yukon (1987).

In British Columbia, prior to the introduction of a (1983) government-restraint budget leading to the repeal of the Human Rights Code and the dissolution of the commission enforcing it, complaints based on the ground of sexual orientation could be dealt with under the general rubric of 'reasonable cause' provisions. In the rest of Canada, the human rights of homosexual persons have been and remain unprotected as there is at present no jurisdictional basis under which legal complaints can be lodged.

The following cases summaries, drawn from Canadian jurisdictions with different mandates regarding 'sexual orientation' (no protection, implicit protection, and explicit protection), may serve to illustrate my thesis that *explicit* legal protection is necessary if the human rights of stigmatized minorities are to be adequately recognized and protected.

No protection
CASE 1 – (Federal jurisdiction) Canadian Human Rights Commission (CHRC)
The CHRC was compelled to dismiss a complaint by a Toronto gay-rights group concerning a discriminatory article that appeared in the May 1983 Canadian edition of *The Evangelist* magazine. The article in question,

written by a United States–based evangelist, argued against the employment of homosexuals in the public sector and quoted a biblical verse describing such persons as 'worthy of death.' The complainant was advised that the CHRC has no jurisdiction over the magazine and that the Canadian Human Rights Act does not prohibit discrimination on the basis of sexual orientation. Nevertheless, the complainant insisted on filing.

The commission was of the opinion that the wording and inference in the article were deplorable, and the members of the commission took the view that this complaint, and others like it, reinforced the need to specify sexual orientation among the prohibited grounds in the federal act (CHRC, *Summary of Decisions* taken at 19–20 September 1983 meeting).

Implicit protection
'Reasonable Cause' Provision (British Columbia Human Rights Code)
Until its (1983) repeal, the British Columbia Human Rights Code offered limited protection to homosexuals and other minorities not enumerated in the non-discriminatory grounds of the Code under the 'reasonable cause' provision applicable in Section 3 (public facilities, accommodations, or services), Section 8 (employment), and Section 9 (membership in trade unions and occupational associations). No protection was provided in other areas, including the purchase and leasing of property, wages, advertising of employment, requesting information on application forms and in job interviews.

In the February 1983 report of the British Columbia Human Rights Commission (BCHRC) on extensions to the Code, support was given by the commission to the position argued in a brief to the commission by the BC Civil Liberties Association on the advantages of explicit, *enumerated* protections over implicit protections under 'reasonable cause' provisions. The most obvious advantage of explicit protection, it was argued, is that a general 'reasonable cause' type of provision is open to a wide range of subjective interpretation. Accordingly, it could be interpreted at some future time in a very narrow sense, which would exclude particular minority groups from protection. Explicit protection, however, eliminates such a possibility (Report of the BCHRC, February 1983: 18).

Explicit protection
Because the amendments to the Ontario and Manitoba human-rights codes, and the prohibited grounds of the Yukon Human Rights Act, which now include sexual orientation in their list of enumerated grounds, have been enacted so recently (1986 and 1987), exemplary cases from these jurisdictions are not, as yet, forthcoming. Alternatively,

sexual orientation has been included in the enumerated, non-discriminatory grounds of the Quebec Charter of Human Rights since 1977, and there is an ample file of cases settled under this provincial jurisdiction to draw upon for illustrative purposes. A small, but typical sample of these cases should serve to demonstrate the superiority of explicit (enumerated) protection for human rights over more general protection (such as 'reasonable cause' provisions).

CASE 2 – (Quebec jurisdiction) Quebec Human Rights Commission (QHRC) (*Reference*: File No. M-M00888–1)
The complainant, a lesbian professor in a private college in the Montreal area, claimed that her teaching contract had been cancelled and that she had been dismissed by the college because of her sexual orientation. She claimed that her life-style differed from that of the other professors and that this difference had evoked marked disapproval from the administrator of the college. The latter had reproached the complainant, before witnesses, for living with two females and three males who were known homosexuals.

The Quebec Human Rights Commission (QHRC) undertook an investigation of the allegation lodged by the complainant against the college (respondent). Initially, the college refused to co-operate, but after a great deal of pressure was brought to bear by the QHRC upon the procurator of the college, a response was forthcoming. The procurator claimed that the cancellation of the complainant's teaching contract could not be contested because the terms of the contract allowed such cancellation at the discretion of either party. The QHRC, however, asserted that the province's Charter of Rights did not permit the practice of discrimination in this kind of discretionary action.

Negotiations were undertaken by the QHRC in order to reach a settlement of the matter between the complainant and the college. Eventually, the college offered the complainant the sum of $4,000, which represented the equivalent of four months' (lost) salary, after benefit deductions. The complainant accepted the settlement, withdrew the complaint, and desisted from further recourse.

CASE 3 – (Quebec jurisdiction) QHRC (*Reference*: File No. M-M00772–1)
The complainant, an openly gay male employee, claimed that the hospital he worked for had demanded his resignation because of his sexual orientation. The complainant had been employed at the hospital for about five years.

The respondent (hospital) argued that the complainant had recently begun to 'flaunt' his sexual orientation, notably in wearing earrings and in coming to work with his boy-friend. These behaviours were determining factors in the decision of the hospital to ask the complainant for his resignation.

A process of mediation was opened by the QHRC with the aim of leading the parties to a mutually agreeable settlement. The final agreement involved the following conditions: 1 / the hospital (respondent) agreed to assign to the complainant the sum of $10,000 as compensation for the remainder of his salary in the annual contract and 2 / the hospital furnished to the complainant a positive letter of reference addressed 'to whom it may concern.' The complainant accepted these conditions and accordingly agreed to drop all charges against the hospital.

CASE 4 – (Quebec jurisdiction) QHRC (*Reference*: File No. QQ00590–1)
A gay rights organization claimed that the Service des Loisirs-Dance du Québec in a particular municipality had published a discriminatory notice that violated the human rights of homosexuals. The notice in question advertised a particular dance club and announced that enrolment in the club's program was restricted to 'male and female' couples. The complainant deemed it unacceptable that a municipality, operating on public funds, should discriminate against a class of human beings (homosexuals) by publishing such a notice, and demanded that both the notice and the discriminatory requirement of the dance studio publicized in it be retracted.

The enquiry established that the dance club in question was a non-profit organization administered by and operating solely through the funds of its members. The only part played by the municipality was that it lent the premises to the organization and it announced the club's activities in its brochure.

The authorities representing the dance club explained that the 'couples only' requirement was designed to ward off individual enrolments. These, they argued, tended to disrupt the organization of the lessons, as the dances taught at the club were designed to be performed in couples. As regards the requirement concerning 'male-female' couples, the club authorities argued that the rules of the province-wide dance competitions for which club members eagerly prepared restricted these events to male-female couples.

The Fédération Loisirs-Dance du Québec (the sponsors of the province-wide dance competitions) was approached about the matter, and, in response, they agreed to accept same-sex couples in the competition.

Consequently, the dance club decided to delete the words 'male and female' or 'boy and girl' after the words 'Requirement: Couples only' in their advertisement. They also agreed not to engage in any further practices that would contravene the non-discriminatory grounds of the Quebec charter.

The retractions were duly carried out and the case was closed.

Sexual orientation and minority rights: reflections on the case summaries

The foregoing synopsis of cases drawn from the files of three Canadian human-rights commissions with quite different jurisdictional mandates regarding 'sexual orientation' lends support to my thesis that *explicit* legal protections for human rights provide the strongest and most reliable safeguards against minority discrimination. A few additional observations, pertaining to the cases drawn from Quebec, may serve to clarify the scope and the limitations of human-rights protections afforded under *explicit* provisions.

With regard to cases 2 and 3, both involving discrimination in employment, the reader should note that in neither instance did the complainant return to the job in question. Here, the *limits* of the protections provided by the process of legal negotiation and settlement between opposing parties in human-rights cases are revealed. As so poignantly put by Dr Daniel Hill: 'You can't legislate a change in people's hearts.'[3] Human-rights laws cannot compel heterosexist employers to love homosexual employees, nor can they compel the minority victim to love the majority discriminator. What they can do, and what they are realistically designed to do, is to ensure minorities equal/equivalent treatment despite feelings of prejudice, distrust, and even hatred on the part of potential majority discriminators.

Human-rights laws set out non-discriminatory standards for human behaviour in public life. They cannot, however, compel parallel standards for human thought and feeling. Accordingly, in the cases referred to and in many others like them, the antipathy between the opposing parties did not disappear once a settlement was reached; hence the complainant preferred to seek new employment rather than to continue to work for an overtly prejudiced employer.

3 This position has been argued by a number of human-rights activists, notably, Dr Daniel Hill and Alan Borovoy, QC. A useful summary of this line of argumentation is found in the BC Human Rights Commission Report on extensions to the provincial Code (February 1983: 11–14).

Case 4 illustrates quite a different point. What this case shows is that explicit legal protections can serve to destigmatize, and to officially legitimize the identified minority condition. Consequently, minority members may gain acceptance in public life by law-abiding individuals and groups. Moreover, once legitimacy is bestowed upon a minority, it may extend even to the private domain, a sector of life normally exempted from constraints of legal provisions. In the example of case 4, both respondents apparently were persuaded of the legitimacy of the Quebec Charter's provisions. Most significantly, concerning the dance club in the case, this respondent was a privately run and funded organization whose members might have sought exemption from the Quebec Charter's provisions (under Section 20, the 'exceptions' clause) as an educative, non-profit organization. Instead, the clubs' representatives chose to act in accordance with the human-rights *principles* of the Quebec Charter. Accordingly, they agreed to retract the club's discriminatory requirement for membership and to desist from further acts that would violate the provincial Charter's legal provisions.

The persuasive, educative function of human-rights legislation illustrated in the foregoing example should not be taken lightly, particularly in a country like Canada with a long-standing reputation (or, at least a pervasive myth) of 'law-abidingness' among its citizens.

In addition to the implicit educative function of non-discriminatory legislation per se, human-rights commissions generally have an explicit public-education function within their mandate. Indeed, one of the most severe criticisms levied against the British Columbia government's repeal of the provincial human-rights code and its replacement by the BC Human Rights Act was that the latter revoked the strong educational mandate of the former (*Globe and Mail*, 19 August 1983).

Protections for the physically and mentally disabled

The minority rights of physically and mentally disabled Canadians are constitutionally recognized and protected under the enumerated grounds of Section 15 of the CRF. Notwithstanding this constitutional mandate for parallel statutory law, fewer than half of Canada's jurisdictions have brought their human-rights legislation into conformity with CRF guidelines. Physically disabled minorities are afforded specified protection (applicable at least in some spheres of public life) under human-rights legislation in all Canadian (federal and provincial) jurisdictions. However, the mentally disabled are protected through explicit provisions (under handicap) only in five jurisdictions: federal (and the Yukon), British Columbia, Manitoba, Ontario, and Quebec.

A perusal of a cross-section of cases drawn from the files of human-rights commissions across Canada suggests that cases involving physical disabilities tend to be more clear-cut and more amenable to fair and equitable solution than are cases involving mental disabilities. In the latter, a major problem lies in accurately measuring the impairing potential of the disability, and in assessing its demonstrable handicapping effects.

The following case summary may serve to illustrate the kinds of difficulties involved in fairly resolving cases where the complainant is mentally retarded.

CASE 5 – (Quebec jurisdiction) QHRC (*Reference:* File No. M-M00660–3)
A case was brought before the QHRC by the Centre for Social Services acting on behalf of a mentally retarded man, allegedly exploited by his live-in girl-friend. The respondent was said to have extorted over $12,000 from the complainant by various means. The complainant worked at a regular job with a good salary. Before cohabiting with the respondent, he had held a term deposit, in a public bank, worth over $12,000.

What seemed incontestable to commission members was that from the time that the complainant and the respondent began to live together the respondent had spent large sums of the complainant's money, notably for the purchase of two automobiles and for a trip to Florida. Where a difference of opinion was evident among commissioners was on the question of the estimated value of services rendered to the complainant by the respondent during the period of their cohabitation.

The complainant claimed that the respondent had neglected him, that she did not provide him with adequate food or clothing, and that she made his life intolerable. However, the respondent claimed that her time had been fully occupied in caring for the complainant, that the automobiles purchased were necessary in order to do the shopping and house-keeping for the complainant, and that the trip to Florida was well earned and deserved as a reward for her many services in caring for a mentally retarded person.

The QHRC found it difficult to determine whether or not the services rendered by the respondent justified the expenditures she had made. There were many imponderable factors to consider in this connection, such as the part played by (or the influence of) the bonds of affection in the intimate relationship between the complainant and the respondent.

Most important, it was necessary to ascertain whether or not the degree of mental deficiency of the complainant was sufficiently severe to justify the application in this case of Section 48 of the Quebec Charter (this section of the legislation prohibits the exploitation of handicapped persons).

A number of aspects of the case cast doubt upon the severity of the condition of mental retardation of the complainant. For example, the complainant had held a regular job for a long time, and he had saved a substantial sum of money. The committee concluded that while the complainant clearly was mentally retarded to some degree, he certainly was not profoundly retarded.

After much deliberation, the Centre for Social Services, acting on behalf of the complainant, persuaded the commission of the importance of obtaining a guarantee from the respondent to the effect that she would not look for or have any further contact with mentally retarded persons.

The commission was able to verify the fact that the respondent had no immediate means of paying any fine that might be levied against her in the final judgment of the case, for she had no job and no income at the time. They therefore sought to obtain a formal written statement from the respondent that she would not seek to meet or to see or to speak with mentally retarded persons from this time onward. A written guarantee, satisfactory to all, was obtained. Further, the commission extended its regrets to the Centre for Social Services that it was not possible to retrieve for the complainant any part of the sums of money spent by the respondent.

The accurate determination of the nature and extent of the handicapping effects of a given disability is central to virtually the whole spectrum of cases involving alleged discrimination on the grounds of disability or 'handicap' (mental or physical). The following case summary with regard to physical disability may serve to shed light on the issues involved in the process of resolution in such cases.

CASE 6 – (Federal jurisdiction) Canadian Human Rights Act, Human Rights Tribunal (January 1982)
The complainant charged that he was denied summer employment with CN Express because of a non-relevant job requirement that discriminated on the basis of physical handicap. The repondent countered that the requirement in question, namely that CN Express warehousemen possess a 'functional hand' (one with at least two fingers), was a bona fide occupational requirement. They argued that the complainant could not

perform the duties of a warehouseman as safely as could a non-handicapped employee.

The tribunal found that the evidence presented by the respondent failed to show that the CN Express 'functional hand' requirement represented a bona fide occupational requirement. The tribunal noted that the complainant had previously been employed in a similar capacity, that he had had no difficulty performing his duties, and that he had no record of injury to himself or his co-workers. The tribunal concluded that the respondent's assumption that applicants lacking fingers on a hand would be unable to perform the job safely was not supported 'in fact and reason' in this case.

The complainant, a man with a fingerless hand, was awarded $1,446 for lost wages and $2,000 for damages to hurt feelings and self-respect. With regard to the latter, the tribunal took into consideration the fact that this was the first time the complainant had been explicitly labelled as a handicapped person. Prior to this experience, the complainant had not considered himself 'handicapped.' Accordingly, the tribunal argued that the complainant's experience of degradation in this situation was particularly severe.

An important point to note, with regard to the settlement of the foregoing case, is that compensation was provided to the disabled complainant not only for violation of economic rights but also for violation of social rights. Human-rights legislation is unique in this respect: it is dedicated primarily to the protection of the fundamental right to human dignity. In connection with the present case, it goes without saying that the disabled minority ranks foremost among those Canadians whose right to human dignity has been most consistently and heartlessly violated.

The accurate assessment of the handicapping effects of a given disability on job performance clearly is a central issue in cases involving alleged handicapism in employment. Another central issue in cases involving disabilities is that of provision of equivalent treatment, where appropriate. Human-rights legislation should ensure the provision of parallel and equitable services and facilities in cases where standard forms deny equal access and opportunity to disabled persons. The next two cases focus on this issue.

CASE 7 – (Manitoba jurisdiction) Manitoba Human Rights Code (MHRC) (reported in *Canadian Human Rights Advocate* [CHRA, III/9, October 1987])

The complainant, parents of a six-year-old girl with cerebral palsy, alleged that the Winnipeg School Board had refused to accept their daughter in the regular kindergarten class at the neighbourhood school, which her brother and all the other neighbourhood children were attending. The school-board allegedly had ruled that the disabled girl should attend a segregated class for handicapped children at another school. The complainant (parents) argued that sending their daughter to a segregated class in a distant school would be the first step on a path to social isolation and exclusion for her. They contended that it was their daughter's right to be integrated into a regular class so that she could become part of the school and the community like everybody else. In response to the parents' filing of the complaint with the MHRC, the Winnipeg school trustees voted to reverse the board's original decision and to allow the disabled girl to attend her neighbourhood school. The board agreed to let the youngster into the regular (at this time, Grade 1) class and to provide a full-time aide to help her in the class-room.

CASE 8 – (Saskatchewan jurisdiction) Saskatchewan Human Rights Code (SHRC) (Board of Inquiry, August 1981)
The complainant, a disabled man reliant on a wheelchair, alleged that the respondent, Canadian Odeon Theatres, discriminated against chair-bound theatre-goers. The complainant alleged that, in the case of a particular Odeon theatre, persons in wheelchairs can gain entrance to the premises and can use the wash-room facilities, but that films can be viewed only from in front of the front row of seats. On this evidence, the complainant charged that, as a wheelchair-user, he was provided with a service or facility in a manner that was different from an inferior to the manner in which the service of facility is provided to others.

The board of inquiry conducted an investigation of the allegation. They concluded that the respondent discriminated against the complainant on the grounds of physical disability. The board rejected the respondent's argument that because the theatre was constructed prior to the enforce-ment of the provisions of the Human Rights Code relevant to the matter, the board could not find an act of discrimination. Subject to any deletions deemed necessary to avoid undue hardship for the respondent, the board directed the respondent to undertake renovations so as to accommodate six wheelchair spaces in two groups of three or three groups of two, in the rear two-thirds of the regular viewing area, placed so as to allow independent mobility of wheelchairs. Further, the respondent was or-dered to advertise these spaces.

The respondent did not accept the ruling of the board and filed an appeal in the Saskatchewan Court of Queen's Bench (CHRA, 1/3, April 1985). The presiding judge ruled in favour of the respondent, supporting his decision with the argument that the provincial human-rights code did not require that the particular needs of physically disabled persons be catered to by those who provide services and facilities to the public. In his view, the Code requires that the physically disabled be afforded the same facilities as are offered to the public, 'no more and no less' (ibid: 2).

The complainant and the SHRC appealed this decision in the Saskatchewan Court of Appeal. The court, in a precedent-setting decision, upheld the complaint. The justices categorically rejected the narrow interpretation of the lower court that provision of the same service to the physically disabled as to others means non-discrimination. They argued that such an interpretation would make the protections in the Code, intended to preserve human dignity, meaningless for persons with a physical disability. Disabled persons, they contended, are entitled to have their special needs taken into consideration and their human dignity preserved in all existing services and facilities. On the basis of this argument, the court restored the original decision of the board of inquiry ordering the respondent to make the required changes in theatre facilities in order to provide equivalent accessibility to the physically handicapped.

The foregoing two cases highlight the enforcement of the human-rights principle of equivalence as a statutory obligation in the treatment of disabled minorities. The principle that *same treatment does not mean equal treatment* requires accommodation of the special needs of the disabled by the providers of services, facilities, and employment opportunities to the public. The impact of these human-rights decisions clearly extends well beyond the particular cases involved. As a general standard, the principle of equivalence is applicable to all parallel situations involving minorities with special needs.

Protection for the alcohol-disabled

At present, only two jurisdictions in Canada, federal and Prince Edward Island, provide legal protection for recovering/recovered alcoholics. In both cases, human-rights legislation affords protection under the rubric of physical disability or handicap. With regard to the remaining jurisdictions, several reportedly have received no complaints in this area, while others have dealt with such complaints (or conceivably could deal with them) under a variety of general (implicit) grounds: Quebec (social condition), Newfoundland (social origin), British Columbia (reasonable cause), Manitoba (physical or mental handicap), Saskatchewan (physical disability).[4]

CASE 8

The issue of whether or not alcoholism might be considered a physical disability came before the Prince Edward Island Human Rights Commission when a man filed a complaint, early in 1982, alleging that he had been fired because he entered the provincial Addiction Services Centre Treatment Program. In this case, the commission ruled that the employer was within his rights to fire the complainant because the man did not complete the treatment, in spite of being allowed to enter the centre on an unscheduled basis.

In settling the complaint, the commission defined alcoholism as a form of disability suffered as the result of an illness and agreed to accept complaints of discrimination on the grounds of alcoholism under the general grounds of physical disability. The PEI Human Rights Commission has since formally defined alcoholism as a form of disability suffered as a result of an illness, and has placed it in the same category as such chronic diseases as asthma, diabetes, and high blood pressure (PEI Human Rights Commission, 1986: 28–31). The commission has stipulated, however, that protection applies only to rehabilitated alcoholics and those trying to cure their addiction. This means that an employer continues to have the right either to refuse to hire or to fire an individual if his or her drinking problem adversely affects job performance.

In making their decision, the PEI Human Rights Commission accepted the *Annals of Internal Medicine* description of alcoholism, which considers it as a 'chronic, progressive and potentially fatal disease' for the following reasons:

1 It is irreversible: that is, it cannot be cured; it can only be treated.
2 It is a potentially terminal illness. If the alcoholic does not stop drinking, s/he will more likely die at an earlier age.
3 It is progressive and will not go away if left untreated.
(PEI Human Rights Commission, 1986)

Insofar as alcoholism can give rise to, or can be intimately associated with,

---

4 This section is based on written responses to questions I posed in form letters to human-rights commissions across Canada during 1983.

mental and/or physical disabilities of various kinds, human-rights cases involving alcohol-related discrimination can be fraught with ambiguities of definition and problems of assessment that defy equitable resolution. The following example provides a case in point.

CASE 9 – (Quebec jurisdiction) QHRC and Superior Court of Quebec (*Reference*: File No. 450-05-00856–78)
The complainant, a female recovering alcoholic, alleged that she had been discriminated against by her employer, a general hospital, on the grounds of 'social condition' (alcohol history). Specifically, the complainant alleged that she had been unfairly dismissed from her new job at the hospital because of her 'social condition.' The complainant had entered employment at the hospital in the position of part-time assistant nutritionist. The position in question was subject to (conditional upon) the results of a medical examination carried out by a doctor employed by the hospital.

The medical report submitted by the examining physician stated that the complainant suffered from chronic alcoholism, that she had made several suicide attempts, and that she had endemic psychological problems pertaining to dependency and immaturity. For these reasons the examining physician turned in an unfavourable job recommendation. On the basis of this negative medical report, the complainant was dismissed from her job by the respondent (hospital).

Following her lodging of the complaint with the QHRC, an investigation was undertaken by the commission. The commission recommended that the complainant be reinstated in her job or in an equivalent position within forty-eight hours, that she be reimbursed in full for the salary lost from the time of dismissal, and that she be awarded the sum of three hundred dollars damages for being subjected to moral prejudice.

The decision was rejected by the respondent, who filed an appeal in the Superior Court of Quebec. The Tribunal of the Superior Court expressed the opinion that the arguments in the case hinged critically on the exact meaning of the term 'social condition' under the Quebec Charter's provision. As the relevant legislation (Quebec Charter) did not define the term, the tribunal agreed to interpret it in its usual sense, as used in common parlance. While prevailing dictionary definitions were found to be exceedingly narrow ('social rank or class'), the expert consulted by the complainant found that, in popular parlance, the term 'social condition' referred not only to social rank or class position in society but also to the class or category to which one belongs by birth, by income, by education, by occupation, or by a set of circumstances and events that caused an individual or a group to occupy a particular situation or position in the society. The tribunal accepted this broader interpretation of the term.

The critical question that remained to be answered was whether or not the complainant's dismissal was predicted on her social condition of alcoholism. The tribunal's ruling was that this was not the case. The tribunal argued that for the complaint to be justified, it would have to be demonstrated that the complainant was not dismissed for *medical* reasons or for her *medical* condition (physical or mental disability). The medical report upon which her dismissal was based, however, had revealed persistent mental problems. Therefore, the tribunal was of the opinion that the facts that the complainant was (apparently) a recovering alcoholic and that she was following an alcohol-treatment program were irrelevant considerations. Accordingly, the tribunal rejected the complaint.

The foregoing case draws attention not only to the complexities involved in alcohol-related cases but, more generally, to the problems of fair assessment in instances involving multiple minority status. It also reveals, once again, the weakness of protections offered under unspecified (implicit) grounds such as 'social condition,' which are open to varying, subjective interpretations (in this case, by two separate judicial bodies, the QHRC and the superior court tribunal). All of these points, in my view, reinforce the argument for *explicit* human-rights protections under the enumerated grounds of non-discrimination in legal instruments.

The limits of the case-by-case approach to human rights

The cases addressed in the foregoing pages represent examples of personal complaints of discrimination brought forward to human-rights commissions by individual members of stigmatized minorities or by others acting on their behalf. This case-by-case method of redressing human-rights violations is designed to provide remedies for individual complainants against individual and institutional forms of discrimination. However, it is not designed to provide redress for the long-term, *collective* disadvantages suffered by minorities, *as collectivities*, as a result of systemic or structural discrimination. Strategies for change, designed to afford collective redress against the adverse impact of structural discrimination upon minorities as entire entities, will provide the focus of the analysis in the section to follow.

Beyond case-by-case remedies: the need for affirmative action

Systemic discrimination and its effects
In the last decade there has been a marked increase in public awareness and understanding of the damaging effects of systemic or structural discrimination on Canadian minorities *as collectivities*. This mounting recognition of the pervasive discriminatory effects of long-term inequality of opportunity on *whole* categories of people, as opposed to on single individuals, has had an important impact on human-rights legislation. At the most fundamental level, it has led to an expansion of the legal definition of discrimination.

Until the 1970s, in legal terms discrimination tended to be equated with isolated acts, motivated by prejudice (individual discrimination). Yet, the cumulative experience of Canada's various human-rights commissions in administering anti-discriminatory legislation over the years was demonstrating beyond doubt that the most pervasive discrimination often results from unconscious, seemingly neutral practices and unexamined traditions that have become embedded, even unintentionally, in the everyday operations of employment, education, and other social institutions (systemic or structural discrimination). Human-rights commissioners, practitioners, and lawmakers alike increasingly have come to realize that systemic forms of discrimination impact adversely upon minorities as entire groups, and thereby guarantee the preservation through time of their collective, disadvantaged minority status (self-fulfilling prophecy). Accordingly, human-rights legislation no longer defines discrimination simply as individual acts; nor does it identify discrimination simply by intent or motive (prejudice). Increasingly, anti-discriminatory legislation defines discrimination as systemic, and identifies it by collective adverse impact.

Section 15 of the Charter of Rights and Freedoms (CRF) in the Canadian constitution (1982) not only prohibits individual discrimination but also recognizes the validity of laws, programs, or activities designed to ameliorate the disadvantaged conditions of individuals or groups. Section 15(2) guarantees that affirmative-action programs designed by federal and provincial agencies to provide forms of collective redress against the adverse impact of systemic discrimination upon disadvantaged (minority) groups will be allowed. This guarantee provided by Section 15(2) of the CRF is imperative in order to ensure that special measures of affirmative action will not constitute 'reverse discrimination' under the non-discriminatory provision of Section 15(1).

Following the guideline afforded by Section 15(2) of the Charter, human-rights codes across Canada's various jurisdictions have increasingly incorporated provisions allowing for programs of affirmative action. In the broader North American context, affirmative-action programs and legislation operate throughout both Canada and the United States. The major difference between the Canadian and u.s. experience lies in the mandate of the regulatory agencies. In the United States, affirmative action is compulsory; in Canada (as yet) it is voluntary.[5]

Systemic discrimination and adverse impact: discussion

The concepts of *systemic discrimination* and *adverse impact*, now articulated in law, are well illustrated in the matter of accessibility to services in the case of disabled persons. Inaccessibility of buildings and transportation systems has an *adverse impact* on a whole class of mobility-disabled persons. Yet, there is little or no evidence to show that such an effect was intended. That is to say, the designers of buildings and transportation systems did not intentionally make them inaccessible to mobility-impaired persons in order to exclude members of this minority group. Nevertheless, the collective effect of many traditional architectural designs is to exclude them, and that *effect* is now held to be discriminatory (Saskatchewan Human Rights Commission [SHRC] *Newsletter*, IX/1, January/February 1980). Structural discrimination, through long-term inaccessibility to institutions of education, work places, and employment offices, prevents mobility-impaired minority members from acquiring and/or using skills through which they could contribute to society as participating citizens. As a result, they become categorically and *systemically* economically disadvantaged and dependent on welfare handouts (self-fulfilling prophecy). Thus, as a *social category*, the disabled become locked out of the productive economic life of the society and locked into their dependent-minority status.

The mechanism that has been developed to provide immediate, group-level redress against the collective, disadvantaging, long-term

5 The 1984 Report of the Royal Commission on Equality in Employment, headed by Judge Rosalie Abella, strongly recommended that all federally regulated employers be required by legislation to implement 'employment equity' (affirmative-action programs) for four target populations: women, disabled persons, aboriginal peoples, and visible minorities. This recommendation for *mandatory* affirmative action was not wholeheartedly endorsed by the federal government and has not, as yet, been implemented.

effects of systemic discrimination on minority categories is called 'affirmative action.'

The rhetoric of affirmative action

Glaser and Possony (1979: 24) interpret the concept of affirmative action as a system of positive discrimination in favour of collectivities hitherto discriminated against; compensatory discrimination in favour of disadvantaged collectivities in the society (ibid: 57).

Programs of affirmative action may be instituted in response to three kinds of minority claims based on categorical rights: 1 / claims for *temporary compensatory* treatment because of *institutional* discrimination; 2 / claims for *temporary compensatory* treatment because of *structural discrimination*; and 3 / claims for *permanent compensatory* treatment because of institutional and structural discrimination, and taking into account *special needs*, previously neglected.

The first kind of claim applies in cases where an *equally* or *better* qualified applicant is rejected in favour of another applicant for a given position because of institutional discrimination against members of his or her minority group.

These claims represent the kinds of cases typically brought before human-rights commissions. While individual cases can be dealt with by such commissions, the larger problem of *collective* disadvantage because of institutional discrimination against particular minorities, at the group level, is not addressed. It is this larger problem that affirmative action seeks to remedy by temporary programs designed to achieve proportionate representation of minorities at all positional levels. The long-range goal of such programs is *equal* (standard) treatment. That is to say, once proportionate representation of designated minorities is achieved, the individual-merit principle applies equally to all.

The second kind of claim applies in cases predicated on structural or systemic discrimination where minority victims of the self-fulfilling prophecy of stigmatization lack the requisite qualifications and skills with which to compete in the Canadian educational or job market. What are required here are programs of affirmative action that provide special education and job training. Minorities whose members have long been denied educational and training opportunities accorded majority Canadians need 'catching up' programs designed to provide them with a level of qualifications and skills equal to that of their majority counterparts.

Such programs rest on claims for *temporary* (compensatory) treatment. However, as is the case for the first kind of claim addressed, the long-range goal is one of equal (standard) treatment. Once minorities have acquired a level of skills equal to that of majority Canadians, the individual-merit principle applies equally to all.

The third kind of claim applies in cases of institutional and structural discrimination where equal (standard) treatment is inappropriate, even as a long-range goal, because of the permanent, handicapping effects of an authentic mental or physical disability. In these cases, affirmative-action programs, in addition to providing immediate redress against institutional and/or structural forms of discrimination, where appropriate, also must provide permanent, compensatory mechanisms. Accommodation of the special needs of the disabled may require permanent architectural modifications to buildings, provision of medical and technological aids, parallel transportation services, and/or other adjustments to existing institutional arrangements, all of which are specifically designed to reduce or to overcome the handicapping effects of particular disabilities. The long-range goal of such programs is to achieve *equivalence* of treatment, through the provision of *permanent* compensatory devices, rather than to achieve a goal of equality based upon sameness or standard treatment for all. In the case of disabled persons, the merit principle cannot be fairly applied unless compensatory devices are put in place, for standard treatment (unadapted buildings, lack of special aids) indirectly discriminates against disabled minorities.

Affirmative action: majority response to categorical minority claims
The fact that a great many historical traditions and public practices embedded in the everyday operations of Canadian public institutions have had and continue to have an adverse impact on whole categories of people clearly demonstrates the need for *intervention*, if these minorities are to enjoy *in fact* the equality promised by human-rights legislation. Even if all minorities were to be afforded explicit protection under the enumerated grounds of non-discriminatory legislation, only future non-discrimination would be assured; no remedies for past human-rights violations would be provided. The strategy of intervention that has been developed in the last decade both to counteract and to provide immediate redress for the disadvantaging effects of systemic discrimination is that of affirmative action.

Affirmative action is a method for identifying and eliminating systemic practices that act as barriers to equality of opportunity across different population categories. It also is a method for assisting minority victims of systemic discrimination to overcome its long-term disadvantaging effects, through the provision of special measures. Both of these components (elimination of discriminatory practices and provision of special measures) are deemed necessary in order for affirmative-action programs to be effective (SHRC *Newsletter*, IX/2, March/April 1980).

Identification of practices of systemic discrimination

In the area of employment, a number of systemic practices have been identified as barriers to equality of opportunity for aboriginal peoples, women, non-whites and disabled persons. For example, 'old-boys' networks' among white males have been found to provide convenient channels for word-of-mouth job recruitment in some employment sectors, ensuring that knowledge of job vacancies is confined to the in-group. Women and non-whites are thereby excluded. It should be noted, here, that insofar as such employment grapevines are controlled by *heterosexual* insiders, gay men as well as lesbian women are also among the minority groups excluded.

Another systemic barrier is that imposed by inaccessibility to work sites, employment centres, and educational institutions, which prevents persons with mobility disabilities from obtaining the qualifications for jobs and/or from working at jobs for which they are fully qualified.

Additionally, inflated or non–job-related requirements have been found to pose systemic barriers for some minorities. Inflated educational requirements serve to bar competent (but poorly educated) aboriginal peoples as well as some classes of competent mentally retarded persons.

Finally, certain non-essential height and weight standards have been found to discriminate against women, some ethnic minorities, and aboriginal peoples (SHRC, 1980).

Public education: practices of omission and commission

In the area of education, systemic barriers can discriminate against particular minorities by practices of omission or commission. For example, a number of research studies (Barrie, 1982) have identified sex-stereotyping of occupational roles (commission), while others (McDiarmid and Pratt, 1974) have revealed the absence of materials dealing with aboriginal peoples' languages, cultures, and histories in standard course curricula (omission).

The reader should easily be able to identify other, similar discriminatory practices. For example, with specific regard to the minorities focused upon in this book, one could point to omission in the area of sex education, noting that what really is taught is *heterosexual* sex.[6] Again, one could point to omission in the area of physical education, noting that standard programs are only for the able-bodied. With regard to commission, it might be suggested that the stereotypes of the wife-beating, car-wrecking alcoholic and the stumble-bum skid-row alcoholic are vividly reinforced through the very educational techniques used to *prevent* alcoholism, namely, the employment of forceful media images. Regarding omission, one might ask: does public education, anywhere in Canada, provide factual information on the alcoholic minority or on the recovering/recovered alcoholic?

Public education: rooting out prejudice

It has been argued previously that *legislation* is needed to combat and eradicate acts of discrimination. In this section, I will argue that *education* is needed to counteract and eradicate the ideas and attitudes of prejudice that lie behind them.

To meet any kind of reasonable goals, public education must be based on accurate, up-to-date information; hence adequate resources must be allocated to fund research projects designed to provide such information. Further, unless potential victims are informed about human-rights principles, legislation, and investigative and conciliation procedures, they may well be unaware of the help available to them in an instance of discrimination. Hence, there is a need for much greater publicization of human-rights materials, including codes, cases, decisions, and so on, as well as the findings of research studies on human-rights issues.

6 In this connection, the reader might note a (1986) decision of the Toronto Board of Education, taken before the December 1986 enactment of the amendment to the Ontario Human Rights Code, which includes sexual orientation among the enumerated grounds of non-discrimination. Allegedly in response to the mandate of the equality-rights provision of the CRF, as well as to the recent, brutal murder of a homosexual Toronto school librarian by high-school students out to 'beat up a fag,' the board decided to take steps to combat teenage heterosexism. They voted to implement a series of measures within the school system to combat discrimination against gay and lesbian students. Measures included the development of a curriculum dealing with sexual orientation and programs to sensitize students to the human rights of homosexuals. Ironically, in light of the then pending amendment to the provincial Code, the one proposed measure that was defeated (by a tied vote) called for the prohibition of discrimination on the basis of sexual orientation to be part of board policy (CHRA, II 6, June 1986).

Probably the most glaring case of *omission* in this area lies in the neglect of formal instruction about human rights in the curricula of public-education institutions in this country. It is essential that textbooks, at all educational levels, be reviewed regularly for errors of omission and commission so as to ensure that they accurately reflect the historical and contemporary character and conditions of Canada's minority groups. Similarly, school facilities, programs, and guidance counselling need to be brought into line with human-rights principles. They must be based on equity of access and equity of opportunity for all. The latter point draws attention to the importance of teacher training in the area of human rights. At present, however, this represents another large lacuna in human-rights education throughout Canada.

Special measures: active recruitment and training programs

The objective of special affirmative-action programs is to create a more equitable distribution of opportunities and benefits across diverse social and cultural groups in Canada. Towards this end such measures as active recruitment and hiring strategies already have been undertaken by various governments and private bodies to move qualified aboriginal peoples, women, and physically disabled persons into labour-force positions that they have previously been prevented from attaining.

Another special measure already undertaken at various levels of government is training programs, designed to equip members of long-disadvantaged minorities with skills and qualifications previously unavailable to them.

Planning for affirmative action

In both employment and education – the two key areas in which affirmative-action programs have been developed – the planning of special programs involves, at the outset, the establishment of a measuring structure and the specification of goals and of timetables to meet specified goals. The measuring structure is designed to ascertain, on a statistical basis, the distribution of opportunities and associated benefits across the various population groups in the relevant locale (society, region, organization, etc.). Once identification of group disadvantage has been established, corrective action is undertaken through programs designed to redress the identified disadvantaged condition of the target population(s).

The following example may serve to illustrate the way in which this process operates in practice.

In 1981, approval was granted to the Saskatchewan Piping Industry Joint Training Board to implement a special training program in the North that would increase the number of men and women of Indian ancestry in the plumbing and pipefitting trade. Evidence was provided to show that persons of Indian ancestry composed 11.5 per cent to 14.7 per cent of the working-age population. Statistics revealed that of the 512 journeymen in the pipe trades in Saskatchewan, 9 (1.74 per cent) were persons of Indian ancestry. These data clearly demonstrated an underrepresentation of approximately 13 per cent, which supported the need for a special program in the plumbing and pipefitting industry. The program was designed to recruit 30 men and women of Indian ancestry each year into the pipe-trades apprenticeship program. It was estimated that by 1989, 14 per cent of the apprentices would be persons of Indian ancestry.

The statement of approval of the program also established specific conditions to ensure that measures be taken to gain a further understanding of 'physical disability,' with a view to the potential recruitment of disabled persons of Indian ancestry into this new program (BCHRC, *Newsletter*, IV/4, Spring 1983).

Contract compliance: an alternative to voluntary affirmative action

One of the alternatives to voluntary affirmative action already in use by the federal and some provincial governments is 'contract compliance.' What this means is that an employer must have an affirmative-action program in place in order to be a successful bidder for a government contract. The Government of Saskatchewan, for example, has done this with AMOK, making the employment of a fixed percentage of Northerners a condition of the surface lease that allows the company to mine at Cluff Lake. Flin Flon Mines and Key Lake Mining Corporation have similar requirements tied to their surface leases (BCHRC, 1983).

Contract compliance, under the regulations of human-rights legislation, clearly provides more forceful leverage for affirmative action than does 'permissive' legislation simply *allowing* voluntary programs.

One example of human-rights compliance regulations is provided by Section 19 of the Canadian Human Rights Act, which gives the Government of Canada the power to make regulations providing for the placing of terms and conditions relating to anti-discrimination in contracts, grants, or licences from the federal government. Under such regulations, organizations would be *required* to comply with the affirmative-action provisions of the Canadian Human Rights Act (s. 9–15).

AFFIRMATIVE ACTION AND HUMAN RIGHTS IN THE 1980s[7]

Despite some variation in the scope of human-rights legislation and in the powers of different commissions, human-rights legislation in Canada is largely permissive, rather than prescriptive. Section 15.2 of the Constitutional CRF, and parallel legislation throughout the country, *permit* affirmative action by stating that it is not a discriminatory practice to implement special programs for (minority) groups disadvantaged through the effects of systemic discrimination.

While legislation is essentially permissive, federal and provincial governments increasingly have gone on record in favour of affirmative action. The constitutional sanction for affirmative action, given by its incorporation within the CRF, makes Canada one of the few countries in the world where programs of affirmative action, including special measures, have gained status recognition under the provisions of the supreme law of the land.

These positive accomplishments notwithstanding, when it comes to assessing the concrete results of voluntary affirmative-action programs, their inherent weakness comes to the fore.

For more than a decade, the federal government has been actively promoting voluntary affirmative-action programs through the Affirmative Action Division of the Canada Employment and Immigration Commission. Since 1979 that division has made contact with approximately nine hundred employers across Canada – employers in federally and provincially regulated industries, or those having contracts with the federal government. Yet, of the nine hundred firms, only thirty-four have instituted voluntary affirmative-action agreements with the Canada Employment and Immigration Commission.

Accordingly, despite the government's commitment to affirmative action, as late as 1982, the Public Service Commission's Annual Report said that women make up only 4.3 per cent of the management ranks of the civil service, while they hold 81.6 per cent of the administrative

7 Data for this section were excerpted from a keynote seminar address given by Gordon Fairweather, then chief commissioner of the Canadian Human Rights Commission, in March 1983, and published in the Saskatchewan Human Rights Commission *Newsletter* (*XII*, 1, March/April 1983).

support jobs. The number of women in the administrative support category increased by 1 per cent from 1980 to 1981, while the number of women in the management groups increased by 0.2 per cent from 1980 to 1981. The inferior position of women compared to men in the public service is also reflected in their salaries. Seventy per cent of the women in the public service earned less than $20,000 in 1981 while only 28 per cent of the men earned under $20,000.

At the provincial level, we may look at Ontario, which heralds its affirmative action in the civil service as a model for its voluntary private-sector program. Ontario's civil-service program had its roots in 1973 as a 'women into management' plan. After ten years, however, 58 per cent of the female civil service in the province is still in the traditional women's office and clerical categories. In maintenance, there are 189 women, compared to 6,180 men; in technical services, there are 729 women and 4,546 men.

In Ontario, again, there are about 266,000 companies in the private sector; yet only 0.053 per cent of them have affirmative-action programs. These examples are paralleled throughout the country.

The general picture, in all regions of Canada, reveals that while employers may have expressed an interest in actively complying with affirmative-action provisions, few have voluntarily initiated programs of affirmative action. At best, it appears that the voluntary approach is working with exceeding slowness and the results remain obscure.

MANDATORY AFFIRMATIVE ACTION:
RED HERRING OR AN OPTION FOR THE FUTURE?

Before I undertake a consideration of the policy option of mandatory affirmative action in Canada, it is important to address the basic issues that have plagued the controversy surrounding the policies and programs of mandatory affirmative action in the United States, since their inception twenty years ago.

The issues in the debate involve discussion at two levels: the level of ideology and the level of public practice.

The ideological debate focuses on the meritocracy principle and on the contradictions to this principle posed by programs of affirmative action. Weinfeld (1981) suggests that Canadian principles of affirmative action as bases for policy-making largely have followed the American model. These principles, he points out, have involved a threefold shift in policy emphasis regarding human rights:

1 a shift from an emphasis on individual discrimination to an emphasis on institutional and structural discrimination;

2 a shift from an emphasis on individual rights to an emphasis on collective rights (which involved a shift from the individual merit principle to a modified merit principle qualified by differential cultural considerations); and

3 a shift towards the employment of statistical indicators of proportionate underrepresentation of population categories as a measure of group inequality (categorical rights). Underrepresentation of social categories in various positions and at various positional levels was taken as indicative of structural discrimination necessitating redress through affirmative-action programs.

At the level of ideology, the first issue to be addressed in relation to the meritocracy principle is that of the legitimacy of collective redress against the adverse impact of systemic discrimination (categorical rights claims). Opponents argue that when compensation is offered to groups (rather than to individual complainants) it is because of some collective characteristic (disadvantage) members (assumedly) share, not because of demonstrable evidence that, as *individuals*, they were victims of discrimination. Affirmative-action programs accordingly are open to criticism on the ground that evidence has not been provided to show that all minority members have been (equally) subject to structural discrimination. The possibility exists, therefore, that some minority members without need of affirmative-action programs may be unjustly advantaged by them.

Opponents of affirmative action, such as the late sociologist John Porter (1980), have argued that American-style affirmative action, with its imposition of quotas for minorities, represents a retreat from the dogmas of universalism, the protection of individual rights, and the merit principle – the fundamental democratic principles behind North American society. Porter (ibid) suggests further that affirmative action may have an effect that is opposite to its intention, namely, to force individual minority members to identify, perhaps unwillingly, with their minority collectivity, thus crystallizing the subordinate status of the group and *reducing* its members' prospects for upward mobility.

At the level of public practice, critics argue that problems in determining the extent of group disadvantage caused by structural discrimination are manifold (see especially, Block and Walker, 1981). For example, critics point out that it cannot be safely assumed that in every situation where disproportionate group representation (or underrepresentation) exists it is the result of structural discrimination. For, even without systemic discrimination, it is unlikely that a random distribution of different groups would be evident in various sectors of society. Clearly, other variables, such as education, religion, and place of residence, can affect differential outcomes for both individuals and groups. Therefore, before affirmative-action programs can be deemed appropriate measures of redress, research must be conducted to identify all the causes of disproportionate representation of minorities within Canadian societal sectors and institutions.

Another set of issues, arising from the u.s. experience with mandatory affirmative-action programs, relates to their unintended, harmful, psycho-social consequences. Such programs have been perceived to have negative effects on the self-image of the minority participants and on the quality of intergroup relations. With regard to the first point, opponents of affirmative action have argued that minority participants in these programs are deprived of the feeling of self-worth and accomplishment that comes from achieving one's social position through one's own merit. As there will almost inevitably be some members of any minority target group who have achieved parallel social positions on their own merit, those members given 'special treatment' may come to see themselves as less worthy, less meritorious, than those have made it on their own.

The other side of the coin of 'special treatment' lies in its potentially negative repercussions on individuals and groups who do not receive such benefits. Both minority and majority members excluded from or by affirmative-action programs may harbour resentment towards minority participants and may feel that they have been discriminated against. The u.s. experience reveals that co-workers and fellow students in the institutional settings where affirmative-action programs have been put in place have tended to look down upon minority participants and to see them as less meritorious than themselves. These attitudes, in turn, have reinforced the negative self-image(s) of the minority participants.

Finally, in the cases where unqualified or less-qualified minority participants are selected for an affirmative-action program (in the u.s. experience, in order to fill arbitrary quotas) the outcome, in many cases, has been the failure of the participant to fulfil the objectives of the program. The negative consequences of failure have been psychologically devastating for the participant, in many instances. In these particular cases, which represent an abuse of the goals of affirmative action, hostile majority backlash has been all but inevitable. The failure of minority members has rendered these programs counterproductive: they have served to reinforce and 'justify' stereotypes of minority inferiority.

In light of the u.s. experience, Glaser and Possony (1979: 325) argue that the mounting injustice not only to victims of 'reverse discrimination' but even to the beneficiaries of positive programs under policies of mandatory affirmative action renders them inappropriate as a means of achieving equality of opportunity for minorities.

Other critics (Block and Walker, 1981) adopt a more positive, yet cautionary approach towards mandatory affirmative-action programs in Canada. Some support the view that small pilot projects should be initiated and should be tested for costs and benefits before large-scale affirmative-action programs are put in place. A major reason behind this cautionary approach is that costs of mandatory affirmative-action programs would be borne largely by the taxpayer, through public funding. Before public resources are formally allocated, it is argued, taxpayers should be able to have a reasonable expectation of demonstrable social benefits from mandatory affirmative-action programs.

Mandatory affirmative action: pros and cons/costs and benefits

Opponents of mandatory affirmative action have argued against this policy option on both ideological and practical grounds. Ideologically speaking, critics have argued that special measures of *collective redress* against the adverse impact of systemic discrimination upon minorities as a whole offend one of the most fundamental principles of North American democratic society, the individualistic principle of meritocracy.

From a practical view, two routine arguments have been raised against legislating mandatory affirmative action in Canada: first, the financial cost and difficulties of implementation of programs, and second, the alleged negative results of such legislation in the United States.

The financial cost of affirmative action, I will argue, must be weighed against the tremendous social costs of maintaining the status quo: the cost of systemic discrimination is demonstrably greater than the expense of redressing historic wrongs. In financial terms alone, Canadians pay very high welfare costs when employers categorically exclude various minorities from employment, not to mention the concomitant costs of poor human-resources planning and utilization. Accordingly, the Canadian economy suffers when women, the disabled, and other minorities are categorically excluded from various sectors of the work force.

As regards the second point, in the United States the implementation of mandatory affirmative action has not produced uniformly negative results as its critics are prone to suggest. It has met mixed reactions and has generated vigorous debate. A particular target of attack has been the negative consequences of the imposition of compulsory 'quotas' designed to increase the representation of particular minorities in the employment and education sectors. As alluded to earlier, in order to fill arbitrary quotas, unqualified or underqualified minority members were accepted in many instances (see Kallen, 1982: 234–40).

In the Canadian case, what must be considered at the outset is that Canada's legal, social, and economic situation is very different from that of the United States. Moreover, Canadians are at present in a position to learn from the *cumulative* American experience. The negative results of early, affirmative-action programs with imposed quotas led to marked policy changes in the United States, favouring the setting of 'reasonable goals.' Canada's voluntary affirmative-action programs have followed this later course, rather than the earlier quota system, and also have adopted monitored recruitment, hiring, and promotion strategies in order to reach projected goals. Most important, Canada's emphasis has been on education and training programs designed to assist target minority populations in the attainment of trade skills and professional certification that will provide them with legitimate qualifications for jobs. In this way, some of the major problems encountered south of the border, specifically the filling of educational and occupational 'quotas' with *unqualified* or *underqualified* minority members, have been circumvented.

BEYOND AFFIRMATIVE ACTION: COMMUNITY ADVOCACY FOR MINORITY RIGHTS

The human-rights provisions of constitutional and statutory law, together with policies and programs of affirmative action, are designed to eliminate institutional and systemic forms of discrimination, to remedy the disadvantaging effects of past discrimination, and to ensure the equitable representation of minority members as full participants in all sectors of public life.

Yet, all of these human-rights–oriented measures cannot guarantee that the minority rights of Canada's stigmatized populations will be recognized and respected in everyday public practice.

In order to identify human-rights issues as they affect all minority groups, in all areas of the country, it is incumbent upon citizens' groups, non-governmental organizations, coalitions of interested groups, and the like, to undertake programs of community advocacy. Initiatives for such programs may be taken by human-rights commissions by setting up public meetings and by establishing liaison mechanisms with majority and minority organizations, but the identification of specific minority needs, and the development of objectives and programs designed to meet those needs, should not be imposed by outside (majority) agencies or bodies. The identification of needs and issues, and of the mechanisms for meeting and resolving them, should stem from the will and the decision of the *minority collectivity*. This strategy recognizes and respects the right of each minority group to determine its own collective destiny.

Where citizens' organizations composed of interested majority members can play a significant part is in the area of community advocacy. This is not to suggest that minority groups abandon their burden of self-advocacy. Insofar as they seek to become self-determining entities, minorities themselves must come out of the closet and assume the tasks of public education, lobbying, and so forth, in co-operation with majority sympathizers. It goes without saying, however, that minority collectivities differ markedly in their internal resources and in their members' ability to promote their own collective cause; thus, the scope of the role played by (majority) community advocacy groups will vary with the particular minority or minorities served.

For example, in the cases of very young children, severely mentally or physically disabled persons, and the institutionalized elderly, community advocacy may be essential if the rights of these minorities, who cannot forcefully speak for themselves, by themselves, are to be recognized and protected. In all of these cases, advocacy groups across Canada have been established to vocalize minority members' expressed needs and concerns and to seek ways and means of addressing them.

Concerned Friends of Ontario Citizens in Care Facilities (CFOCCF), established some seven years ago, is a non-funded, entirely volunteer-staffed organization of over five hundred members that operates on the mandate: *Residents First*. This community advocacy group maintains a 'watchdog approach,' when permitted, in Ontario's nursing homes. Because nursing homes in the private sector are deemed private property, some owners and administrators have barred CFOCCF members from their premises. In CFOCCF's view, this restriction constitutes a direct violation of paying residents' right to access to advocates who speak out against any practices within the home that violate their human rights (CHRA, II/3, March 1986). CFOCCF uses the media to draw public attention to human-rights abuses such as proposed drug experimentation on the elderly incompetent, the dehumanizing use of restraints and medication as controlling mechanisms on nursing-home residents, laxity in meeting hygienic requirements, and costs cut to the point of inadequacy in the area of nutrition. With regard to last named, it was to CFOCCF that information was leaked of a budgetary expenditure of less than $2 per day per resident for food in one private nursing home (ibid: 13).

As well as maintaining a vigilant presence in Ontario's nursing homes, CFOCCF members also are engaged in working for reform in public policy and legislation in order to improve protection for the minority rights of the institutionalized elderly and other vulnerable people. During 1986, CFOCCF compiled a list of over one thousand complaints of abuse and neglect of the elderly in Ontario institutions. In some cases, documented abuses carried allegations that could involve offences under the Criminal Code. The CFOCCF is lobbying for the enforcement of criminal charges against anyone who abuses institutionalized elderly persons through assault, theft, negligence, and restraining procedures.

In light of the appalling documentation of human-rights violations of the institutionalized elderly amassed by the CFOCCF, members of the organization identified a pressing need for an advocacy system to assist vunerable people who, because of their age and/or disability, are less able to secure for themselves their full entitlements as citizens. Based on the group's wealth of experience and their research into systems elsewhere, the CFOCCF submitted to the attorney general of Ontario a proposal to establish *Advocacy Ontario*. This proposal provided the impetus for the *Review of Advocacy for Vulnerable Adults*, chaired by the Reverend Sean O'Sullivan, whose recent (September 1987) report, *You've Got A Friend*, recommends an advocacy system for Ontario (*Concerned Friends*, No. xix, Autumn 1987).

The concept of advocacy in the O'Sullivan report is 'non-legal' or *social advocacy*. An advocate would advise the client and assist him or her to decide upon the best course of action and would pursue that course with vigour and commitment. *Individual advocacy* would be undertaken on behalf of a person. *Systemic advocacy* would be undertaken to effect reforms in the systems and government that affect many people. The vulnerable people for whom advocacy services are needed include 'frail elderly, physically handicapped, psychiatrically disabled, and developmentally handicapped persons,' people with some type of physical, emotional, or cognitive impairment, whether they reside in the community or in institutions (*Concerned Friends*, Autumn 1987: 1).

It is interesting to note, at this juncture, that as the process of lobbying for an advocacy system progressed, the identified target population expanded from an initial, narrow focus on the institutionalized elderly to include a broad spectrum of age- and disability-related minorities, within and outside of institutional confines.

The O'Sullivan report recommended that the Province of Ontario set up an independent commission to help train and certify volunteers and to be responsible for seven regional offices, staffed by civil servants, that would co-ordinate the advocacy efforts of these volunteers and community groups. This network of voluntary advocates (volunteers and community groups) would speak up for vulnerable people, expressing their concerns to governments and institutions through sustained lobbying efforts. The immediate goals of the advocacy network would be to empower vulnerable people to take charge of their own lives, and to ensure that their human rights were fully protected.

O'Sullivan's report was welcomed by advocacy groups such as the CFOCCF and the Advocacy Resource Centre for the Handicapped (ARCH), but with a few pointed reservations. The CFOCCF expressed concern that the model relies too heavily on volunteers, with insufficient professional support. They also criticized the recommendation that regional offices be operated by a community-elected board of directors, the majority of whom would be consumer representatives. In response, they argued that 60 per cent of board members should be consumers or advocates, and that persons affiliated with organizations providing services to consumers should be excluded from the board because of conflict of interest. ARCH criticized the O'Sullivan model for not going far enough on the vital issue of consumer control. They responded with the assertion that a majority of primary consumers *must* be on both the Provincial Advocacy Commission and regional boards (CHRA, III/10, November 1987). Despite the reservations noted, both advocacy groups are vigorously lobbying the Ontario government to take action to implement the report.

Before concluding this discussion of community advocacy for vulnerable minorities, an important consideration needs to be addressed, that of economic disadvantage. Minority groups lacking in economic resources (children, skid-row alcoholics, the institutionalized disabled, and the elderly) lack the necessary means with which to begin to organize on their own behalf. Here, community advocacy is essential in order to lobby effectively for the provision of economic resources out of public funds. In order to bring about equivalence of economic maintenance across differentially disadvantaged minorities, the equivalent allocation of public resources must be secured.

In this context, the fundamental right of self-determination (freedom to decide) might best be interpreted as the collective right of the minority as a whole to designate those areas of need where resource allocation from public funds is deemed essential. For the physically disabled minority, architectural modifications to transport and building facilities as well as medical and technological aids may assume priority; for other minorities, such as recovering alcoholics, or gays and lesbians, public-information campaigns designed to destigmatize the public image of the minority and to accord legitimacy to its members' alternative life-styles may assume priority. Whatever the area of need pinpointed as essential *by the minority group*, it is essential that public resources be distributed equitably if the long-range goal is to ensure equivalence of opportunity and equal respect for human dignity across minority collectivities.

To recapitulate, community-advocacy systems designed to promote recognition and protection of minority rights must address two major tasks: public education (to reduce prejudice) and legislative/policy change (to eradicate discrimination). While the education and public-relations mandate of Canada's human-rights commissions encourages the promotion of human rights through various programs and activities, in practice this mandate can be ineffectual if it is pursued 'in a vacuum' (BCHRC, *Newsletter*, IV/2, Fall 1982). Human-rights commissioners cannot always be aware of the myriad concerns of the whole spectrum of minority groups within their area of jurisdiction. The role of minority advocates in identifying and articulating minority concerns to human-rights commissioners and other authoritative bodies is thus a critical one.

With regard to legislative change, community advocates must vigorously pursue legislative changes designed to secure *explicit* protections for minority rights through the enactment of *specified* constitutional and legal provisions recognizing both the individual and collective rights of minorities. It is in the latter area that we find the most glaring omission in Canada's current, constitutional CRF and in parallel, statutory provisions.

CONCLUDING COMMENTS

To protect minority rights fully, across Canada, strategies for change need to be formulated and implemented in all relevant societal spheres: legislation, public policy, and public practice. Chart 3 schematizes the areas in which protections for minority rights must be addressed.

At the time of writing, the real impact of Canada's constitutional CRF (with or without the anticipated effects of the MLA upon its minority-rights provisions) remains to be demonstrated. While the Constitution Act became law in April 1982, it was not until April 1985 that the equality-rights provisions of Section 15 of the CRF came into legal effect. Accordingly, cases brought forward under the provisions of Section 15 only recently are beginning to emerge. At the time of writing, two court

CHART 3 Promoting minority rights in Canada

LAW

Constitution CRF
Statutory Legislation
• enumeration of minority status criterion: protections at individual and group
  levels

PUBLIC POLICY

• non-discrimination
• affirmative action
• compensation for authentic disabilities
• equitable distribution of resources across minorities

PUBLIC PRACTICE

• minority self-advocacy
• community advocacy
• human-rights coalitions
• liaison with human-rights commissions

PUBLIC ATTITUDES

• public information
• public education at all levels
• elimination of negative stereotypes, prejudiced language, and labels from all
  forms of public communication

challenges under Section 15 of the Charter, both involving alleged
discrimination on the grounds of sexual orientation in federal-government
employment (Department of National Defence and Royal Canadian
Mounted Police), are being funded by the Court Challenges Program of
the Canadian Council on Social Development (CHRA, III/3, March 1987).
   The extent to which federal and provincial jurisdictions will bring their
existing non-discriminatory legislation into line with the CRF provisions is
yet an open question. In this connection, an important task for community-
advocacy groups would be to lobby their provincial governments to
dissociate themselves officially from the 'opting out' provision of the CRF
(under Section 33).

Yet, even if the human-rights principles constitutionally entrenched in the CRF are endorsed throughout the nation, what this book has attempted to demonstrate is that until such an endorsement is accompanied by parallel changes in public attitudes, policies, and practices, the full recognition of the minority rights of stigmatized populations in Canada will remain a 'dream deferred.'

In closing, I express the hope that governments, community-advocacy groups, and minorities themselves will continue to formulate and to press for the adoption of measures of social change designed to ensure the recognition and protection of the individual and collective rights of all minorities, in law, in policy, and in practice, throughout the Canadian state.

Addendum:
Suggestions for future research

My investigation, in preparation for this book, revealed clearly that further research is needed in two main areas: the experience of stigma (in the closet) and the process of coming out (out of the closet). Current theorizing and explanatory models in the labelling, ethnic-relations, and social-movements literature have been well developed to account for the processes of becoming a minority (going into the closet) and the evolution of minority protest (contention and revitalization movements). The transitional processes between these phenomena, however, need further investigation and explication.

A real scholarly lacuna exists in the explanation of the social-psychological impact of stigmatization and ostracization on the individual bearer of stigma and on the stigmatized minority as a social collectivity. Before cogent models can be developed in this area, it is imperative that empirical research studies be conducted among members of stigmatized minorities and within organized aspects of minority communities. Because of the highly sensitive nature of such research, it is crucial that investigators respect the right to privacy of respondents through ensuring strict confidentiality of data and through maintaining full accountability to minority respondents and communities.

Another glaring lacuna that remains is in the exegesis of the social and social-psychological processes involved in coming out of the closet. Here, the literature on the homosexual minority provides seminal models that are well developed to explain the nature of coming out of the *invisible closet*. Parallel models, designed to explain the psycho-social ramifications of coming out of the *institutional closet* (prison, psychiatric hospital, home for the disabled, and the like), are not as well developed. The literature on the process of deinstitutionalization provides an appropriate beginning for analysis, but, again, empirical research is needed in order fully to explicate and document the nature of the coming-out experience for formerly institutionalized minority members.

In this book, I have conceptualized the entire sequence of social processes implicated in going into and coming out of the closet of stigma in terms of a human-rights–oriented framework. It is hoped that future scholars working in this area will utilize this scheme in their analyses and will build upon and refine the conceptual design.

Universal Declaration of Human Rights

Adopted and proclaimed by United Nations General Assembly resolution 217 A (III) of 10 December 1948

PREAMBLE

Whereas recognition of the inherent dignity and of the equal and inalienable rights of all members of the human family is the foundation of freedom, justice and peace in the world,

Whereas disregard and contempt for human rights have resulted in barbarous acts which have outraged the conscience of mankind, and the advent of a world in which human beings shall enjoy freedom of speech and belief and freedom from fear and want has been proclaimed as the highest aspiration of the common people,

Whereas it is essential, if man is not to be compelled to have recourse, as a last resort, to rebellion against tyranny and oppression, that human rights should be protected by the rule of law,

Whereas it is essential to promote the development of friendly relations between nations,

Whereas the peoples of the United Nations have in the Charter reaffirmed their faith in fundamental human rights, in the dignity and worth of the human person and in the equal rights of men and women and have determined to promote social progress and better standards of life in larger freedom,

Whereas Member States have pledged themselves to achieve, in co-operation with the United Nations, the promotion of universal respect for and observance of human rights and fundamental freedoms,

Whereas a common understanding of these rights and freedoms is of the greatest importance for the full realization of this pledge,

Now, therefore,

The General Assembly

Proclaims this Universal Declaration of Human Rights as a common standard of achievement for all peoples and all nations, to the end that every individual and every organ of society, keeping this Declaration constantly in mind, shall strive by teaching and education to promote respect for these rights and freedoms and by progressive measures, national and international, to secure their universal and effective recognition and observance, both among the peoples of Member States themselves and among the peoples of territories under their jurisdiction.

Article 1

All human beings are born free and equal in dignity and rights. They are endowed with reason and conscience and should act towards one another in a spirit of brotherhood.

Article 2

Everyone is entitled to all the rights and freedoms set forth in this Declaration, without distinction of any kind, such as race, colour, sex, language, religion, political or other opinion, national or social origin, property, birth or other status.

Furthermore, no distinction shall be made on the basis of the political, jurisdictional or international status of the country or territory to which a person belongs, whether it be independent, trust, non-selfgoverning or under any other limitation of sovereignty.

Article 3

Everyone has the right to life, liberty and security of person.

Article 4

No one shall be held in slavery or servitude; slavery and the slave trade shall be prohibited in all their forms.

Article 5

No one shall be subjected to torture or to cruel, inhuman or degrading treatment or punishment.

Article 6

Everyone has the right to recognition everywhere as a person before the law.

Article 7

All are equal before the law and are entitled without any discrimination to equal protection of the law. All are entitled to equal protection against any discrimination in violation of this Declaration and against any incitement to such discrimination.

Article 8

Everyone has the right to an effective remedy by the competent national tribunals for acts violating the fundamental rights granted him by the constitution or by law.

Article 9

No one shall be subjected to arbitrary arrest, detention or exile.

Article 10

Everyone is entitled in full equality to a fair and public hearing by an independent and impartial tribunal, in the determination of his rights and obligations and of any criminal charge against him.

Article 11

1. Everyone charged with a penal offence has the right to be presumed innocent until proved guilty according to law in a public trial at which he has had all the guarantees necessary for his defence.
2. No one shall be held guilty of any penal offence on account of any act or omission which did not constitute a penal offence, under national or international

law, at the time when it was committed. Nor shall a heavier penalty be imposed than the one that was applicable at the time the penal offence was committed.

Article 12

No one shall be subjected to arbitrary interference with his privacy, family, home or correspondence, nor to attacks upon his honour and reputation. Everyone has the right to the protection of the law against such interference or attacks.

Article 13

1. Everyone has the right to freedom of movement and residence within the borders of each State.
2. Everyone has the right to leave any country, including his own, and to return to his country.

Article 14

1. Everyone has the right to seek and to enjoy in other countries asylum from persecution.
2. This right may not be invoked in the case of prosecutions genuinely arising from non-political crimes or from acts contrary to the purposes and principles of the United Nations.

Article 15

1. Everyone has the right to a nationality.
2. No one shall be arbitrarily deprived of his nationality nor denied the right to change his nationality.

Article 16

1. Men and women of full age, without any limitation due to race, nationality or religion, have the right to marry and to found a family. They are entitled to equal rights as to marriage, during marriage and at its dissolution.
2. Marriage shall be entered into only with the free and full consent of the intending spouses.
3. The family is the natural and fundamental group unit of society and is entitled to protection by society and the State.

Article 17

1. Everyone has the right to own property alone as well as in association with others.
2. No one shall be arbitrarily deprived of his property.

Article 18

Everyone has the right to freedom of thought, conscience and religion; this right includes freedom to change his religion or belief, and freedom, either alone or in community with others and in public or private, to manifest his religion or belief in teaching, practice, worship and observance.

Article 19

Everyone has the right to freedom of opinion and expression; this right includes freedom to hold opinions without interference and to seek, receive and impart information and ideas through any media and regardless of frontiers.

Article 20

1. Everyone has the right to freedom of peaceful assembly and association.
2. No one may be compelled to belong to an association.

Article 21

1. Everyone has the right to take part in the government of his country, directly or through freely chosen representatives.
2. Everyone has the right of equal access to public service in his country.
3. The will of the people shall be the basis of the authority of government; this will shall be expressed in periodic and genuine elections which shall be by universal and equal suffrage and shall be held by secret vote or by equivalent free voting procedures.

Article 22

Everyone, as a member of society, has the right to social security and is entitled to realization, through national effort and international co-operation and in accordance with the organization and resources of each State, of the economic, social and cultural rights indispensable for his dignity and the free development of his personality.

Article 23

1. Everyone has the right to work, to free choice of employment, to just and favourable conditions of work and to protection against unemployment.
2. Everyone, without any discrimination, has the right to equal pay for equal work.
3. Everyone who works has the right to just and favourable remuneration ensuring for himself and his family an existence worthy of human dignity, and supplemented, if necessary, by other means of social protection.
4. Everyone has the right to form and to join trade unions for the protection of his interests.

Article 24

Everyone has the right to rest and leisure, including reasonable limitation of working hours and periodic holidays with pay.

Article 25

1. Everyone has the right to a standard of living adequate for the health and well-being of himself and of his family, including food, clothing, housing and medical care and necessary social services, and the right to security in the event of unemployment, sickness, disability, widowhood, old age or other lack of livelihood in circumstances beyond his control.
2. Motherhood and childhood are entitled to special care and assistance. All children, whether born in or out of wedlock, shall enjoy the same social protection.

Article 26

1. Everyone has the right to education. Education shall be free, at least in the elementary and fundamental stages. Elementary education shall be compulsory. Technical and professional education shall be made generally available and higher education shall be equally accessible to all on the basis of merit.
2. Education shall be directed to the full development of the human personality and to the strengthening of respect for human rights and fundamental freedoms. It shall promote understanding, tolerance and friendship among all nations, racial

or religious groups, and shall further the activities of the United Nations for the maintenance of peace.

3. Parents have a prior right to choose the kind of education that shall be given to their children.

Article 27

1. Everyone has the right freely to participate in the cultural life of the community, to enjoy the arts and to share in scientific advancement and its benefits.
2. Everyone has the right to the protection of the moral and material interests resulting from any scientific, literary or artistic production of which he is the author.

Article 28

Everyone is entitled to a social and international order in which the rights and freedoms set forth in this Declaration can be fully realized.

Article 29

1. Everyone has duties to the community in which alone the free and full development of his personality is possible.
2. In the exercise of his rights and freedoms, everyone shall be subject only to such limitations as are determined by law solely for the purpose of securing due recognition and respect for the rights and freedoms of others and of meeting the just requirements of morality, public order and the general welfare in a democratic society.
3. These rights and freedoms may in no case be exercised contrary to the purposes and principles of the United Nations.

Article 30

Nothing in his Declaration may be interpreted as implying for any State, group or person any right to engage in any activity or to perform any act aimed at the destruction of any of the rights and freedoms set forth herein.

(CONSTITUTION ACT, 1982, PART I)

Canadian Charter of Rights and Freedoms

Whereas Canada is founded upon principles that recognize the supremacy of God and the rule of law:

Guarantee of Rights and Freedoms

1 The *Canadian Charter of Rights and Freedoms* guarantees the rights and freedoms set out in it subject only to such reasonable limits prescribed by law as can be demonstrably justified in a free and democratic society.

Fundamental Freedoms

2 Everyone has the following fundamental freedoms:
(a) freedom of conscience and religion;
(b) freedom of thought, belief, opinion and expression, including freedom of the press and other media of communication;
(c) freedom of peaceful assembly; and
(d) freedom of association.

Democratic Rights

3 Every citizen of Canada has the right to vote in an election of members of the House of Commons or of a legislative assembly and to be qualified for membership therein.

4 (1) No House of Commons and no legislative assembly shall continue for longer than five years from the date fixed for the return of the writs at a general election of its members.

(2) In time of real or apprehended war, invasion or insurrection, a House of

Commons may be continued by Parliament and a legislative assembly may be continued by the legislature beyond five years if such continuation is not opposed by the votes of more than one-third of the members of the House of Commons or the legislative assembly, as the case may be.

5 There shall be a sitting of Parliament and of each legislature at least once every twelve months.

Mobility Rights

6 (1) Every citizen of Canada has the right to enter, remain in and leave Canada.

(2) Every citizen of Canada and every person who has the status of a permanent resident of Canada has the right

(a) to move to and take up residence in any province; and

(b) to pursue the gaining of a livelihood in any province.

(3) The rights specified in subsection (2) are subject to

(a) any laws or practices of general application in force in a province other than those that discriminate among persons primarily on the basis of province of present or previous residence; and

(b) any laws providing for reasonable residency requirements as a qualification for the receipt of publicly provided social services.

Legal Rights

7 Everyone has the right to life, liberty and security of the person and the right not to be deprived thereof except in accordance with the principles of fundamental justice.

8 Everyone has the right to be secure against unreasonable search or seizure.

9 Everyone has the right not to be arbitrarily detained or imprisoned.

10 Everyone has the right on arrest or detention

(a) to be informed promptly of the reasons therefor;

(b) to retain and instruct counsel without delay and to be informed of that right; and

(c) to have the validity of the detention determined by way of *habeas corpus* and to be released if the detention is not lawful.

11 Any person charged with an offence has the right

(a) to be informed without unreasonable delay of the specific offence;

(b) to be tried within a reasonable time;

(c) not to be compelled to be a witness in proceedings against that person in respect of the offence;

(d) to be presumed innocent until proven guilty according to law in a fair and public hearing by an independent and impartial tribunal;

(e) not to be denied reasonable bail without just cause;

(f) except in the case of an offence under military law tried before a military tribunal, to the benefit of trial by jury where the maximum punishment for the offence is imprisonment for five years or a more severe punishment;

(g) not to be found guilty on account of any act or omission unless, at the time of the act or omission, it constituted an offence under Canadian or international law or was criminal according to the general principles of law recognized by the community of nations;

(h) if finally acquitted of the offence, not to be tried for it again and, if finally found guilty and punished for the offence, not to be tried or punished for it again; and

(i) if found guilty of the offence and if the punishment for the offence has been varied between the time of commission and the time of sentencing, to the benefit of the lesser punishment.

12 Everyone has the right not to be subjected to any cruel and unusual treatment or punishment.

13 A witness who testifies in any proceedings has the right not to have any incriminating evidence so given used to incriminate that witness in any other proceedings, except in a prosecution for perjury or for the giving of contradictory evidence.

14 A party or witness in any proceedings who does not understand or speak the language in which the proceedings are conducted or who is deaf has the right to the assistance of an interpreter.

Equality Rights

15 (1) Every individual is equal before and under the law and has the right to the equal protection and equal benefit of the law without discrimination and, in particular, without discrimination based on race, national or ethnic origin, colour, religion, sex, age or mental or physical disability.

(2) Subsection (1) does not preclude any law, program or activity that has as its object the amelioration of conditions of disadvantaged individuals or groups including those that are disadvantaged because of race, national or ethnic origin, colour, religion, sex, age or mental or physical disability.

Official Languages of Canada

16 (1) English and French are the official languages of Canada and have equality of status and equal rights and privileges as to their use in all institutions of the Parliament and government of Canada.

(2) English and French are the official languages of New Brunswick and have equality of status and equal rights and privileges as to their use in all institutions of the legislature and government of New Brunswick.

(3) Nothing in this Charter limits the authority of Parliament or a legislature to advance the equality of status or use of English and French.

17 (1) Everyone has the right to use English or French in any debates and other proceedings of Parliament.

(2) Everyone has the right to use English or French in any debates and other proceedings of the legislature of New Brunswick.

18 (1) The statutes, records and journals of Parliament shall be printed and published in English and French and both language versions are equally authoritative.

(2) The statutes, records and journals of the legislature of New Brunswick shall be printed and published in English and French and both language versions are equally authoritative.

19 (1) Either English or French may be used by any person in, or in any pleading in or process issuing from, any court established by Parliament.

(2) Either English or French may be used by any person in, or in any pleading in or process issuing from, any court of New Brunswick.

20 (1) Any member of the public in Canada has the right to communicate with, and to receive available services from, any head or central office of an institution of the Parliament or government of Canada in English or French, and has the same right with respect to any other office of any such institution where

(a) there is a significant demand for communications with and services from that office in such language; or

(b) due to the nature of the office, it is reasonable that communications with and services from that office be available in both English and French.

(2) Any member of the public in New Brunswick has the right to communicate with, and to receive available services from, any office of an institution of the legislature or government of New Brunswick in English or French.

21 Nothing in sections 16 to 20 abrogates or derogates from any right, privilege or obligation with respect to the English and French languages, or either of them, that exists or is continued by virtue of any other provision of the Constitution of Canada.

22 Nothing in sections 16 to 20 abrogates or derogates from any legal or customary right or privilege acquired or enjoyed either before or after the coming into force of this Charter with respect to any language that is not English or French.

Minority Language Educational Rights

23 (1) Citizens of Canada
   (a) whose first language learned and still understood is that of the English or French linguistic minority population of the province in which they reside, or
   (b) who have received their primary school instruction in Canada in English or French and reside in a province where the language in which they received that instruction is the language of the English or French linguistic minority population of the province,
have the right to have their children receive primary and secondary school instruction in that language in that province.

   (2) Citizens of Canada of whom any child has received or is receiving primary or secondary school instruction in English or French in Canada, have the right to have all their children receive primary and secondary school instruction in the same language. ·

   (3) The right of citizens of Canada under subsections (1) and (2) to have their children receive primary and secondary school instruction in the language of the English or French linguistic minority population of a province
   (a) applies wherever in the province the number of children of citizens who have such a right is sufficient to warrant the provision to them out of public funds of minority language instruction; and
   (b) includes, where the number of those children so warrants, the right to have them receive that instruction in minority language educational facilities provided out of public funds.

Enforcement

24 (1) Anyone whose rights or freedoms, as guaranteed by this Charter, have been infringed or denied may apply to a court of competent jurisdiction to obtain such remedy as the court considers appropriate and just in the circumstances.

   (2) Where, in proceedings under subsection (1), a court concludes that evidence was obtained in a manner that infringed or denied any rights or freedoms guaranteed by this Charter, the evidence shall be excluded if it is established that, having regard to all the circumstances, the admission of it in the proceedings would bring the administration of justice into disrepute.

General

25 The guarantee in this Charter of certain rights and freedoms shall not be construed so as to abrogate or derogate from any aboriginal, treaty or other rights or freedoms that pertain to the aboriginal peoples of Canada including

(a) any rights or freedoms that have been recognized by the Royal Proclamation of October 7, 1763; and

(b) any rights or freedoms that may be acquired by the aboriginal peoples of Canada by way of land claims settlement.

26 The guarantee in this Charter of certain rights and freedoms shall not be construed as denying the existence of any other rights or freedoms that exist in Canada.

27 This Charter shall be interpreted in a manner consistent with the preservation and enhancement of the multicultural heritage of Canadians.

28 Notwithstanding anything in this Charter, the rights and freedoms referred to in it are guaranteed equally to male and female persons.

29 Nothing in this Charter abrogates or derogates from any rights or privileges guaranteed by or under the Constitution of Canada in respect of denominational, separate or dissentient schools.

30 A reference in this Charter to a province or to the legislative assembly or legislature of a province shall be deemed to include a reference to the Yukon Territory and the Northwest Territories, or to the appropriate legislative authority thereof, as the case may be.

31 Nothing in this Charter extends the legislative powers of any body or authority.

Application of Charter

32 (1) This Charter applies

(a) to the Parliament and government of Canada and to all matters within the authority of Parliament including all matters relating to the Yukon Territory and Northwest Territories; and

(b) to the legislature and government of each province and to all matters within the authority of the legislature of each province.

(2) Notwithstanding subsection (1), section 15 shall not have effect until three years after this Act, except Part VI, comes into force.

Citation

33 This Part may be cited as the *Canadian Charter of Rights and Freedoms*.

Declaration on the Rights of Mentally Retarded Persons

Proclaimed by the General Assembly of the United Nations on 20 December 1971 (resolution 2856 (xxvi))

The General Assembly,

Mindful of the pledge of the States Members of the United Nations under the Charter to take joint and separate action in co-operation with the Organization to promote higher standards of living, full employment and conditions of economic and social progress and development,

Reaffirming faith in human rights and fundamental freedoms and in the principles of peace, of the dignity and worth of the human person and of social justice proclaimed in the Charter,

Recalling the principles of the Universal Declaration of Human Rights, the International Covenants on Human Rights, the Declaration of the Rights of the Child and the standards already set for social progress in the constitutions, conventions, recommendations and resolutions of the International Labour Organisation, the United Nations Educational, Scientific and Cultural Organization, the World Health Organization, the United Nations Children's Fund and other organizations concerned,

Emphasizing that the Declaration on Social Progress and Development has proclaimed the necessity of protecting the rights and assuring the welfare and rehabilitation of the physically and mentally disadvantaged,

Bearing in mind the necessity of assisting mentally retarded persons to the develop their abilities in various fields of activities and of promoting their integration as far as possible in normal life,

Aware that certain countries, at their present stage of development, can devote only limited efforts to this end,

Proclaims this Declaration on the Rights of Mentally Retarded Persons and calls for national and international action to ensure that it will be used as a common basis and frame of reference for the protection of these rights:

1. The mentally retarded person has, to the maximum degree of feasibility, the same rights as other human beings.

2. The mentally retarded person has a right to proper medical care and physical therapy and to such education, training, rehabilitation and guidance as will enable him to develop his ability and maximum potential.

3. The mentally retarded person has a right to economic security and to a decent standard of living. He has a right to perform productive work or to engage in any other meaningful occupation to the fullest possible extent of his capabilities.

4. Whenever possible, the mentally retarded person should live with his own family or with foster parents and participate in different forms of community life. The family with which he lives should receive assistance. If care in an institution becomes necessary, it should be provided in surroundings and other circumstances as close as possible to those of normal life.

5. The mentally retarded person has a right to a qualified guardian when this is required to protect his personal well-being and interests.

6. The mentally retarded person has a right to protection from exploitation, abuse and degrading treatment. If prosecuted for any offence, he shall have a right to due process of law with full recognition being given to his degree of mental responsibility.

7. Whenever mentally retarded persons are unable, because of the severity of their handicap, to exercise all their rights in a meaningful way or it should become necessary to restrict or deny some or all of these rights, the procedure used for that restriction or denial of rights must contain proper legal safeguards against every form of abuse. This procedure must be based on an evaluation of the social capability of the mentally retarded person by qualified experts and must be subject to periodic review and to the right of appeal to higher authorities.

Declaration on the Rights of Disabled Persons

Proclaimed by the General Assembly of the United Nations on 9 December 1975 (resolution 3447 (xxx))

The General Assembly,

Mindful of the pledge made by Member State, under the Charter of the United Nations; to take joint and separate action in co-operation with the Organization to promote higher standards of living, full employment and conditions of economic and social progress and development,

Reaffirming its faith in human rights and fundamental freedoms and in the principles of peace, of the dignity and worth of the human person and of social justice proclaimed in the Charter,

Recalling the principles of the Universal Declaration of Human Rights, the International Convenants on Human Rights, the Declaration of the Rights of the Child and the Declaration on the Rights of Mentally Retarded persons, as well as the standards already set for social progress in the constitutions, conventions, recommendations and resolutions of the International Labour Organisation, the United Nations Educational, Scientific and Cultural Organization, the World Health Organization, the United Nations Children's Fund and other organizations concerned,

Recalling also Economic and Social Council resolution 1921 (LVIII) of 6 May 1975 on the prevention of disability and the rehabilitation of disabled persons,

Emphasizing that the Declaration on Social Progress and Development has proclaimed the necessity of protecting the rights and assuring the welfare and rehabilitation of the physically and mentally disadvantaged,

Bearing in mind the necessity of preventing physical and mental disabilities and of assisting disabled persons to develop their abilities in the most varied fields of activities and of promoting their integration as far as possible in normal life,

Aware that certain countries, at their present stage of development, can devote only limited efforts to this end,

Proclaims this Declaration on the Rights of Disabled Persons and calls for national and international action to ensure that it will be used as a common basis and frame of reference for the protection of these rights:

1. The term 'disabled person' means any person unable to ensure by himself or herself, wholly or partly, the necessities of a normal individual and/or social life, as a result of a deficiency, either congenital or not, in his or her physical or mental capabilities.

2. Disabled persons shall enjoy all the rights set forth in this Declaration. These rights shall be granted to all disabled persons without any exception whatsoever and without distinction or discrimination on the basis of race, colour, sex, language, religion, political or other opinions, national or social origin, state of wealth, birth or any other situation applying either to the disabled person himself or herself or to his or her family.

3. Disabled persons have the inherent right to respect for their human dignity. Disabled persons, whatever the origin, nature and seriousness of their handicaps and disabilities, have the same fundamental rights as their fellow-citizens of the same age, which implies first and foremost the right to enjoy a decent life, as normal and full as possible.

4. Disabled persons have the same civil and political rights as other human beings; paragraph 7 of the Declaration on the Rights of Mentally Retarded Persons applies to any possible limitation or suppression of those rights for mentally disabled persons.

5. Disabled persons are entitled to the measures designed to enable them to become as self-reliant as possible.

6. Disabled persons have the right to medical, psychological and functional treatment, including prosthetic and orthetic appliances, to medical and social rehabilitation, education, vocational training and rehabilitation, aid, counselling, placement services and other services which will enable them to develop their capabilities and skills to the maximum and will hasten the process of their social integration or reintegration.

7. Disabled persons have the right to economic and social security and to a decent level of living. They have the right, according to their capabilities, to secure and retain employment or to engage in a useful, productive and remunerative occupation and to join trade unions.

8. Disabled persons are entitled to have their special needs taken into consideration at all stages of economic and social planning.

9. Disabled persons have the right to live with their families or with foster parents and to participate in all social, creative or recreational activities. No

disabled person shall be subjected, as far as his or her residence is concerned, to differential treatment other than that required by his or her condition or by the improvement which he or she may derive therefrom. If the stay of a disabled person in a specialized establishment is indispensable, the environment and living conditions therein shall be as close as possible to those of the normal life of a person of his or her age.

10. Disabled persons shall be protected against all exploitation, all regulations and all treatment of a discriminatory, abusive or degrading nature.

11. Disabled persons shall be able to avail themselves of qualified legal aid when such aid proves indispensable for the protection of their persons and property. If judicial proceedings are instituted against them, the legal procedure applied shall take their physical and mental condition fully into account.

12. Organizations of disabled persons may be usefully consulted in all matters regarding the rights of disabled persons.

13. Disabled persons, their families and communities shall be fully informed, by all appropriate means, of the rights contained in this Declaration.

References

Abbot, S.; and Love, B. 1972. *Sappho Was a Right-on Woman*. New York: Stein & Day

Adam, B.D. 1987. *The Rise of a Gay and Lesbian Movement*. Boston: Twayne

Al-Anon Family Groups, n.d. *A Guide for the Family of the Alcoholic*. Pamphlet no. 7. New York

– n.d. *Understanding Ourselves and Alcoholism*, Pamphlet no. 48. New York

– n.d. *What Do You Do about the Alcoholic's Drinking?* Pamphlet no. 19. New York

Alcoholics Anonymous World Services Inc. 1952. *Twelve Steps and Traditions*. New York

– 1976. *Alcoholics Anonymous*. 3rd ed. New York

– 1981. *The AA Grapevine*. New York, March

Altman, D. 1971. *Homosexual: Oppression and Liberation*. Sydney (Australia): Angus & Robertson

– 1982. *The Homosexualization of America and the Americanization of the Homosexual*. New York: St. Martin's Press

American Sociological Association. 1982. 'Report of the ASA's Task Group on Homosexuality.' *The American Sociologist*, 17 (August): 164–80

Antze, P. 1976. 'The Role of Ideologies in Peer Psychotherapy Organizations: Some Theoretical Considerations and Three Case Studies.' *The Journal of Applied Behavioral Science*, 12 (3): 323–46

Barrie, M. 1982. *Images of Women*. Report of the Task Force on Sex-Role Stereotyping in the Broadcast Media. Hull, Que.: Minister of Supply and Services Canada

Baureiss, G. 1982. 'Towards a Theory of Ethnic Organizations.' *Canadian Ethnic Studies*, 14 (2): 21–37

Beatty, H.; Carden, S.; and Spindel, P. 1986. *A Proposal to Establish Advocacy Ontario*. Brief submitted to the Honourable Ian Scott, Attorney General (July)

Becker, H.S. 1963. *Outsiders: Studies in the Sociology of Deviance*. New York: The Free Press

Beckton, C. 1987. 'Section 27 and Section 15 of the Charter.' In Canadian Human Rights Foundation, 1987

Bell, A.P.; and Weinberg, M.S. 1978. *Homosexualities: A Study of Diversity among Men and Women*. New York: Touchstone Books (Simon and Schuster)

Berger, T.R. 1981. *Fragile Freedoms: Human Rights and Dissent in Canada*. Toronto/ Vancouver: Clarke, Irwin & Company Ltd

Berkeley, H.; Chadfield, C.; and West, G., eds. 1978. *Children's Rights: Legal and Educational Issues*. Toronto; OISE

Biklen, D. 1979. 'The Case for Deinstitutionalization.' *Social Policy*, May/June: 48–54

Binavince, E.S. 1987. 'The Juridical Aspects of Race Relations.' Paper presented for Canada 2000, a conference held at Carleton University, Ottawa, 1 November

Blatt, B.; Bogdan, R.; Biklen, D.; and Taylor, S. 1977. 'From Institution to Community: A Conversion Model.' In *Educational Programming for the Severely and Profoundly Handicapped*. Reston, Va: Council for Exceptional Children

Block, W.E.; and Walker, M.A., eds. 1981. *Discrimination, Affirmative Action and Equal Opportunity*. Vancouver: The Frazer Institute

Body Politic, The. A Magazine for Lesbian/Gay Liberation, published monthly by the Pink Triangle Press, Toronto

Boydell, C.L.; Grindstaff, C.F.; and Whitehead, P.C., eds. 1972. *Deviant Behaviour and Societal Reaction*. Toronto: Holt, Rinehart & Winston

Breton, R. 1964. 'Institutional Completeness of Ethnic Communities and the Personal Relations of Immigrants.' *The American Journal of Sociology*, 70 (2; September): 193–205

Brown, J.C. 1977. *A Hit and Miss Affair: Policies for Disabled People in Canada*. Ottawa: The Canadian Council on Social Development

Cairns, A.; and Williams, C., eds. 1986. *The Politics of Gender, Ethnicity and Language in Canada*. Royal Commission on the Economic Union and Development Prospects for Canada, vol. 4. Toronto: University of Toronto Press

Calendino, M. 1975. 'Control of Employee Alcoholism.' *Resources Protection*, 4 (8): 27–37

Canada. House of Commons. 1981. *Obstacles*. Report of the Special Committee on the Disabled and Handicapped. February

Canadian Council on Children and Youth. 1978. *Admittance Restricted: The Child as Citizen in Canada*. Ottawa

Canadian Human Rights Commission. 1979. *Sexual Orientation: A Policy Planning Report*. Prepared for the CHRC, August

Canadian Human Rights Foundation. 1987. *Multiculturalism and the Charter: A Legal Perspective*. Toronto: Carswell

Canadian Rehabilitation Council for the Disabled. 1980. A Brief Presented to the Special Committee for the Disabled and Handicapped, July

Case, F.I. 1977. *Racism and National Consciousness*. Toronto: Plowshare Press

Clark, S.D.; Grayson, J.P.; and Grayson, L.M. 1975. *Prophecy and Protest: Social Movements in Twentieth-Century Canada*. Toronto: Gage

Clinard, M.B.; and Meier, R.F. 1979. *Sociology of Deviant Behaviour*. 5th ed. New York: Holt, Rinehart & Winston

Coalition for Gay Rights in Ontario. 1978. *Discrimination and the Gay Minority*. A Brief to the Members of the Ontario Legislature, March

– 1981. *The Ontario Human Rights Omission*. A Brief to the Members of the Ontario Legislature, June

– 1986. *Discrimination against Lesbians and Gay Men: The Ontario Human Rights Omission*. A brief to the members of the Ontario legislature. Toronto, October

Coalition of Provincial Organizations of the Handicapped. 1987. COPOH's Preliminary Position on Fiscal Arrangements Affecting Disabled Canadians. Winnipeg, November

[The] Commission on Emotional and Learning Disorders in Children. 1970. *One Million Children*. Toronto: Leonard Crainford

Concerned Friends of Ontario Citizens in Care Facilities. 1987. *Concerned Friends*. A Quarterly Newsletter. No. XIX, Autumn

Conrad, P.; and Schneider, J. 1980. *Deviance and Medicalization: From Badness to Sickness*. St Louis: C.V. Mosby

Cook, G., ed. 1976. *Opportunity for Choice: A Goal for Women in Canada*. Ottawa: Statistics Canada in association with C.D. Howe Research Institute

Cruickshank, D.A. 1979. 'The Rights of Children.' In MacDonald and Humphrey, 1979

Csicsai, R. 1983. 'From Alienation to Integration: A Sociological Analysis of Alcoholics Anonymous.' A paper submitted to the CSAA Annual Meeting, Vancouver, BC, June

Dear, M.J.; and Taylor, S.M. 1982. *Not on Our Street: Community Attitudes to Mental Health Care*. London: Pion Ltd

D'Emilio, J. 1982. 'Dreams Deferred: The Early American Homophile Movement.' In Jackson and Persky, 1982

Derksen, J. 1985. 'The Consumer Movement of the Disabled.' *The Central Courier*, September

Eberts, M. 1979. 'The Rights of Women.' In MacDonald and Humphrey, 1979

Edgerton, R. 1967. *The Cloak of Competence: Stigma in the Lives of the Mentally Retarded.* Berkeley: University of California Press

Edgerton, R.; and Bercovici, S. 1976. 'The Cloak of Competence – Years Later.' *American Journal of Mental Deficiency,* 81: 485–97

Eisener, M. 1982. 'An Investigation of the Coming Out Process, Life-Style and Sex-Role Orientation of Lesbians.' PhD dissertation (unpublished), Faculty of Graduate Studies, Department of Psychology, York University, Downsview

Elliott, P. 1983. 'Lesbian Identity and Self-disclosure.' *Resources for Feminist Research,* March: 51–2

Fadiman, A. 1983. 'The Double Closet.' *Life,* May: 76–100

Feintuck, A. 1958. 'Sheltered Workshops: A Conceptual Framework.' *Journal of Rehabilitation,* 24 (1): 9–10

Felming, T. 1983. 'Mad Dogs, Beasts and Raving Nutters: The Presentation of the Mentally Disordered in the British Press.' In Fleming and Visano, 1983

Fleming, T.; and Visano, L.A., eds. 1983. *Deviant Designations: Crime, Law and Deviance in Canada.* Toronto: Butterworths

Foster, M.; and Murray, K. 1972. *A Not So Gay World: Homosexuality in Canada.* Toronto: McClelland & Stewart Ltd

Freedberg, E.J.; and Johnston, W.E. 1978. 'Effects of Various Sources of Coercion on Outcome of Treatment of Alcoholism.' *Psychological Reports,* 43: 1271–8

Freeman, D. 1972. *Creeps.* Toronto: University of Toronto Press

Gays of Ottawa. 1983. *Cleaning Up the Acts: Selected Discrimination Issues Affecting the Gay Minority.* A Report for the Secretary of State. February

Gellman, J.P. 1964. *The Sober Alcoholic: An Organizational Analysis of Alcoholics Anonymous.* New Haven, Conn.: College and University Press

Gibbins, R.; and Ponting, J.R. 1986. 'An Assessment of the Probable Impact of Aboriginal Self-Government in Canada.' In Cairns and Williams, 1986

Giffen, P.J. 1966. 'The Revolving Door: A Functional Interpretation.' *The Canadian Review of Sociology and Anthropology,* 3 (3): 154–66

Glaser, K.; and Possony, S.T. 1979. *Victims of Politics: The State of Human Rights.* New York: Columbia University Press

Goffman, E. 1961. *Asylums.* New York: Anchor Books

– 1963. *Stigma: Notes on the Management of Spoiled Identity.* Englewood Cliffs, NJ: Spectrum Books

Government of Canada. 1982. *The Charter of Rights and Freedoms: A Guide for Canadians.* Ottawa: Minister of Supply and Services Canada

– 1986. *Toward Equality: The Response to the Report of the Parliamentary Committee on Equality Rights.* Ottawa: Minister of Supply and Services Canada

Hannon, G. 1980. 'No Sorrow, No Pity: A Report on the Gay Disabled.' *Body Politic,* February: 19–22

Heshusius, L. 1981. *Meaning in Life as Experienced by Persons Labelled Retarded in a Group Home*. Springfield, Ill.: Chas. C. Thomas

Hughes, D.R. 1982. Introduction to Kallen, 1982

Hughes, D.R., and Kallen, E. 1974. *The Anatomy of Racism: Canadian Dimensions*. Montreal: Harvest House

Human Rights Commission of British Columbia. 1983. *I'm Okay: We're Not So Sure about You: A Report of the B.C. Human Rights Commission on Extensions to the Code*. Victoria: Queen's Printer for British Columbia, February

Humphrey, J. 1973. 'The International Law of Human Rights in the Middle Twentieth Century.' In Bos, ed., *The Present State of International Law*. The Netherlands: Kloner

Humphreys, L. 1972. *Out of the Closets: The Sociology of Homosexual Liberation*. Englewood Cliffs, NJ: Prentice-Hall

Isaacs, H.R. 1977. *Idols of the Tribe: Group Identity and Political Change*. New York: Harper & Row

Ishwaran, K., ed. 1976. *The Canadian Family*, rev. ed. Toronto: Holt, Rinehart & Winston

Jackson, E.; and Persky, S. 1982. *Flaunting It: A Decade of Gay Journalism from the Body Politic*. Vancouver: New Star Books: Toronto: Pink Triangle Press

Jay, K. 1983. 'Life in the Underworld: The Lesbian Bar as Metaphor.' *Resources for Feminist Research*, March: 18–20

Jenkins, M.; and Shain, M. 1982. *Alcoholism, Intoxication and Employer Responsibility: Trends in Worker's Compensation Law*. Toronto: Addiction Research Foundation of Ontario, January

Kallen, E. 1982. *Ethnicity and Human Rights in Canada*. Agincourt, Ont.: Gage
– 1988. 'The Meech Lake Accord: Entrenching a Pecking Order of Minority Rights.' In *Canadian Public Policy*: XIV Supplement, September

Kallen, E.; and Kelner, M. 1976. 'Parents and Peers: Who Influences Student Values?' In Ishwaran, 1976

Kessel, J. 1962. *The Road Back: A Report on Alcoholics Anonymous*. New York: Alfred A. Knopf

Killian, L.M. 1968. *The Impossible Revolution?* New York: Random House

Kinloch, G.C. 1979. *The Sociology of Minority Group Relations*. Englewood Cliffs, NJ: Prentice-Hall

Kissin, B.; and Begleiter, H., eds. 1976. *Social Aspects of Alcoholism*. New York: Plenum Press

Klapp, O.E. 1969. *Collective Search for Identity*. New York: Holt, Rinehart & Winston

Krauter, J.F.; and Davis, M. 1978. *Minority Canadians: Ethnic Groups*. Toronto: Methuen

Kurtz, E. 1979. *Not-God: A History of Alcoholics Anonymous*. Centre City, Minn.: Hazelton Educational Services

Lauristen, J.; and Thorstad, D. 1974. *The Early Homosexual Rights Movement (1864–1935)*. New York: Times Change Press

La Violette, F. 1948. *The Canadian Japanese and World War II*. Toronto: University of Toronto Press

Leavy, J. 1979. 'Working Paper for a Series of Regional Conferences on Minority Rights.' For the Canadian Human Rights Foundation, October

Lee, J. 1978. *Getting Sex*. Don Mills, Ont.: Musson Book Co. (General Publishing)

Lemert, E.M. 1967. 'The Concept of Secondary Deviation.' In *Human Deviance, Social Problems and Social Control*. Englewood Cliffs, NJ: Prentice-Hall

Lincoln, C.E. 1961. *The Black Muslims in America*. Boston: Beacon

Lumsden, D.P., ed. 1984. *Community Mental Health Action: Primary Prevention Programming in Canada*. Toronto: The Canadian Public Health Association

MacDonald, R.St.J.; and Humphrey, J.P., eds. 1979. *The Practice of Freedom*. Toronto: Butterworths

Mackie, M. 1974. 'Ethnic Stereotypes and Prejudice: Alberta Indians, Hutterites and Ukrainians.' *Canadian Ethnic Studies*, (1–2): 39–52

Magnet, J.E. 1987. 'Interpreting Multiculturalism.' In Canadian Human Rights Foundation, 1987

Matthews, R. 1983. *The Creation of Regional Dependency*. Toronto: University of Toronto Press

McDiarmid, G.; and Pratt, D. 1974. *Teaching Prejudice: A Content Analysis of Social Studies Textbooks Authorized for Use in ontario*. Toronto: OISE

Meigs, M. 1982. *Lily Briscoe: A Self-Portrait*. Vancouver, BC: Talonbooks

Mewett, A.W. 1979. 'The Rights of the Institutionalized.' In Macdonald and Humphrey, 1979

Moses, A. 1978. *Identity Management in Lesbian Women*. New York: Prager

Neiderhoffer, A. 1967. *Behind the Shield: The Police in Urban Society*. Garden City, NY: Doubleday

Oberschall, A. 1973. *Social Conflict and Social Movements*. Englewood Cliffs, NJ: Prentice-Hall

Office des Personnes Handicappées du Québec. 1981. Reports 1–5

Perrin, B. 1982. 'Misconceptions about the Principle of Normalization.' *Mental Retardation*, 32 (3; summer): 39–42

Pittman, D.J., ed. 1967. *Alcoholism*. New York: Harper & Row

Plummer, K. 1975. *Sexual Stigma: An Interactionist Account*. London: Routledge & Kegan Paul

Ponse, B. 1978. *Identities in the Lesbian World*. London: Greenwood Press

Ponting, J.R.; and Gibbins, R. 1980. *Out of Irrelevance: A Socio-political Introduction to Indian Affairs in Canada*. Toronto: Butterworths

Porter, J. 1979. *The Measure of Canadian Society: Education. Equality and Opportunity*. Agincourt, Ont.: Gage

Prince Edward Island Human Rights Commission. 1986. *Tenth Annual Report of the Prince Edward Island Human Rights Commission*. Charlottetown

Prus, R. 1983. 'Deviance as Community Activity: Putting "Labeling Theory" in Perspective.' In Fleming and Visano, 1983

RFR (Resources for Feminist Research). 1983. *The Lesbian Issue*. 12 (1; March)

Rioux, M. 1971. *Quebec in Question*. Toronto: James Lewis & Samuel

Safilios-Rothschild, C. 1976. 'Disabled Persons' Self-Definitions and Their Implications for Rehabilitation.' In *The Sociology of Physical Disability and Rehabilitation*, ed. G.L. Albrecht. Pittsburgh: University of Pittsburgh Press

Sagarin, E., ed. 1971. *The Other Minorities: Nonethnic Collectivities Conceptualized as Minority Groups*. Toronto: Ginn and Co.

Sagarin, E.; and Montanino, F., eds. 1977. *Deviants: Voluntary Actors in a Hostile World*. New York: General Learning Press

Sanders, D. 1987. 'Article 27 and the Aboriginal Peoples of Canada.' In Canadian Human Rights Foundation, 1987

Sepejak, D. 1977. 'The Willingness of Homosexuals to Report Criminal Victimization to the Police.' MA thesis (unpublished), York University

Sherman, M. 1981. *Bent*. A professional stage production operating under the jurisdiction of Canadian Actors' Equity Association

Shibutani, K.; and Kwan, K.M. 1965. *Ethnic Stratification: A Comparative Approach*. New York: Macmillan

Simmons, H.G. 1982. *From Asylum to Welfare*. Toronto: National Institute for Mental Retardation

Stone, S.D. 1983. 'Lesbian/Feminist Protest: A Case Study.' In Fleming and Visano, 1983

Sunahara, A.G. 1981. *The Politics of Racism: The Uprooting of Japanese Canadians during the Second World War*. Toronto: J. Lorimer & Co.

Tanaka, J. 1982. 'Normalization, Social Integration and Community Services' (a review). *Mental Retardation*, 32 (3; Summer): 44–5

Tarnopolsky, W.S. 1982. 'The Equality Rights.' In Tarnopolsky and Beaudoin, 1982

Tarnopolsky, W.S.; and Beaudoin, G.A., eds. 1982. *The Canadian Charter of Rights and Freedoms: Commentary*. Toronto: Carswell

Trice, H.M.; and Roman, P.M. 1970. 'Delabeling, Relabeling and Alcoholics Anonymous.' In *Social Problems*, 17 (4; Spring): 539–46

Turner, R.; and Killian, L.M. 1972. *Collective Behavior*. 2nd ed. Englewood Cliffs, NJ: Prentice-Hall

United Nations. 1978a. *The International Bill of Human Rights*. New York

– 1978b. *Human Rights: A Compilation of International Instruments*. New York

Valverde, M. 1983. 'Beyond Guilt: Lesbian-Feminism and Coming Out.' *Resources for Feminist Research*, March: 65–7

Van den Berghe, P.L. 1967. *Race and Racism: A Comparative Perspective*. New York: Wiley and Sons

Wallace, A.F.C. 1956. 'Revitalization Movements.' *American Anthropologist*, 58 (April): 264–81

Weinfeld, M. 1981. 'The Development of Affirmative Action in Canada.' *Canadian Ethnic Studies*, 13 (2): 23–9

Weitz, D. 1984. '"On Our Own": A Self-Help Model.' In Lumsden, 1984

West, W.G. 1978. 'Children's Rights in the Canadian Context.' In Berkeley, Gaffield, and West, 1978

Wiberg, H. 1981. 'Self-Determination as an International Issue.' Paper presented at the Ninth Conference of the International Peace Research Association, Orillia, Ontario, 21–26 June

Williams, J.I.; Kopinak, M.; and Moynagh, W.D. 1972. 'Mental Health and Illness in Canada.' In Boydell, Grindstaff, and Whitehead, 1972

Wine, J. 1983. 'Lesbian Academics in Canada.' *Resources for Feminist Research*, March: 9–11

Wolfensberger, W. 1972. *Normalization: The Principle of Normalization in Human Services*. Toronto: Leonard Crainford

Wolman, B.B., ed. 1982. *Psychological Aspects of Obesity*. New York: Reinhold

Zigler, E.; and Balla, B. 1977. 'Impact of Institutional Experience on the Behavior and Development of Retarded Persons.' *American Journal of Mental Deficiency* 82: 3

Index